Under the Mango Tree

UNder the MaNgo Tree

AN AdoptioN Story

Erika IsNor

iUniverse

UNDER THE MANGO TREE
AN ADOPTION STORY

This is Erika Isnor's first book

iUniverse books may be ordered through booksellers or by contacting:

iUniverse
1663 Liberty Drive
Bloomington, IN 47403
www.iuniverse.com
1-800-Authors (1-800-288-4677)

ISBN: 978-1-5320-5313-9 (sc)
ISBN: 978-1-5320-5315-3 (hc)
ISBN: 978-1-5320-5314-6 (e)

Print information available on the last page.

iUniverse rev. date: 05/03/2019

For Eveline

Whoever believes in me, as Scripture has said, rivers of living water will flow from within them.
John 7:38

CONTENTS

FOREWORD

Adopting a child from another country is extremely complicated. We were required to comply with the Hague Convention, Alberta's *Child, Youth, and Family Enhancement Act,* Jamaica's legislative requirements, and Canadian immigration simultaneously. We remained committed to navigating through the process even though it felt like we were trying to maneuver a corn maze wearing blindfolds.

The Hague Convention of 1993 regulates adoptions between contracting countries safeguarding procedures ensuring that adoption is in the best interest of the child, the biological parents, and adoptive parents. It also serves to prevent the abduction, sale, or traffic in children. The child's country must make reasonable efforts to place the child domestically before considering International adoption.

Alberta's provincial *Child, Youth and Family Enhancement Act* require compliance with the Hague Convention having implemented it in 1997. Alberta must determine that adoptive parents have been trained and are suitable for adoption. The country of the child's origin and Canada's government must agree that the proposed adoption should proceed.

Alberta recognizes three types of International Adoption:

1) "Hague Convention Adoption is the process when: The child's country is a member of the Hague Convention on Protection of Children and Cooperation in respect of Intercountry Adoption.
2) Government Adoption for Non-Hague Countries is the process when: There is an adoption process established between the child's country and Alberta.

Private International Adoption is the process when: The child's country has not implemented the Hague Convention. The child's country does not have an adoption process with Alberta"

In Jamaica, the Adoption Board is the only body that has responsibility and authority for adoption. The Child Development Agency (CDA) prepares and processes all applications presented to the Adoption Board for their consideration.

There are two processes in Jamaica to adopt a child:

1) An application for an Adoption Order provides for the completion of an adoption in Jamaica. Persons must show family ties to Jamaica, have title to some property on the island, or maintain an account in a Jamaican financial institution.

2) A License for Guardianship is the type of application where the applicant does not meet the requirement to be granted an Adoption Order. Prospective adopters submit documents to the Adoption Board for consideration. If the Board approves the application, the matter goes before the court. An applicant is allowed to take the child overseas when the court grants a license. The applicant finalizes the adoption overseas.

Immigration Canada regulations require that the applicant secure a permanent resident visa before the child enters Canada.

An applicant finalizes a privately arranged adoption in Canada to comply with the requirements of the Hague Convention, the Alberta Child, Youth and Family Enhancement Act, and Canada's Immigration and Refugee Protection Act.

Alberta does recognize a Private Guardianship order for children originating from counties where there is no legislation to process an adoption. A Private Guardianship Order is issued in the country of origin and the adoption may be finalized privately in Alberta when the adoptive parents obtain permanent status for the child.

Immigration regulations require a permanent resident visa for the child to enter Canada to finalize an adoption in these circumstances. Families who obtain Private Guardianship Orders or Private Guardianship Certificates for children who live abroad must deal directly with Citizenship and Immigration Canada to obtain permanent residence status for the child. Alberta Adoption Services had no role in obtaining permanent residency status for children and no authority to provide Letters of No Involvement with Private Guardianship cases.

Here's the catch! Citizenship and Immigration Canada *requires* a Letter of No Involvement through Alberta Adoption Services *before* the child may leave the country of origin. The letter serves to prove that a home study is overseen by and given provincial approval on the adoptive parents.

Welcome to the Bermuda Triangle! If we wanted to complete this convoluted process to offer the opportunity of a home to a child who might never otherwise have one, we would have no choice but to navigate through mysterious unchartered waters.

ONE

INTO THE WATER

Almost everyone warned us not to adopt an older child who would come home with scars that would likely never heal, but you can't talk someone out of an adoption if they have their hearts set on it. My heart was set on the romantic notion of making a difference in the life of a child who may otherwise never have opportunity. I imagined that by providing a nurturing environment we could ease the effects of the initial path littered with malnutrition, abuse and neglect.

I'd read the horrific news report about a boy being sent back to Russia when his adoptive mother caught him starting a fire with papers in his bedroom. She'd feared the child might burn the house down and kill her family. I hadn't yet walked in her shoes. I'd thought we were different because we considered ourselves experienced parents of seven children. We were willing to tread through high waters and walk through fire to give one child a fighting chance for a better life.

I'd recently been hired as a flight attendant for a young Canadian airline and looked forward to traveling with the four of our children still living at home. The two eldest had both married and were already themselves parents, while my third born and I were not on speaking terms. I wanted to spend every spare minute I had exploring life and its promising possibilities before the rest of them grew up and away.

We did not go to Jamaica with the intent of adopting a child. We wanted to escape our cold Canadian winter, and Jamaica was one of a hand full of exotic hot destinations where my company flew. Jamaica perpetuated a reputation for being dangerous, but I soon suspected that the expensive resorts fed off the paranoia they instilled in travelers to keep the tourist dollar well within the gates of their perimeter. We rented a small villa rather than to pay the exorbitant per person price for an all-inclusive vacation. After a quick Internet search, we located a villa complete with a pool, cook, and private driver to keep us safe.

Angie, our cook at the villa, supported her extended family on forty-five dollars a week in 2009, and the gratuity she received from the houseguests often exceeded her meager salary. I understood what it meant to live from paycheck to paycheck having been a single parent. There were many times that I ate only what was left on my children's plates, so I could easily imagine stealing a roast, or a jar of peanut butter to provide a few days of leftover dinners or sandwiches to put in my children's lunch bags.

Segregation was not a new experience either; I'd lived in the state of Georgia where both the black people and the white people separated themselves like fancy meal courses. However, my kids and I felt uncomfortable at the dinner table when we learned that Angie kept her children out of view until my family finished our dinner. We invited them to join us in the dining room to share the evening meal after that.

The second night, while sharing a Jamaican feast of callaloo, stuffed fish, and rice and peas, Angie confessed concerns about how many Jamaicans were going hungry and homeless on the island. She admitted to picking up the five-year-old twins, Rej and Duj, after finding them begging on a street corner. She'd unofficially adopted them, providing a home because their birth mother couldn't manage. "There are many orphanages in Montego Bay and all over the island," Angie said prompting me to visit one.

I asked why Rej stayed behind at the villa during the day when all the others headed off to school wearing brown khaki pants and yellow uniform shirts each morning. "He doesn't have 'polishable' brown shoes," replied Angie.

We moved poolside after dinner to watch over our children as they swam. It amazed me how quickly children made friends. I prayed that Angie's daughter and my Alyssa would treasure their newfound relationship and that it would be long lasting. I hoped the color of their skin would never come between them. I sat under the stars wondering how much 'polishable' brown shoes cost. Eventually, I extracted by boys from the pool and we padded off to the master bedroom. The boys and I soon fell asleep together in a king-sized bed gazing at the stars through the slats in the roof above.

The next day Angie drove us to town in her little beat-up Toyota to a strip mall where we would buy shoes for Rej. Afterward, we dropped him off at Sam Sharpe Square, where he caught his bus to go to school. His enormous smile spoke volumes, he sincerely desired an education.

We then maneuvered the pothole riddled streets to the orphanage Angie had spoken of at dinner. Blossom Gardens was situated high on Brandon Hill overlooking Montego Bay. We arrived unannounced at their gates, rang the bell and waited. A professional woman dressed in a skirt and jacket came out of the building to speak to us through the iron bars.

"We were hoping to visit the children," I said.

"You can't just show up and expect to be let in," the woman said.

I was embarrassed to have entertained the notion. "No problem," I replied as I turned to leave.

She unlocked the padlock. "Well, since you are here, you might as well come in."

We followed the woman inside down a narrow hallway to an office where we were handed a bottle of Purell and told to disinfect our hands. We were then led to a large open room where there were three rows of cribs in the middle, and a row of toddler beds lined up against the wall facing us. Beautiful black babies filled the cribs. Some slept, some cried, some stood.

"Let's hold them," I suggested.

The babies clung to us, but when we put them down they each shriveled up into a tight fetal position. I wondered if we were doing more harm than good as we moved from crib to crib. Sidney clutched onto a single child the entire time we were there so that he would only have to experience putting a baby down once. I carried Shaneka, a girl with obvious physical limitations who never spoke despite being more substantial and older than the other toddlers in the room. Shaneka wrapped her arms tightly around my body when it came time to put her down.

We then visited a smaller room where the babies were as young as six-weeks old. I picked up baby Katherine and rocked her in my arms while I paced the room. She cooed quietly until I gently placed her back in her crib. And then, she began wailing like a banshee. What a set of lungs! A

3

caregiver, I've come to know as Auntie Joy, scooped baby Katherine into her arms and purred into her tiny ear. The incident became the first of many innumerable acts of kindness I would witness of Auntie Joy. The woman who was escorting us through the orphanage lovingly chastised Auntie Joy. "You can't go spoilin' them," she said shaking a finger.

The older children had been playing outside in the yard when we first arrived. They'd moved inside to a staff room while we were holding the babies. I was reluctant to visit with the older children at first because I was worried about what they would think. Would they think we were there to pick out a child to take home with us as if we were choosing a puppy from the Humane Society? I could only imagine the path that had brought each of the children to their present circumstance, the last thing I wanted was to create false hope in any of those little minds.

We poked our noses through the door to say goodbye to the kids we'd seen outside when we were invited in. We obediently entered the room and took seats in folding chairs along the wall facing the children. They were playing a game that included lots of body movement, singing and smiling.

A precious boy with sparkling eyes and shoulder length dreadlocks jumped across the room to stand before me. He stuck out his hand saying, "Pleased to meet you. My name is Irishun." I later learned Irishun was the son of a Rasta man. I hadn't expected to find social graces in an orphanage.

A fiery lanky girl with a ferocious smile also ran across the room towards me and jumped into my lap. This girl had the most perfect straight white teeth I'd ever seen. I didn't know it yet, but this little firecracker was Ashley, the girl we would adopt. Anyone could tell that all of the children inside those walls craved attention. In that instant, I thought about Darwin's origin of the species; theorizing that in nature only the strongest survived. Ashley possessed an innate ability to propel her way into the foreground.

We remained with the older children until I suspected we had overstayed our welcome. Our chaperone then escorted us back to the iron gates where we thanked her for her time and said our goodbyes. She secured the padlock behind us leaving me to wonder what atrocities the children inside were being protected from.

"I wish we could take one home," Sidney said in his quiet way.

"They're not puppies," I replied.

My children and I piled into our expensive chartered van and drove away from Blossom Gardens towards the villa in Ironshore. We splashed in the pool, ate jerk chicken prepared by our own private chef, and slept in comfortable beds with iron gates surrounding the property to keep us safe at night.

Two distinctly Jamaican sounds woke me up in the morning; crickets singing beneath my window and the neighborhood dogs barking. The purposeful howling somehow sounded like an SOS call.

I've always loved the stillness of the early morning. It is my think time. I sat alone by the pool with thoughts whirling through my head like a Van Gogh painting. A flock of small green parrots chattered overhead. "They're not puppies," kept moving through my head.

I pictured our home in Canada where we maintained three dogs, four children, and a tank full of tropical fish. My husband was accustomed to my bringing home strays, but our house was full to the gills. And yet, I couldn't help but think about the possibility of taking one of those sweet deserving orphans home with us.

My youngest son, Kaiden, interrupted my thoughts by climbing into my lap to burrow his downy head into my breast. We mutually enjoyed our morning cuddling ritual before he asked permission to jump into the pool. Kaiden swam as I sat speculating about the difficulty of the Jamaican adoption process. It was a lazy day that rolled in and out of my mind like the tide.

Meanwhile, the wafting smell of bacon emerged from Angie's kitchen. I would learn that bacon was a luxury in Jamaica rarely gracing the breakfast table, yet all of our Angie-prepared breakfasts reminded me of a Sunday Easter brunch. It embarrassed me how decadent we were eating knowing that there were so many little ones going without food on the island. Angie daily prepared an abundance of cut fruit, bacon, eggs, pancakes, and freshly squeezed orange juice.

Angie agreed to keep the boys at the villa, so that they could swim, while Alyssa and I went into Montego Bay to visit the Child Development Agency. We'd arranged for our driver, Easten, to pick us up after breakfast.

We arrived at 4 Kerr Crescent Street, climbed the two stories of concrete stairs, and found a glass door with block lettering on it marking the entrance to Children's Services. Inside was a small waiting area, thankfully cooled by an oscillating fan.

A scattering of folding chairs lined one wall. I sat in front of the fan for a brief moment hoping to dry my back before a distinguished black man in his late sixties walked through a Dutch door that separated the social worker's cubicles from the waiting area. We were the only white people in the room commanding his immediate attention. I felt as though I'd made a spectacle of myself looking quite like vanilla ice cream, melting before his eyes.

May I help you? He asked.

I explained my intentions.

"International adoptions can be very long and drawn out. There is not an aspect of your life that they will not look at. Even Madonna has been told *no.*" Only a month earlier, on April 3, 2009, a Malawian court had ruled against the pop music singer, Madonna, from taking a three-year-old girl away from Malawi on residency grounds.

Mr. Sidney Grant handed me an international pre-application form along with his business card that read Regional Director of Adoptions. I took the pleasant surprise meeting as a sign of divine intervention, accepting both the card and the form graciously.

We took the short application form back to the villa where our Jamaican friends helped us fill it out by the pool. Angie the cook, Easten the driver, and Avian the pool boy, each encouraged me to write down their names as the required Jamaica references. The next day I returned the completed application to Mr. Grant to be reviewed. If we were approved, we could expect an application package mailed to our home in approximately six weeks.

Two

THE GREAT WHITE NORTH

Back in Canada, my husband Sid reluctantly agreed to investigate a Jamaican adoption. Our protagonist, the process was set to motion when I turned in the single page pre-application form. Sid thought I'd set my sights on a specific child, but Alyssa helped explain that we'd been placed on a list, and were waiting to be matched to an available child.

The next step in the early stages of the adoption was to wait four to six weeks to receive a response to our application. The answer would be provided acknowledging receipt of the form, as well as to inform us whether our request was denied or approved. If the request passed, we would receive a formal application and a list of required documents. We would need to supply proof of income, character references, birth certificates, medicals, and pictures as proof of identity. But first, we would be required to produce a letter from a licenced adoption agency in Alberta proving we had an affiliation with them, and that they were committed to providing our home study.

The first time I approached my husband about the possibility of bringing another child into our lives he declared me of an unsound mind, having finally gone completely nuts. Usually we saw eye to eye, but on this issue were polar opposites because we fundamentally disagreed about adopting. One of us was going to lose this argument because compromising was not an option. Either we did, or we did not. He couldn't possibly understand how deeply I was affected by the visit to the orphanage.

There are two factions to the experience of every adoption; there is what you go through emotionally and what you can *do* to make it happen.

The hardest part is the emotional side of things including the insufferable waiting. I can now empathize with people who so desperately want to be parents, yet may not be able to conceive a child naturally. The last couple of weeks of most pregnancies inevitably seem to crawl by, but with an adoption the time goes on with no definite due date. Our adoption took twenty-four months from the time we turned in our paperwork to the time Ashley left the island. That's as long as the gestation period of an elephant!

Interestingly, in preparing for an adoption one often experiences a psychological pregnancy. Potential adoptive parents may create a fantasy child in their heads about who they've envisioned joining their family. The child in my head was a girl who wore a yellow strapless sundress, had wiry shoulder length hair, and played on a warm sandy seashore.

I soon shared hopes of adopting with other flight attendants I worked with, including Donna K., whom I connected with immediately because we were both raising teenage daughters. One morning we were in the aft galley of the airplane. We'd finished service, restocked our carts, and sat down in our jump seats to take a break before securing the cabin for landing. Donna sat flipping pages through *O, the Oprah Magazine* as we talked. I'd already explained where we were in the adoption process. Suddenly, Donna thrust the magazine towards me, "Here's the little one in your head!" The photograph showed my fantasy child including her yellow sundress and untamed hair. Donna ripped the page out and gave it to me. I've carried Oprah's little girl with me ever since.

I decided to focus on what I could take action with rather than what was beyond my control. The first step in the process, in Canada, was to make an International Adoption Application with Alberta Children's Services. The information we provided on the form was collected under the authority of the Child, Youth and Family Enhancement Act.

Once the document was stamped with the official seal of approval we were required to provide it to a specific licenced agency that would request a child intervention record check, known as a CYIM. It is a review to determine whether an adult has an existing intervention record with Children and Youth Services.

I did not initially realize how critical the relationship between adoptive parents and a licenced agency was. It proved to be so much more than merely having someone oversee our completion of the required pre-adoption training and providing a home study report. We would need to affiliate with an organization that would *believe* in us and make a recommendation to the Alberta Adoption Services for approval of the home study. It was not at all as easy as it sounded.

The first adoption agency we chose required being paid seven hundred and fifty dollars in *cash* at the initial visit. I delivered the money and the signed the CYIM request. The counsellor assured me that we were not the first family they'd worked with that had experienced troubles with a teenager. They provided me with the Letter of Affiliation and promised to govern the adoption procedure including providing a home study. The counsellor also gave me the first SAFE questionnaire with instructions for Sid and me to complete it, independently of each other, before returning it at our earliest convenience.

Alberta implemented the Structured Analysis Family Evaluation, or SAFE model, for the home assessment process in 2008. It is a methodology that provides standardized practices for the description and evaluation of prospective adoptive parents. It is a structured evaluation process that assists practitioners in identifying and addressing strengths, and areas of concern, that may impede safe and effective parenting.

Sid reluctantly agreed to participate in the questionnaire. We shared our responses only after completing the forms. One of the strongest contributing factors to the success of our marriage is our appreciation for each other's sense of humour. The first question asked, "What do you like most about your wife?"

Sid answered, "My wife is driven and headstrong, when she gets something in her head she forges forward until she completes the task."

The second question asked, "What do you like least about your wife."

"My wife is driven and headstrong, when she gets something in her head she forges forward until she completes the task."

I returned the completed SAFE questionnaire in good faith. I'd also assembled the stack of requested documents that needed notarization before being included in the dossier for the Jamaican government. The counsellor promised the task would be completed by the end of the month before we headed back to Jamaica. She also advised me that the home study would be delayed because the person assigned to our case was on summer holiday.

The completed questionnaire is the first point of contact introducing applicants hoping to adopt with an agency to support them through the process. It also assists the social worker in determining which questions need more detailed discussion during the home study. It is considered to be "respectful of an applicant family's expectation for open, transparent, and fair treatment in a sensitive area of their lives."

The SAFE questionnaire leads the respondent into describing themselves and their spouse. There is also significant focus on the couple's original families. The content gathered informs the adoption agency intimate self-described details about the individuals, family, its characteristics and capabilities.

It is the affiliated adoption agency's duty to provide a comprehensive examination of the prospective adoptive parents. The home study being the primary hurdle in the adoption process. No adoption, whether private, domestic, or international will come to pass until it is completed and approved. The cost of the home study is about $3,000, and the financial burden falls solely on the shoulders of the prospective parents.

A provincially licensed adoption practitioner conducts the home study but is not authorized to approve a placement. They make a recommendation as to the parents' suitability for adoption. In Canada, only a Director of the Provincial Ministry in charge of adoption makes the final decision. Once the documentation receives approval from province, the Government of Alberta provides it to the foreign country and Citizenship and Immigration Canada.

The social worker explores the prospective parents reasons to adopt, expectations for the child, and any specific needs a child might have. In our case, we intended to bring an older child into our home with a long history of abuse in her formative primary years. We would have to discuss malnutrition, physical and emotional trauma, deprivation, institutional care, the fact that we had limited social and medical information about our child, and how she would have to adjust to a new country and language. *Who in their right mind would volunteer for such a project?*

Two days before our return to Jamaica I learned that the dossier documents continued to sit negligently on the counsellor's desk, waiting for notarization. I should have followed up with the small warning I'd felt nagging at my heart, but I wasn't receptive to the voice of the Holy Spirit's instant words, yet. I located a paralegal at the last minute who completed the necessary task for a four hundred dollar fee. I picked the dossier up on the way to the airport, and stuffed it inside my big red bag, to take to the Government of Jamaica.

Three

Under The Mango Tree

The boys, Alyssa, and I took the red-eye back to Montego Bay in June when school let out for the year. Natural consequences dictated that Nadia remain in Calgary to redo Science ten. In Jamaica, we wound our way through the long yellow corridor leading to the row of previously intimidating immigration officers. We brought fewer bags on that trip intending on wearing less in the Caribbean sun.

Easten stood among the hordes of taxi drivers to take us back to the villa where Angie and her family awaited our arrival under the mango tree. Excited girl scream pierced the air with Alyssa and Charnelle jumping up and down doing puppy circles around each other. That night, we shared the first of many vivacious meals around the family dining table where Kaiden would fall asleep in my arms. I would carry him to the master bedroom to tuck him in, beside me, where we would sleep like kittens.

Each morning I pushed aside the protective iron gates and unfolded the bedroom's wooden accordion doors that Avian always closed at night when we were sleeping. I padded my way past the pool towards the kitchen to make coffee. Angie always set out a cup, a spoon, and a small pitcher of sweetened condensed milk, covered by a cloth, to keep the pesky little ants away. She put the grounds in the filter and filled the percolator with water. Random thoughts wandered freely through my head as I brewed the Blue Mountain coffee. I tried to take it all in using all of my senses, smelling coffee, and trash burning. I took my mug poolside to mentally prepare for the day, willing myself to find the fluid rhythm of Jamaica.

The rest of the house began stirring. Avian arrived to sweep and clean the swimming pool for us. I could tell by his glazed eyes that he enjoyed smoking marijuana; in Jamaica they call it 'ganja.' We never saw Avian smoke, and it never seemed to keep him from doing his duties around the villa. He was always the first person I'd see working in the morning. I knew he picked up the towels and lounge chair pillows, put away the pool toys, and closed up the house long after we went to bed. Avian had a quick genuine smile and always treated my family respectfully.

Soon after, Kaiden cannonballed his way into Avian's clean pool. I'm certain it was the sound of the splash that always drew Sidney out of bed. Sidney would plant a quick sleepy peck on my cheek before joining his brother in the pool for a game of Marco Polo.

Angie and Duj soon returned from the open-air market lugging several bags of fruit out of the hatch back of Angie's vehicular clunker. I thanked Angie for the coffee as I poured a second cup. "Good morning, Erika, what would you like for breakfast?"

"We want to eat Jamaican. Whatever you normally fix for your own family we would love to try."

"Do you want ackee and saltfish?"

"We'd love ackee and saltfish," I replied.

The boys swam, I read, and Alyssa slept."

Once our bellies were stretched beyond imagination, Alyssa and I returned to Montego Bay with the adoption papers while the boys continued swimming under Angie's watchful eye. The city smelled like sewage. It was dirty and hot. Sweat dripped uncomfortably down my spine as Easten maneuvered through the traffic and the city's winding streets. We drove on the left side of the road, unless we needed to avoid the deep potholes.

Cobblestone pavers surrounded Sam Sharpe Square, a central area named after a Baptist deacon who was hung during the 'Christmas Rebellion' in 1894. Tall bronze statues depicting a group of slaves stood in permanent readiness and seemed to be listening to the freedom fighters' message. A tall clock tower hovered over Humber Avenue, no longer working, yet a firm reminder of the city's youth and more prosperous times. Still further up the mountainous slope, in the center of the street, sat a water tower also constructed of cobblestone. The tower, now in a permanent state of idleness, once provided fresh spring water for the entire metropolis. I used these markers time and time again to lead me back to the Childhood Development Agency (CDA) where I fought to bring Ashley home.

Easten parked his van on the side of the road, promising to keep an eye out for Alyssa and me. We had no expectations as to how long we might be waiting inside the CDA. We bound up the concrete stairwell through the glass doors, right into Mr. Grant, the Adoptions Director. The words, "Madonna got her baby!" tumbled out of my mouth, announcing that the pop singer had been granted adoption privileges of a three-year-old girl named Mercy James.

I felt like a kid waiting for Christmas morning my holding my bundle of paperwork to turn in to Mrs. O'Connor; the sole adoption agent for Montego Bay and its surrounding area. Alyssa and I sat for several minutes in the small waiting room immensely grateful for the oscillating fan drying our backs.

Apparently, it was intake day at the CDA, because I saw a handful of adults arriving with children and then leaving without them. I began to bear witness to the effects of trauma on a child. I would observe tiny bodies walking self-sufficiently at the orphanage where the children were often sick, didn't seem to gain weight on schedule, and showed signs of emotional disturbance, cognitive delays, and disabilities. The environment seemed so overwhelmingly dismal that it almost discouraged me from even trying to do anything to help. I naively thought that love could change anything at all.

Mrs. O'Connor summoned me into her office using quick drawing movements of her hand. I complied instantly, entering her workspace carrying my red shoulder bag stuffed with our papers. We sat, waited, and watched as she opened a manila folder on her desk. "Ms. Isnor, you have been approved at this stage, now we need to acquire documents." She handed me an approval letter with the list of requirements.

"I have them prepared for you." We made eye contact for the first time.

One at a time she asked for, and received the notarized papers. Ms. O'Connor smiled apparently satisfied. Then, she picked up and waved a letter in her hand. "This reference letter is not signed."

I'd provided childcare for my friend Christina in our home the year before Kaiden started school. Christina provided us the reference letter via email, and no it was not signed. I scoured through the bag looking for my address book and cell phone. Then prayed as I dialed, hoping someone on the other end would answer. Trent, Christina's husband picked up on the third ring.

"Hello Trent, this is Erika. I'm in Jamaica turning in documents," I said suspecting that I was racking up a phone bill that would cost Sid a small fortune. "I have Christina's reference letter, but it is not signed. Do you have a fax machine?"

"Yes." Thank God. The line crackled as I repeated the number twice before the words *call ended* appeared on the cell phone screen.

Ms. Bradford, another social worker, entered the cubicle to hand the signed reference letter to Mrs. O'Connor that had arrived by facsimile. "This is the fastest that anyone has ever turned in all the necessary paperwork."

I shrugged. I got things done when I wanted something.

"You will now be placed on the waiting list for any available children. When a child comes up that we think is a match for the kind of child you have requested we will contact you."

"What is the normal time frame? How long should we expect to wait? So many questions danced through my mind.

"There is no telling. There are so many people on the waiting list; since you are looking for an older child it should not be long."

There was no more I could do for the moment. I intended on picking up the boys at the villa and heading straight to the beach to play with my children. Until then, I'd been on a mission specifically focused on the adoption. It was high time we relaxed and enjoyed ourselves in the Jamaican sun.

I'd no sooner opened a Red Stripe beer back at the villa than there was a phone call for me from Ms. O'Connor. "Ms. Isnor, I have a child on the list, a boy who is seven-years-old." *My God that was fast!*

"Yes…?" I said, waiting for more information.

"He is available now for adoption. He lives in a foster home here in Montego Bay. Would you be able to come into the office at around ten in the morning?

"May I bring my children?"

"Yea mon. Bring your children."

"Very well…see you in the morning. *Oh,* what is his name?

"Tejah mon. His name is Tejah."

I hung up the phone feeling a bit shell-shocked. My children swam in the pool until Angie called us in for super where Kaiden, once again, fell asleep at the table. My little energizer bunny had run out of gas. I wasn't worried that Kaiden hadn't eaten much of his dinner, knowing he would make it up for it at breakfast. I carried him to the master bedroom followed by his weary big brother.

The rain started falling at midnight. I've always loved the rhythm of rain tapping on the roof and leaving a fresh bouquet in its departure. It rained nearly every afternoon when we lived in the state of Georgia. We often lost our electricity, lit candles, and pulled out a deck of cards to play gin rummy until it let up. The rain didn't caress my heart that night but gripped it. Soon a torrential downpour accumulated a good three inches of water on the slippery white tile floor.

Rej, Duj, and Alyssa ran through the water unplugging the lights. "*STOP!*" I yelled. "Everyone get off the floor! Jump on my bed! Don't touch the plugs!" I didn't trust the wiring in the house on a dry sunny day; in this rain I *feared* it. Thankfully, everyone listened to me finding higher ground on the bed and couches.

The night sky went white with simultaneous lightning and thunder. I wasn't exactly sure what God was saying, but He was speaking loudly. His omnipresence could not be ignored. Even Kaiden woke up. He curled against me as tight as a roly-poly bug, sticking his fingers in his ears to block out the noise. I covered a boy on each side of me holding my arms over their backs like a mother bird protecting hatchlings. We huddled close beneath the storm that raged above our heads until finally falling asleep tangled together like knotted fishing lines.

The morning sky snuck through the wooden accordion doors of our bedroom, shimmering brightly like the inside of an albacore shell. I woke up earlier than usual because I'd planned on going to the open-air market with Angie and Rej. I'd promised to bring fresh fruit back to the orphanage.

The rain saturated the streets of Mobay, it stunk, and I wasn't entirely sure what the brown gunk was that I walked through. Angie and I maneuvered the suspicious puddles while we inspected the carts of hopeful vendors.

There were no other white women at the market so I stuck out remarkably pale. I followed Angie like a wide-eyed child from stall to stall as she bartered for our food. I smelled ganja for the first time since arriving on the island. I snapped photographs of the colourful vegetables and interesting people. I took a picture of a Rasta man who stared straight into my lens before demanding money for his image. I was out of my element, but never felt unsafe or uncomfortable.

Angie explained that the sellers on the outside of the market asked less for their wares and produce that the people inside who had paid rent for their stalls The outside vendors took the chance of getting goods impounded in the event of a police sweep. I listened to Angie as she bargained for mangos, watermelon, and papayas...all the fruit my chiLdren and I devoured each morning at her breakfast table. I spent only $3,500 JMD, or thirty-five US dollars, feeding seventy-two children at the orphanage.

We finished our grocery shopping before seven o'clock in the morning, returning to the villa where Angie, Rej, Duj, and Avian cut it up in the tiny kitchen. Those beautiful people filled two large coolers with Ziploc baggies of fresh fruit, giving so freely of their hearts and time. My babies continued sleeping as the Jamaicans around them made preparations to feed some of the less fortunate children on the island.

Alyssa, the boys, and I delivered the fruit before returning to the CDA to see Tejah's file. We dragged the heavy coolers to the front gates at Blossom Gardens, rang the bell, and were greeted warmly by Carmelina, the same woman who had initially opened the gates for us. This time, we were allowed to stay with the children as long as we wished. I felt torn between playing with the orphans and learning about a boy named Tejah. We relinquished the coolers to the aides in the kitchen, who promptly set out great grey aluminum trays on the tables for us to fill plastic bowls with fruit.

Ms. Matthews and the Mennonite volunteers, Rhonda and Mandy, were in the yard supervising the toddlers. Ms. Matthews ordered the toddlers to sit on the picnic bench prior to giving them fruit. Thirteen toddlers, none of which came up to my kneecaps, climbed up onto the bench wordlessly to wait for their treat.

"I don't know how she does it. I can't get my own children to sit at a table quietly," I complained.

"Fear," Ronda explained. They fear Ms. Matthews." Ms. Matthews began handing me the plastic bowls to give to the children.

Miss Mathews was a small spindly woman with lean arms and legs who stood no more than five-foot-three inches tall, but maintained an intimidating presence. Her eyes darted quickly, as did her hand when she slapped the back of a child's head or legs. She reminded me of a spider biding time waiting for an unsuspecting victim to be entangled in her web.

"Give this one to a small child," Ms. Matthews instructed. She made it perfectly clear that she preferred the smallest children by giving them the biggest bowls of fruit. Ms. Matthew was capable of touching a child gently one moment and back handing another in the blink of an eye.

Naturally, the children's clothing took a beating from the juicy fruit that quickly disappeared from the plastic bowls. Ms. Matthews brought a bucket of water and a couple of cloths for us to clean up the little faces. An aide appeared from behind the concrete building carrying a Tupperware bin full of clean clothing. We were instructed to take off the children's dirty clothes, wipe down their sticky bodies, and redress them. I watched Ms. Matthews harshly wipe one little boy's face, and then chastise him for crying.

The quality of the clothes in the Tupperware bin surprised me. "The clothing is all donated; much of it is the outgrown clothing of the wealthy," Rhonda, one of the Mennonite girls explained.

Ms. Matthews tossed me a pink shirt for the child whose face I was cleaning. "But he is a *boy!*" I challenged. Ms. Matthews shrugged and walked away. I threw the pink shirt back into the bin and grabbed one with a picture of a truck on it. The small defiance felt delightful.

The older children spilt into the yard after having finished their morning studies. Each child accepted a bowl of fruit and ate it with their hands before running away to play in the dirt yard.

The only time we were ever warned against using a camera was on our first visit. Afterwards, we watched many of the visiting volunteers taking pictures without reserve. I hesitated before pulling out my digital camera to document our stay. I snapped photos of several of the children under the mango tree growing in the middle of the dirt play yard. The girls flocked towards me beneath the tree to get their pictures taken. I made mental notes hoping to remember something specific about each child; Ashley wore a pink rayon skirt and a simple yellow cotton t-shirt. She climbed up on the bench, posed, and gave me a perfectly practiced smile. Julieanne and Jodianne were identical twins; Julieanne demonstrated a fierce protectiveness over her sister who suffered from cerebral palsy. Jodieanne warmed up slowly to strangers, keeping her eyes down and hiding her mouth when she smiled. Daysha seemed a bit cunning, always fighting with Ashley to be in the forefront. Kimeshya, the round pistol, needed a good tickle. The girls all had unique pasts and special unaddressed needs; they all deserved a hand up in life.

The older children in the yard formed two lines to go inside the cafeteria for their lunch. Kaiden and Sidney joined the boys' line just as they would after recess at their own school. I held a finger up to my lips hoping to keep the girls I'd photographed quiet and out of trouble. I walked behind Ashley as the line made its way into the washroom where the children cleaned up for lunch. And then, I turned around in time to see Ms. Matthews grab Sidney's arm.

"What's going on?" I asked calmly.

"I told him to give me the bag," Ms. Matthews stated.

I looked down at the heavy red bag I'd asked Sidney to carry for me. He knew what it contained and that it was important. He'd taken the responsibility seriously and I valued his trustworthiness. My spidey senses tingled. I felt both instinctively protective of my young son and intensely proud of him for possessing the courage to stand up against that miserable woman.

Ms. Matthews leaned forward to spit her words at me. "He refused to do what I asked. He should listen to adults." I became fixed on the yellowness of her eyes, posturing as tall as a mother bear protecting her cub.

"I am his mother, he need only listen to me," I stated never taking my eyes off Ms. Matthews. I felt Sidney's warm breath behind me. I wondered what he was thinking when he saw Ms. Matthews grab my wrist.

"Your skin is white, my skin is black, but our blood is the same colour." Sidney instinctively stuck very close to me, but I noticed that none of the other children were bothered by the commotion. I assumed that they must

19

have been accustomed to such chaotic confrontations. We soon filed into the cafeteria where Sidney and Kaiden remained glued to my side.

Ashley sat next to Alyssa, leaning those long, svelte, dark arms around my teenage daughter. They both looked up and smiled just before the camera captured what would become our *ahh haa* moment. Later, in Canada when I printed it, I realized that what we had hoped to find had been right in front of our faces all along. The thing I liked most about the photograph was how it captured Alyssa's content spirit and radiated her angelic kindness. These girls belonged together. They *looked* like sisters.

The children at Blossom Gardens were never permitted to make a peep of sound in the cafeteria. They were all aware of the rules and they followed them. Ms. Matthews paraded between the tables tapping the back of the children's chairs with a long yardstick. Ironically, the godless woman led the gentle children in mealtime prayers.

Sidney stayed beside me holding tightly onto the red adoption bag. Once prayers were finished, Ms. Matthews headed to the kitchen to get the large serving trays. Those trays were as big as four extra-large pizza boxes put together. Each tray held thirty or more plastic bowls of food. Ms. Matthews handed me a tray instructing me to disperse the meals to the children. And then, Ms. Matthews tried to hand Sidney another full tray of food. "He should help," she stated.

Sidney's eyes grew wide. He understood Ms. Matthews expected him to follow her instructions. He also knew she expected him to drop the tray of food, and that it would clatter to the tile floor and make a huge terrible mess.

"He will help me pass out the bowls from my tray," I responded firmly. Ms. Matthews shrugged. She set down the second tray and retreated towards the kitchen. And then, I handed the food bowls to Sidney who gave them to the children.

Lunch was Spam spread inside white bread, cut twice into perfectly shaped triangles that Kaiden called sailboats. Hormel Foods introduced the pre-cooked meat product during the US Military occupation after World War II, since fresh meat was difficult to get to the soldier. It is often a food associated with economic hardship because of its relative low cost. There wasn't a scrap of Spam left in the children's lunch bowls.

We prepared to leave after lunch promising to have our driver bring us back soon. Our private chauffeur waited in the van outside the gates. A 'charter driver' would sit for hours as tourists experienced daily excursions on the island. It was nine forty-five in the morning, and it was already stinking *hot!* I learned to carry a cooler in the van with water and soda chilling over ice. My kids and I drank water like fish in Jamaica to keep hydrated, but I never saw Easten take a single sip of anything. It amazed me how he sat in the heat, wearing a pressed long-sleeved shirt and pants, with endless patience. We left Blossom Gardens headed downtown into the sweltering city to see Tejah's file before returning to the villa where we planned on cooling off in the pool.

I wasn't nervous anymore climbing the stairwell back up to the CDA. I tried imagining what the little boy was like that was being proposed to us as we sat and waited for Ms. O'Connor. I honestly hadn't considered adopting a boy, my thoughts had always been of Oprah's wild haired girl wearing the yellow dress. I looked down at my youngest son, whose little body still had so very much growing to do. The only thing we actually knew about Tejah was that he was born in the same year as Kaiden.

Mrs. O'Connor suddenly breezed through the waiting room. She handed me a file and invited us to move to her cubicle before exiting through the glass door. "I'll be right back with Tejah." I stood straight up. Did I hear her right? Was the boy here? So close? I thought we were there to look at a manila file, not to visit with a child.

I learned, from the file, that Tejah lived with the superintendent of his school in a foster home. I examined a small collection of his work samples, and read the comments on his report card. "Tejah has a hard time focusing and staying on task." *Red flag, red flag, red flag!*

A commotion erupted in the waiting room that prompted me to glance over the partition. Ms. O'Connor was dragging a very large boy towards us who literally held onto the walls with his fingernails. My children looked back and forth between each other without speaking a word.

I took in a deep breath hoping to make a connection with Tejah, finally getting his attention when I drew nine stick figures of the members of our family. I wrote down a name beside each sketch on paper in my green journal. "Can you draw your family too Tejah?" I asked.

He drew four detailed stick figures complete with curly hair and clothing. He wrote "Tom" under his first drawing, just as I had labeled mine "Sid."

"Who is Tom?" I asked.

"He mi Papa," Tejah answered speaking Patois.

Tejah enjoyed drawing, yet remained isolated in his own world, not interested in letting us in. Ms. Wilton agreed to our taking him back to the villa for a good meal and a swim that afternoon after we promised to return him to the CDA by four pm.

Tejah told me that his favourite food was dumplings on the drive to the villa. Upon our arrival, I passed that information on to Angie who immediately disappeared into her kitchen to make them for him.

"Race to get your swim trunks on!" I challenged the boys. I pulled out a pair of red and white Hawaiian print swim trunks from Sidney's suitcase for Tejah, but when I turned around to give them to him he looked positively green.

"Mi sick." Tejah goaned. I considered that he might truly be ill due to all of the excitement surrounding his outing with us, but soon realized that he was absolutely terrified of the water. It took me over an hour to get him into the pool. First, he touched the water with his toes and fingers. I slowly coaxed him into sitting on the first step of the pool, and then finally held him on my hip the way that I would a small child, blowing bubbles into his face, and twirling him about, before he even cracked a smile. I glanced towards the deep end of the pool where my boys were swimming like fish receiving very little of my attention.

The three boys sat together on the diving board for a picture. Sidney who would be turning nine in October had inherited his father's athletic physique; he was a bit bigger and taller than most of his peers. Kaiden on the other hand, was of average size for his age, but thin and wiry. Interestingly, Tejah was the largest of the three boys despite supposedly being chronically the youngest.

I suspected that Tejah had more issues than we were prepared to deal with. Assimilating Tejah into our family would have been at the expense of our own children. We shared an afternoon with a sweet boy, but we all knew right away that he would not become a family member. Alyssa and the boys stayed with Angie while I returned an exhausted Tejah to Ms. Wilton. I hoped he might find less difficulty getting into a swimming pool after that. Later, I learned that Tejah, along with siblings, had been adopted by an American couple in Florida, where I am confident he has learned how to swim.

We intended on devoting the entire next day to Doctor's Cave beach in Montego Bay, arranging to have Easten pick us up right after breakfast. I packed the cooler with refreshments, grabbed towels and sunscreen for a relaxing day by the water. Doctor's Cave, a hidden gem, was a small stretch of land first opened in 1906 that could initially only be accessed through a cave. The $1,200 JMD, or twelve US dollar entrance fee allowed us to spend an afternoon on one of the most serene places in the world.

We set our towels out on the shore where I sat in a rented beach chair watching my children bury each other up to the neck in the sand. I noticed a fair-headed mother playing with two similarly fair-haired girls and a third small black child close to me. Black children with white people attracted attention. "Is that your son?" I asked while reapplying sunscreen to Kaiden's vulnerable back and nose.

"Not yet, we're in the process of adopting him."

"Really? We just turned in our dossier and have begun visiting with children on the waiting list." The red headed woman smiled. Later, I learned that in Jamaica there is no *real* waiting list. "We have been volunteering at Blossom Gardens." I said.

The woman's smile warmed. She extended a freckled hand to me in greeting. "My name is Meghan. I am the Adoptions Coordinator for 'Embracing Orphans.' You need to meet Carl." She dug through a handbag to find a pen to write down Carl's phone number. There are no accidents; meeting Meghan on the beach and having her give me Carl's contact information was a gift from God. My sister calls those precious gifts diamonds from heaven.

I imagined myself walking down an endless stretch of beach after Meghan and her brood left. I saw a glimmer of beautiful white light on a specific place in the sand. I bent down and picked up a handful of it, letting the ordinary sand sift through my fingers, until nothing was left but the rare gift of a precious gem. The gift, meant for me to find, provided a special glimmer of understanding. It propelled me forward providing an understanding that I was on the right path, even if I didn't know where I was going.

My heart felt a measure of contentment even though my skin felt red. It was time for everyone to get out of the sun. We returned to the villa to another wonderful evening meal of Angie's before retiring.

I left a quick voicemail for Carl from the house phone before we headed back down to the seashore the next day. I referenced my chance encounter with Meghan on the beach, explaining how were looking for a girl around six or seven-years-old. Only a matter of minutes passed before Carl rang back. He was in Montego Bay staying on Gloucester Avenue at the Caribic House. "If you know the hip strip, there is a restaurant right across the street called Margaritaville. I could meet you there, in say about an hour, if that works for you."

"It works perfectly! We'll be on the lower deck near the water."

Carl, a genuine Christian missionary, was also a teacher from Walla Walla, Washington who couldn't stand to see children give up the hope of being loved. He'd founded 'Embracing Orphans' to help the needy children in Jamaica; he'd posted two blogs on the website before we ever met:

> *Current Adoption News*
> *July 5, 2009*
>
> *If you are interested in adopting a six/seven year old girl from Blossom Gardens please email me ASAP*
>
> *July 6, 2009*
>
> *Again, there is a seven-year-old girl, beautiful and well mannered who is ready for adoption, and we are getting the inside track here. If you are interested pray, and then let me know ASAP.*

Ironically, my kids had their minds set on tackling the steep hundred-and-twenty foot water slide at Margaritaville that same afternoon. The intimidating slide wound its way from the rooftop terrace into the warm Caribbean Sea below. The four of us arrived at the top arguing about who would be the first to go down. The majority ruled that I would be their guinea pig.

I sat down, criss-crossed my arms over my chest, and took the plunge. I had to make a quick decision whether to plug my nose, or hold the top of my swimming suit on. I chose the latter, so salt water flushed my nostrils as I shot out of the yellow tube like a clown out of a circus cannon. Shouts of joy followed close behind me when Alyssa and the boys catapulted into the ocean. Kaiden's pure rambunctious giggle sent us all into fits of sputtering laughter, once we accumulated together in the seawater below.

We swam to the floating deck where I laid claim to a lounge chair to work on my tan. I supervised the kids, watching them jump on the two giant water trampolines that were anchored near the base of the slide.

When Carl arrived, I quickly pulled my cover-up on over my bikini, having the impression that he was a man of the cloth. The excitement I heard in Carl's voice on the phone rose as we spoke face to face. He testified, "I just finished praying for a family for Ashley when you called."

Carl agreed to facilitate a formal introduction to Ashley in the morning. He encouraged me to write down contact information for the people of authority in Jamaica. I learned that Mrs. Geneva Brown managed Blossom Gardens, Mr. Bowen headed international adoptions, and the official stamp of approval to adopt came from the Adoption Board in Kingston; specifically Ms. Marjorie Tumming. Most importantly, Carl directed me to embracingorphans.org where we viewed a picture of the little girl known as 'Ashley.'

We left Margaritaville when they closed the slide at dusk, sun kissed and weary.

Early the next morning, we arrived at Blossom Gardens armed with our reference from Carl. "The older children are still in their classroom if you want to join them," directed Carmelina. I noticed that each time we returned as visitors, we were given more and more liberty to move around the orphanage and interact with the children.

Ashley's classroom looked like one from my childhood with a long chalkboard lining the front wall, and a big brown oak desk resting right in front of it. Ms. Cambell, her teacher, had personalized the walls with the children's artwork, filled the shelves with books, and set out a round braided rug beneath an old wooden rocking chair where she read stories to her students. She'd assembled learning centers by pushing sets of four desks together where the children worked.

I watched a group of teenage missionaries present a puppet show from the doorway. The volunteers were instructing the children how to make their own paper bag puppets using crayons, glue, and yarn. My boys joined the morning craft project eagerly, sitting at the first set of tables with Irishun. Alyssa jumped right in as well helping the kids.

I weaved my way through the learning centers in search of the little girl named Ashley. The first child that caught my eye was a stocky five-year-old boy sleeping on the desk despite the noisy chatter in the classroom. I learned his name was Daniel, and that he slept on his desk all day most days.

Ashley sat next to Daniel, holding a polaroid picture of herself with one of the Mennonite volunteers. I recognized her beautiful face from the image that I'd seen on Carl's website. I knew she was one of the girls I'd taken photos of under the mango tree because she was wearing the same clothing. The pink rayon skirt and stained yellow t-shirt, so striking a contrast, next to her dark skin. Her small plastic chair practically swallowed her tiny malnourished body. What I didn't see was the damage caused by emotional abuse behind that practiced smile.

And then, all hell broke loose. Sabrina Williams, the pretty girl with the blackened tooth and light brown hair, grabbed the photograph Ashley held in her hands and ran away with it. Ashley burst into tears and fought like a feral hog trying to get it back. Sabrina taunted Ashley by crinkling the picture up in the palm of her hand, and then throwing it in her face. Ashley seemingly dissolved into a heap on her desk, and hung her head like a wounded animal.

Daniel slept through all of it.

"That wasn't very nice now was it? I said, bending down to her level, and wrapping my arms around her shaking shoulders. "Hey, I took lots of pictures yesterday, and I'm certain I have one of you. I'll bring it back next time I come for a visit," I promised.

That ruckus in the classroom, and Ashley's tears ended as fast as they had begun. I don't know why those little red flags didn't pop up for me then. Hindsight shows me that the distractibility was a clear sign of her primitive reflexes. I was blinded by the cute little puppy syndrome, unaware of the obvious signs of neuro-developmental delay. I had no idea how deeply marred by childhood trauma this beautiful child already was. In that moment, I became smitten with Ashley. Instantly, I made it my mission to fight against all the odds stacked against our favor to bring her to our home.

Our Jamaican vacation soon ended and I had no idea when we might be coming back. Kaiden fell asleep as our plane landed in Calgary. I carried him piggyback style down through the empty airport terminal with a sleepy-eyed Sidney following slowly ten feet behind. My dear husband, compassionate to my wanderlust, stood waiting at the bottom of the escalator where travellers emerged from their globetrotting. He ruffled Sidney's blondness, gathered up our suitcases, and drove home, to deposit us in our own beds where we slept like dogs until the sun rose. I didn't hear the din of crickets first thing in the morning, so I knew I wasn't dreaming, and we were home.

In Canada, the prospective adoption would cause a disruption in our home life threatening our equilibrium. I knew the entire family was about to embark on an adventure that would be life changing for all of us. Most importantly, our marriage found an unexpected crossroad. The proposition of an adoption became both exciting and scary because I didn't know if Sid would be willing to walk down that road or not. Sid would say that I started the process with guns blazing, "Ready, fire, aim!"

The ball started rolling when we identified Ashley. I came home and plastered Ashley's picture all over the refrigerator. They became a constant reminder about how blessed we were living in North America. I couldn't stop thinking about how many children suffered, simply due to the misfortune of where they were born. I hoped that Sid would be willing to take a trip to Jamaica to meet Ashley Parkinson, knowing that if he saw the circumstances of her life, he would change them.

● FOUR ●

PERFECT SERENITY

It took nearly a month to get Sid to agree to return to Jamaica with me. I emailed Mrs. O'Connor advising her of our plans; We would arrive in Jamaica on August 11th for a short five-day visit. I said we'd been assigned a social worker for our home study and expected to have it completed within the month. Most importantly, it had come to my attention that a girl named 'Ashley' at Blossom Gardens might be 'available' for adoption through the CDA. We would greatly appreciate knowing if that was true. If so, we would be very excited about the possibility.

I prayed for patience, and got tested. God will never fail to provide circumstances to help develop what we ask him for in prayer. The Bible says "tribulation worketh patience," (Romans 5:3) meaning, I'm supposed to *delight* in troubles and *rejoice* in sufferings, knowing that pressure, *and* affliction, *and* hardship produce patient *and* unswerving endurance. Dive into that Bermuda triangle with blind faith, and you will be prepared to swim the English Channel!

While my patience simmered on the back burner, I concentrated on preparing for a third trip to Jamaica in as many months. After we'd turned in our SAFE questionnaire, Sid agreed to go with me to meet the little girl whose picture plastered our refrigerator. The monumental gesture meant the world to me.

I planned on turning the trip into a romantic getaway for the two of us. I'd stumbled upon a special bed and breakfast named Polkerris, that fit our budget, and was conveniently located on the hillside facing the Montego Bay, just above the infamous hip strip. According to the Internet,

29

the property featured an extensive garden, a sun terrace with a swimming pool, and breakfast was included.

Sid and I met in the Toronto airport terminal after dispersing our kids to relatives for the week. We were able to take advantage of our standby privileges going in different directions to get our brood where they could spend time with extended family. Sid flew out to Halifax with the boys, so they could stay with Helen and Ed, their paternal Grandparents, while I took the girls to Denver to spend time with my mom. We knew everyone would get some quality family time while we got some couple time. I liked the idea of rushing towards each other to be alone. We flew from Toronto to Montego Bay together, giddy as newlyweds.

The hotel sent their driver, Mr. Dixon, to pick us up at the airport. He instructed us to wait by the curb while he ran to get his parked vehicle, an older VW bus that reminded me of Scooby Doo's mystery machine. We noticed gold fringe dangling from the ceiling edges and a definite lack of air conditioning. My legs stuck to the plastic seat covers. I slid the window open a notch hoping to make Sid more comfortable.

Mr. Dixon continuously wiped his brow with a cloth as he drove us to our hotel. He turned off the Gloucester Avenue, known as 'Bottom Road,' scaling the steep incline of Coral Hill road. The dirt path wreaked havoc on the mystery machine's suspension system as it crept along the ridge over Montego Bay. At the top of the hill, Mr. Dixon turned left onto a silky smooth driveway leading to a distinctly Colonial style home. He unloaded our luggage and placed it inside its grand foyer. We paid his fare after arranging for him to return in an hour to take us to Blossom Gardens.

The proprietors of the Polkerris, Jeremy and Clarissa, were a refined older couple; He English, and she Jamaican. They greeted us with a refreshing chilled glass of pineapple juice served on a silver tray. We were given a set of keys on a tassel for our room, the front door, and the gates to the property. They escorted us to the front of the house where our 'green room' overlooked the bay.

Sid unlocked the bedroom door wearing that sheepish adorable grin of his. "You're going to like this," he said stepping inside. There was a four-poster mahogany bed with chocolates on the pillow tops. Sid took me in his arms, both of us relishing the moment of our arrival. Sid soon retreated to the private bathroom to shower off the lingering smell of airports and diesel while I puttered around the room unpacking our bags and settling in.

The picture window view looked like an airbrushed postcard. The home sat on a hillside dropping abruptly down to the sea where the gentle blue sky paled against the turquoise water. I watched a cargo ship moving quickly through the buoys and out towards the horizon.

I reached Mrs. O'Connor at the CDA on the landline reminding her that my husband had returned to the island with me. We wondered if there might be any other children on the waiting list that we would be able to meet while we were here.

"There is a family of three siblings," said Mrs. O'Connor. I heard Sid turn off the water. He stepped out of the shower and waited for my response.

"Three children, all siblings you say?"

"All under the age of ten," Mrs. O'Connor replied.

"No, I don't think we will be able to do that," I said. Sid sighed. "I think that's a bit more than we are able to do." The word 'no' stuck in my throat. I knew that if I ever met them my resolve would easily dislodge. It was better to say 'no' without faces or names to remember.

"There is also a boy born in 2002. He is the boy I spoke of last time you were here. He lives in SOS. I've spoken to the Director who says the boy is well settled and she would be reluctant to consider him for adoption. I can make an appointment for you to meet that boy if you like."

"Yes, please do so. We would love to meet him," I said, never asking for his name.

"Yea mon, I will do it. I will make arrangements and speak to you in the morning." I replaced the receiver thinking about the tour of the SOS facility that I'd attended on my initial visit. I'd left Alyssa supervising the boys at the villa and gone alone. Mrs. O'Connor had arranged for me to meet with its Director.

SOS Children's Villages offered orphaned and abandoned children permanent homes to prepare them for an independent life. The village created a support system by emulating a family. It was nestled next to a river in Barrett Towne, fifteen kilometers from Montego Bay. I couldn't fathom taking one of the fortunate few who were placed there away from the successful environment.

Mr. Dixon pulled his van into the driveway precisely one hour after he dropped us off. His muffler let out a bang of smoke. We climbed back into the vehicle rejuvenated from our showers anticipating Sid's first visit to Blossom Gardens.

I didn't recognize the person who seemed to take forever when we rang the bell. All she said was, "visiting hours is over," and turned away.

Mr. Dixon had parked expecting to wait a while for us. He was surprised when we came back so quickly asking to be returned to Montego Bay. On the way down the hill we asked where we might find some great local food. He suggested the Port Pit BBQ, and pointed it out to us as we passed it on the way back to our room. We paid him $200 JMD and made arrangements to return to Blossom Gardens at ten the next morning.

It was early evening; we sat near the poolside waterfall to relax until our stomachs required food. We strolled down the driveway, out the gates of our hotel, crossed the dirt road onto another identical driveway where a similar stately home stood. Jeremy had given us instructions as to where we would find a concrete stairwell leading to an access gate to Bottom Road. One of the keys on the tassel fit into the lock. Once through, we would come into the heart of the hip strip.

We stumbled upon a patio restaurant called the Groovy Grouper where the palm trees were wrapped with little white holiday lights. We sat on the deck just in time to watch the sun dip behind the horizon. Sid decided that we should do a pub-crawl along the hip strip ordering an appetizer at each stop. We began with a disappointing Jerk chicken and a couple of luke warm beers to wash it down, before moving on hoping for better food and colder beer.

We sauntered down the wooden boardwalk watching the waves slap their silvery sea foam on the flat beach. We stopped at the Twisted Kilt, an Irish public house in the heart of Jamaica where they served traditional pub style comfort food.

Afterwards, we crossed the street and ate plantains doused in salsa on the porch at the Jamaican Bobsled. We climbed inside the Cool Runnings sled for a picture together because the 1993 comedy had been filmed in our hometown. It was an endearing movie about four Jamaican bobsledders fulfilling a dream of competing in the Winter Olympics, despite never having seen snow.

We walked down the crumbling sidewalk to the Pork Pit, as recommended by Mr. Dixon, for our main course. The open-air hot spot sits directly across the street from the Walter Fletcher Beach. It is arguably the best place on the island to find authentic Jamaican BBQ. We ordered a whole jerk chicken, a large Styrofoam container of rice and peas, a half-pound of pulled pork, and a couple of Red Stripes. We paid for the meal and received a yellow receipt to turn in to the boys at the grill to get our supper. We sat on picnic benches drinking the beer under the stars as it was prepared.

I hadn't ever been out after dark. Jamaica felt different at night, like the pounding of a bass drum beating inside your soul. The faster rhythm of the night air felt warm, sticky, and sexy. The people on the streets became lively and assertive. We returned to our hotel walking past the Coral Cliff Casino, a nocturnal gaming lounge, where the music pulsed loudly. An actual life-sized African elephant statue stood on the corner of the property marking the spot where we would turn to go up the hill towards our hotel. A man sold us chilled Red Stripe out of the trunk of his car, packaging it a brown paper bag for us to take back to the room.

It was only nine o'clock. It seemed like a waste of a night to turn in so early. A single light glowed dimly in the immaculate pool. Sid pulled me close to him with one arm, low and strong behind my back. We pressed our hips together. He grasped my other hand with his free one raising it above my head. We swayed to the music in his head dangerously near to the edge of the pool. I kicked off my sandals allowing the strap of my dress to fall from my shoulder. I unzipped, and then dropped the dress onto the deck before slipping into the quiet water. Sid watched, hesitating only slightly before joining me.

Afterwards, it didn't take long to fall asleep once our heads hit the pillow.

The next morning we woke up when the telephone rang," I looked over at the face of the clock on the nightstand. It wasn't even eight o'clock. "Good morning Mrs. Isnor, What would you like for breakfast?"

"Is it possible to get a pot of coffee and some water before breakfast?"

"Yea mon, I will bring it to you. Today we have a choice of ackee and saltfish with dumplings and fried plantains, a ham and cheese omelet, or French toast."

Sid was by no means a picky eater. He only ever turned up his nose once at my sloppy joes when we both decided to turf the whole skillet into the garbage and ordered pizza. When I'd described our 'Angie meals' he'd pleaded, "Please don't ever make me eat ackee and saltfish, it tastes like salted rubber. It's right up there with your sloppy joes."

"My husband would like the omelet please, and I would like the ackee and saltfish." I replied.

In Jamaica every first morning feels like a Sunday to me, no matter what day of the week it is. It feels like heaven without the TV blaring the morning traffic news. We opened the curtains of the big picture window. Fishing boats were already returning with the morning's catch and the Sandals catamaran was just beginning to troll for the tourist dollar. We'd just rolled out of the four-poster bed when there was a knock on our door to deliver our Blue Mountain coffee.

The house was built around a glassed-in area with French doors that opened wide out onto the porch. The doors could be closed tight for inclement weather allowing someone to sit inside, without fear, when the sky filled with thunder and lightning illuminated heaven.

Soon after breakfast was served, English style, on the beautiful wide wrap around porch. A dark, tall statuesque woman wearing a pressed white uniform carried our breakfast out from the kitchen on an elegant silver tray. She set it down inside the French doors of the atrium on the veranda. We were formally served from the right, with the dishes removed from the left. The beautiful presentation of the scrumptious food was supreme. I doubted we would require sustenance for hours.

I'd tried to get Mrs. O'Connor to agree to let us take Ashley out, like we'd done with Tejah, before Sid and I arrived in Jamaica. I'd hoped the three of us could go to the beach and then grab a bite to eat together. I wanted to see what Ashley would be like away from the other children, imagining she might be shy hiding behind my back until she got comfortable with Sid. I already thought of myself as her mother, her protector.

I was summoned from the breakfast table to our room to take a call from the Adoptions Coordinator. Mrs. O'Connor stated that she needed permission from her supervisor, Mr. Green, before allowing the visit. He was not yet in the office, but was expected shortly. I asked her to please inform Blossom Gardens about our intended morning visit so that we would not get turned away again. She promised to contact us at the orphanage once she'd made arrangements with Mr. Green.

I looked out the window. Mr. Dixon drove through the gates and parked beneath it. He got out of the van on the right side and walked around the vehicle. He removed his t-shirt replacing it with a neatly pressed long sleeved dress shirt that hung in the back of his van. I watched him tuck his shirt into his slacks preparing for an honest days work.

Shortly afterwards, Sid came to the room to tell me that our ride had arrived. I dabbed a small amount of Red Door perfume on my wrist and put some chapstick on my lips. I picked up the red bag that now held books and games for the children at the orphanage.

Carmelina answered the door when we rang the bell at Blossom Gardens. *Thank God* for her familiar face. We were immediately allowed inside the gates. I introduced my husband and was told that the children were in the yard. We walked around the corner of the building where the old wooden picnic table stood. The children ran wildly around in the hot mid morning sun playing in the dirt. The only play structure was the dilapidated metal swing set at the back of the yard. Sid and I sat at the picnic table where the children flocked to us. Interestingly, the boys gravitated to Sid while the girls came to me.

A few of them recognized me from my previous visits, but there were many new faces too. I pulled out the zebra photo album that I carried in the red bag. I'd printed the pictures I'd taken of the children under the mango tree the last time I'd been there. I had pictures of the twins, Deja, Sabrina Williams, Kimeysha, and of course Ashley. The girls all giggled when they saw their own likenesses.

Ashley found her picture tucked behind a plastic page protector with another photograph in front of it. She was still wearing the same pink skirt and yellow t-shirt. She squealed when she discovered it. I'd promised to bring copy of it to give to her when Sabrina Williams snatched another photo out of her hand in the classroom. I wondered if Ashley remembered my promise.

I looked over to see a small boy sitting on Sid's lap. Several other boys also hovered around his shoulders. All of a sudden, one of the larger boys started hitting the boy in Sid's lap with a closed fist. The boy did so with an unbridled vengeance. Sid instinctively reached out and grabbed the boy's wrist. "We do *not* hit," Sid said, holding the boy's arm tight enough not to allow movement of any kind. The large boy's eyes were on fire. He sucked air in and out of his chest like he was hyperventilating. He'd wanted possession of the cheap plastic truck in the small boy's hand.

The children had all been given dollar store toys that morning. The boys were given plastic trucks, and the girl's imitation Barbie dolls. The toys all broke within five minutes of being taken out of the cheap cellophane wrappings. Ashley instantly undressed her doll, and then whined incessantly as she tried to get me to help her put the clothes back on. Ashley chewed the shoes when we couldn't get them back on the doll's feet. She spit them across the picnic table when I scolded her for putting plastic in her mouth.

The large boy's name was Orlando. He was the oldest boy at the orphanage. We learned he had a younger brother there named David. I assumed that they allowed Orlando to stay at Blossom Gardens in an attempt to keep the siblings together. Later, Sid and I would both describe the crazed look in Orlando's eyes as demonic. We agreed that we were probably looking at the face of a twenty-year-old criminal in a nine-year-old body. What violent atrocities had occurred in his young life to make him so angry? I envisioned future acts of violence this young man would commit as I sat on that bench. It saddened me to think that some of these children were so badly damaged that they were already beyond any human help.

Carmelina came into the yard to get me for a phone call. Again, it was Mrs. O'Connor from the CDA. I answered it in the Director, Mrs. Brown's office. "Did you get permission for us from Mr. Green to take Ashley to the beach?" I asked.

"No mon. Mr. Green is not yet available. I am calling to tell you that you are expected at SOS to visit with the boy today.

I hesitated. "Mrs. O'Connor, the boy is settled. I think we would like to work with Ashley Parkinson." *The little girl who spits out shoes.*

"You want to work with Ashley Parkinson?" asked Mrs. O'Connor. You don't want to visit with the boy at SOS? I knew she had gone to great lengths making the arrangements for us.

"No mon. We want to work with Ashley Parkinson. What is the next step that we need to take Mrs. O'Connor?"

"The next step is to run an ad in the paper to see if someone claims her. I see that her social worker is Ms. Wilton, the same worker as the boy you saw before. I will speak to her," said Mrs. O'Connor.

"Thank you very much for your help." I hung up the phone. Mrs. Brown sat behind her desk watching me. She knew more than I how long the road would be. I just sat there for a moment to let it all sink in. I'd asked to adopt a specific child named Ashley Parkinson.

Mrs. Brown gave me permission to give Ashley a gift. I'd packed a couple of dresses in the red bag hoping Ashley would wear one on an outing. "If I give her a dress, will it be her very own?" I asked Mrs. Brown.

"Yea mon. It will be hers."

"Thank you very much," I replied.

I handed Carmelina Mr. Dixon's card and requested that she call our driver to come pick us up. Then, I took Ashley into the washroom to change her clothes. She slipped into the mostly white t-shirt dress that had a splash of green tie-dye marking and a small pink peace sign on the hip. Ashley smiled, looking confused at the unexpected attention she was receiving. Sid took pictures of both of us wearing white dresses together. I could only imagine what that dress would look like after thirty minutes in the dirt. I wanted Ashley to know that someone in the world cared about her. We never saw that dress again.

We intended on leaving Jamaica Friday to attend the wedding of one of Sid's co-workers on Saturday afternoon. I'd checked the flight loads four days earlier before leaving Canada. There had been nine open seats at that point. We learned the return flight to Canada was sold out when we were checking in at the airport. In all of ten years of marriage, I'd never seen Sid so mad. He'd made it clear how important it was to go to the wedding before leaving Canada. We were given boarding passes allowing us to clear immigration and security, but we did not have seat assignments. The ticket agent advised us to check in at the gate at one o'clock to see if we could get on the plane or not.

We passed through immigration not speaking to one another. My mind worked like a hamster on an exercise wheel trying to sort out alternatives. Air Canada's scheduled flight left shortly after ours did. My contingency plan was to pay full fare for a ticket to get Sid home. I walked to the competitors customer service desk at the end of the terminal and learned that their flight was also sold out. I wrung my hands while checking the departures board to see which other airlines flew to Calgary. There were none.

We waited until the one o'clock hour, praying for 'no shows' on the flight. Our chances looked grim. I was pretty sure we were stuck for another night in Montego Bay and would miss the wedding. Unbelievably, there were *five* no shows that day. Sid said that I was just plain lucky. I didn't see it as luck; I knew God was taking care of us. We made it home that night with plenty of time for a leisurely drive to the wedding in Lake Louise, Canada the next day. We rented a two-man canoe after the wedding and paddled around Emerald Lake ending our romantic adventure in perfect serenity.

FIVE

INTERVENTION

The last thing I'd done before heading off for Jamaica was to mail our intervention report requests to social services. The response we received ten days later was not the one we were expecting. The reporting officer had determined "a concern regarding the suitability of the applicants to have care and custody of a child."

None of it made any sense. This was a nightmare. I felt like I was losing control, like in one of those dreams where you keep falling and falling, and then you wake up. The situation seemed hilariously overwhelming. My stomach sank when I read the letter, but I refused to allow it to be discouraging.

The Intervention review, known as the CYIM report assesses the documents that Children and Youth Services maintain. Alberta provided the form for us to fill out, which required us to list all of our children, regardless of whether they lived at home or not. A review of records is run on every person over the age of eighteen, to determine whether an adult of the household has an existing intervention record indicating cause for a child in need of protective services.

I now understand the difficulty this presented for my oldest daughter who lived 3,000 miles, and ten years away. She grew up in an entirely different reality than we were currently living. I needed to work nights then to pay the bills and was often irritable with the burden of the responsibility. Sid had taken the hardship away and given us a lifestyle free from day to day struggle. My focus had changed from trying to pay the electric bill before the shut off notice came to making pancakes on a school day. I believe Erica found herself in a tough spot needing to tell her truth without feeling she was betraying her mother.

The review "revealed an initial assessment in March of 2008 regarding the applicants' children Sidney and Kaiden. There [were] also screenings and investigation from 2004 to 2006 involving the female applicant's daughter Olivia. These matters should be contextualized within the home assessment report. Please contact your agency to have the information released to them by Alberta Children and Youth Services. Please call if you have any questions. Thank you."

I do much sighing over Olivia.

Evil people in the world do horrific things to children. Children need protection from abuse; physical, emotional, sexual, neglect, trafficking and so many more atrocities that my overactive imagination cannot fathom. We were willing to have our lives investigated because we were confident that although our lives were not perfect, we had never committed a single harmful act against a child.

We fully cooperated by signing the 'Freedom of Information Protection' (FIOP) form, allowing the department of Children's Protective Services to share any pertinent information collected by social services about our family between the Adoption Agency, Adoption and Permanency Services, and Alberta Children's Services.

I contacted our adoption agency forewarning them about the content of our CYIM review. They consoled me with assurances that we were not the first family they had dealt with who parented difficult teenagers. I delivered the Intervention Record Check to our adoption agency, and waited to hear when our home study would be completed.

That day, I also received notification from the Calgary Police Service that my police clearance had been conducted and that I was required to pick it up in person. Interestingly, Sid received his by mail. Mr. Grant sure was right, "They look at every aspect of your life." Rightfully so, but *we* had nothing to be ashamed of or to hide!

I arrived at the police station expecting only to collect an envelope with a letter of certification enclosed. I sat waiting for more than an hour before a uniformed policeman called out my name. The officer asked me to follow him up an elevator to the third floor informing me that a warrant had been issued for my arrest. My mouth went dry wondering if he was planning to lock me up or not. Would anyone ever walk into a police station *knowing* about an outstanding warrant?

"I have no idea what you are talking about. Please tell me why I am being arrested." I'm sure he'd heard those words a hundred times before. Did I have an unpaid ticket for going through a red light from one of those cameras hovering above our intersections in Calgary?

"It will take time for me to look it up," said the officer before disappearing. He returned several minutes later, "It appears you a warrant for failure to appear in court for a dog at large."

I'd been issued a ticket for our Great Dane, Stella, running away on Christmas Eve the year before. That dog loved to watch for an opportunity to bolt out the front door to stretch her lanky limbs. She reveled in the ensuing hullabaloo with us chasing behind her. That night, I'd driven the neighbourhood looking for Stella for over two hours. Shortly after giving up and returning home, a neighbour rang my doorbell to return our runaway. Relieved, I thanked him and brought Stella inside. Five minutes later the doorbell rang again. A peace officer gifted me with a one hundred dollar holiday fine. The dog was registered in my name so the ticket belonged to me. Ironically, I bore the responsibility of having a large dog at large.

"Are you able to pay the fine now?" The current officer questioned, jogging my mind back to the present.

I paid the fine and was escorted back down the elevator to an area where I was instructed to wait for my police clearance. An hour later, *two* female police officers led me into a small office where I complied with their request to sit in a chair facing a desk. One of the women sat before me while the other flanked my side.

"We found some items of interest on your police record check," said the seated officer. Incredulously, I stared at them thinking that I was in an episode of the Twilight Zone. The best thing I could do was to stay silent and listen to what they wanted to say.

"Since the purpose of this police clearance is for adoption we have to be especially careful. Your name has come up as a 'Domestic Subject' in several police reports."

I released yet another Olivia sigh.

"Oh, this is about my daughter. We had a tough time with her. I was following the instructions provided by our social worker. May I see the report?"

The answer was unequivocally no because the Freedom of Protection Act protected Olivia. Olivia was being protected from her mother. *I was her mother! I was her protector.* The two women stared at me. I'm confident they had looked into the faces of women who had hurt or beaten their children. I was not one of those women. "If you want to see the reports you need to do so in writing. The FOIP Act will withhold some of the information you want. The information will be severed, or blackened out," informed the hovering officer.

"It's *all* about Olivia, will it be just one big redacted page?" I questioned.

"The essence of the incident will be clear. Is there anything else we can help you with?"

"No thank you. I will show myself out."

I made an official request to access of information on June 25, 2009. Mr. Grant was indeed correct. I was under a microscope. What was next? A rectal exam?

On July 21, 2009, I received a letter stating that the criminal records check confirmed by the National Repository for Criminal Records in Canada indicated that I had no convictions and nothing to disclose on file with the Alberta Provincial Courts. It did, however, reveal local records on file with the Calgary Police Service. The letter instructed me to pick up the specifics of the report back at the police station.

My daughter Nadia agreed to return with me to the place of my humiliation just in case, sitting in the car with the boys while I went inside. I walked right up to the counter and immediately received the thick package that was prepared and waiting for me. A red stamp labeled, "personal and confidential" marked the sealed flap of the envelope. Thank God I didn't have to endure another tête-à-tête with more police.

I returned to the car tempted to rip open the envelope that contained all the dirty laundry of our lives between April 2004 and February of 2008. Prudently, I waited until returning home. I wasn't looking forward to reading about our domestic troubles.

I thought about Olivia as I looked through the thirty pages of police reports feeling numb. Deadened. How did I lose her? When did she start drifting away? None of the papers before me accurately reported Olivia's true nature. Olivia has always been one of the warmest most charming people I have ever known; she is probably most like me of all of my children, having some of my flaws, but the parts in me that are good are even better in Olivia. Still, she must believe that I have wronged her, somehow hurting the very essence of her being. The violation against Olivia may not have been real, but the pain she perceives remains real.

'No one is perfect, not even one.'

I owe a great deal of gratitude to Olivia. I continue missing her physical presence in our lives. I've learned that all adoptions stem from loss and I had to fill a great big hole in my heart when she left. My heart restores itself slowly, and the sharpest pain has subsided, like a piece of sea glass from broken bottles in the ocean losing its sharp edges with repetition of waves kneading it through the sand. I am grateful that He took me to the warm waters in Jamaica to ease my sorrow.

In all fairness, I must admit that I used alcohol to escape the stress, looking forward to the five o'clock hour when I could legitimately open a can of beer to smooth out the rough edges in my life.

It wasn't until August 18, 2009, that I spoke with the Programs Director at the first adoption agency. "We have reservations regarding the longevity of the social services file. Your past involvement with social services raised concerns about a child's welfare. Adoption of an older child requires a strong family unit. We are not willing to do the home study for you. Please return the self-guided international adoption study book. We will refund your fee in the form of a check."

"Would you be willing to come to our home for a dinner to meet with us? You could see, first hand, our interactions with each other."

"That would be a home study."

It sounded ass backwards. The Director made her final decision without ever even meeting us. In her mind, we were not considered suitable parents for an orphan. She stated that Alberta Adoption Services would *never* approve our application. She expressed concerns about maintaining the statistical average of successful placement approvals.

I asked for the refund in cash which was denied. They didn't keep that amount of money in the office. I felt like telling them that I'd been instructed to locate an ATM machine when they wanted funds because

I never kept that amount of money in my wallet. They mailed me a refund check ending our relationship and much-needed agency affiliation. Admittedly, the documents sat at the first agency until mid-October when I was able to coordinate another initial interview at a second agency because I was embarrassed to pick them up.

I finally turned in all of the paperwork to a new agency Director before returning to Jamaica for Ashley's seventh birthday. She changed our initial interview several times before calling me last minute requesting an immediate consultation. Sid was not able to go at such short notice, but like a bull in a china closet I chose to go alone.

The new office was in complete disarray when I arrived. The bookshelves were barren, and the computers were still in the manufacturer's boxes. The paint and carpet had that new car smell. There were even little fuzzies still on the rug, left over from its installation. Director Liz apologized for the disarray. "Don't be silly. It was me that pushed for this appointment. We want to begin the home study as soon as possible."

I laid everything out on the table including several pictures of Ashley and our current family. I answered as honestly as possible when she asked me to describe when and how we'd come to the decision to adopt. "I feel as though God planted a desire in my heart. It feels as if it is a 'calling' of sorts."

"So, you think God speaks to you?" She held a legal pad in her lap and was quickly recording my responses. I noted that her scribbling looked large and messy; perhaps she was taking shorthand. I tried to connect with eye contact, but she never looked beyond her legal pad.

"I think he answers prayers," I said softly. *We know that we abide in him and He is us, because he has given us his Spirit.*

"As you know you signed permission for our agency to review the intervention report with Child Services. According to the report, it says that you sought treatment for alcohol." I nodded.

"Where did you seek treatment?"

"Aventa." It was a voluntary outpatient treatment centre that I attended for thirty days. My hands felt clammy. My temperature seemed to be rising.

"When was the last time you spoke to Olivia?"

"Two years ago when she moved out." My heart sank.

"Is there anything else you want to say to me?" she asked. I teared up.

"Well, I'm nervous because I want this so much. I'm a wonderful mother. It's why I'm here. I want to be Ashley's mother."

I pretty much knew I didn't pass their test before leaving. I believe Liz made up her mind before I ever stepped inside her office. The Director soon texted her decision to me. Didn't Taylor Swift get dumped by text? Here we were making ourselves vulnerable with no other agenda other than to give a child a home. Where was the compassion? Where was the *grace*?

I phoned Liz asking her to explain her decision. "It doesn't come down to one thing. There are too many issues. There is the estrangement with Olivia, the intervention with social services, the number of children in your home, your alcoholism. It wouldn't be fair to ask a social worker to put in the required time and effort for a home study. It isn't fair to subject the children in your home to the scrutiny knowing it won't be approved.

"Well, thank you for your time."

"You are welcome. I will give your documents to the receptionist. Please give her a courtesy call before collecting them."

"I will, I promise."

Everyone always acted so damn polite. Here we were back to square one. The only thing I could do was to write a cathartic letter:

> *To whom it may concern,*
>
> *It is an extreme necessity to be careful in placing a child in an international adoption. It would be unconscionable not to investigate every aspect of prospective adoptees before making a decision whether or not to place a child in such a home.*
>
> *Likewise, it follows that it would be unconscionable not to allow such prospective adoptees every opportunity to fairly and honestly present themselves within the context of an unbiased home study. Failure to provide the opportunity to have a social worker complete the home study prevents any possibility for completing the requirements of the Alberta Government. The home study is the only avenue by which to bring a child and family together for a forever home.*

Director Liz provided several reasons why she would not proceed with a home study for our family.

We appreciate that there is a tremendous commitment of time and effort on the part of the assigned social worker. Liz presents it as being unfair to the social worker to be expected to put the effort forward when the probability of passing the Adoption Board seems slim. Respectfully, the focus of the home study should be on the prospective family instead of the social worker. The onus and responsibility of funding the home study lie in the hand of the family whether it is approved or not.

We expect that the social worker would thoroughly investigate in an unbiased manner. We are confident that when we open the doors to our home, the social worker will make a fair assessment as to the suitability of bringing Ashley home.

Our decision to adopt a seven-year-old girl from Jamaica has been a careful one. Adding children to a family either through adoption or birth is not a decision to come to lightly.

There are no guarantees that all will go as expected. Whether by birth or adoption, one cannot make a return as one might for a damaged item purchased at a local department store. The only guarantee any child comes with is that he or she will have unique attributes and provide challenges and rewards to every member of his or her immediate and extended family.

Our family is not conventional. What is customary these days? We are not exceptional unless you consider the number of children under our roof. We have had the privilege of raising seven children. Four of the seven remain in our care. Things haven't always been perfect, yet we stay constant. Sid and I make each other, our children, and our family our priority. The number of children we have raised and are raising should not be considered a liability. Our seven are children an asset. Carefully consider that Ashley is in an orphanage surrounded by sixty-one other children. Ashley currently shares a bedroom with eight other girls. In our home, Ashley would share a room with only one other. Nadia and Alyssa, the two girls still living in our home, both want to share their rooms with Ashley. Ashley would have brothers to protect her, and sisters to teach her 'girl stuff.' We have more children than usual in our house. We are committed to all of the children in our home.

We are not entering into an international adoption blindly. We have experienced the natural ups and downs of parenthood. Our relationship with Olivia needs careful consideration. Olivia, not unlike her mother, chooses to travel the road less taken. We are confident that with maturity and time Olivia will return phone calls, text messages, acknowledge visits, and come home. These are issues that need, as recommended in the intervention report, "to be addressed with the context of the home study."

We sought help in 2004 by calling social services because we needed support, advice, strategies, and counseling for Olivia. I insisted a file remain open knowing that things had become unmanageable. We consistently maintained two rules that Olivia consistently defied. We needed to know where Olivia was and that she went to school. Unfortunately, five weeks before graduation Olivia decided to move out. She left our home and school severing any communication.

At the same time that Olivia declared emancipation, my eldest son Jonathan spent eighteen months in Iraq. It was a dark and challenging time. I found that I would drink beer to take the edge off the pain. I decided to join AA and follow the twelve-step program voluntarily. I wanted to be present and available to all of my children and found that drinking did not solve or prevent problems from occurring.

Proactively seeking help through social services for a problematic teenager or treatment for any illness should not be treated punitively. My airline has employed me as a flight attendant since July 16, 2007. My employer maintains a zero-tolerance policy for alcohol and drug abuse. I have never had a problem respecting this policy. When asked how I can guarantee that I will not relapse into previous behavior, I can only answer honestly. I cannot make guarantees. I can only move forward with faith and experience. I can use the knowledge, skills and tools I learned during the hard times to manage inevitable stumbling blocks in the future. I find that being generous with my time and attention, genuinely listening to what my children say and don't say keeps the environment of our home calm and safe.

Kind regards,
Erika Isnor

I couldn't bring myself to ever mail that letter. I left the portfolio of personal information at the agency, half-hoping that Sid could somehow talk sense into Liz, making her change her mind about doing the home study.

And yet, I maintained a sense of peace in spite of the news. Our romantic vacation mended the rift that was nagging our relationship; Sid and I returned from Jamaica rejuvenated by our together time. It meant the world to me that Sid met Ashley and knew where my heart lay. You can't go to an orphanage without being affected unless you have a heart of stone, and my husband has a heart of gold. I sat collecting my thoughts before dialing Sid's cell to tell him about the second refusal to proceed with our home study. "I'll be right home," he said. Bless him. He left work in the middle of the day to come home and comfort me. The gesture showed a great concession for Sid who was so thoroughly devoted to his role as a provider for our family. He *never* left work early.

Sid went uncharacteristically ballistic at home, "There is little doubt in my mind that Liz screens prospective adopters much the way a bank screen people who apply for loans. Banks don't really care what kind of a person you are. They only look at the numbers. Horrible as it sounds, I believe they approach things statistically, not compassionately. Our statistics don't seem to fit their criteria."

Looking back, I see how the rejection was an important part of the process. We were where we were meant to be at the time. We grew closer as a couple when the second agency refused us. It strengthened our partnership. Years later when I asked Sid why he changed his mind about adopting. He said, "One of us had to." I think visiting the children at Blossom Gardens showed him how soft hearted his hard headed wife could be.

We were eventually denied by two of the three licensed adoption agencies in Calgary. I'm the mother of seven children with five fathers. Who wouldn't be concerned with that? Mistakes can be hard to come to terms with, and for me, they seem to keep resurfacing until I do. My children were God's gifts that became my life's purpose. My life has been colorful, but I'm comfortable in my skin now. For the first forty years of my life I wandered through wilderness before following the Lord. I've found a person to share my life with who understands the unconventional way I think. I'm accountable, but have found forgiveness. I'm bold and transparent because I am at peace with who I have become.

---• SIX •---

BUILDING TRUST

In fall, I concentrated on getting kids back into the school routine. We traded the quiet spontaneity of summer for busy school schedules. Once the dust settled, I fixed my attention on making progress with the adoption.

I Googled Carl's 'Embracing Orphans' site making myself familiar with Christian volunteers and other people hoping to adopt from Jamaica. I joined a growing affiliation of people all over the world banding together to help orphans.

I became acquainted with Maryam, a single woman from New York, who was in the later stages of adopting three-year-old Daniel, also from Blossom Gardens. Daniels' adoption differed from ours, as it was initiated in the United States and finalized in Jamaica. Although Daniel's adoption was finished, he still needed a visa to leave the island. The decision about the visa was up to the discretion of the US embassy weighing heavily on Maryam.

I looked forward to reading Maryam's daily postings describing their exhausting journey.

> *Daniel and I will be at the US Embassy on Tuesday morning. We will deliver the documents. I made sure that he wears a hat and has plenty of water. Please show my son that America always opens her doors. Let us go home so that Daniel can meet his family and friends; they are all waiting for him. Let him go to school. Please. Help us go home together this week.*

Maryam's words virtually transported me back to the Caribbean, as I envisioned the sweat beading down her back during the long, arduous road trip between Montego Bay and Kingston. I imagined myself sending a cool breeze her way, sweeping the tension off her brow.

I wanted Maryam and Daniel to go home to New York together. However, my need to have Maryam explain to me how she'd accomplished her adoption was of much more importance to me. The morning of September 7, I wrote Maryam with self-serving motivations.

> *We are hoping for the same thing one day with Ashley. I read your story and it gives me strength. I will be returning to Montego Bay for the fourth time with a promise of a visitation on the 15th.*
>
> *Do you have any suggestions? What are the normal guidelines for the paperwork? If you are there next week, I would love to meet you and Daniel.*
>
> *I will be staying at the Polkerris B&B, off Gloucester Avenue, in Coral Cliff. The phone number is 876 XXX-XXXX. Hope we can get together, perhaps with our children, at Doctor's Cave…or there is a beautiful pool at the hotel.*
>
> *Take care,*
> *Erika.*

Maryam wasn't the only one that was frustrated. We encountered constant challenges navigating through ever-changing regulations and policies in Jamaica. The country lacked infrastructure, procedures, and manpower to get the job done effectively. There were technical difficulties reaching officials either by phone or email. Jamaica was 3,000 miles away from our home, and nothing seemed to progress unless we maintained a presence there.

I'd asked Mrs. O'Connor if Ashley's name was on the list of children whom we could visit. She'd said that Ashley was available for adoption, but not yet signed off. I was also told that Ashley had recently been assigned to Ms. Wilton, the same social worker that had introduced us to Tejah.

I reminded Ms. Wilton that she needed to place an ad in the *Jamaican Gleaner* searching for anyone related to Ashley. The local paper would run an advertisement for three consecutive days several times over a six-week period, in adherence to both the Jamaican Government and the Hague Convention. Only then could Ashley be declared 'free for adoption.' I assumed, once this was done, that Ashley would either be in our home, or out of the institution rather quickly.

It bothered the bejesus out of me that I'd been trying for a month to get approval from the CDA to visit Ashley away from Blossom Gardens. I'd go back and forth between Mrs. O'Connor and Ms. Wilton, as each told me that only the other was authorized to give consent to my request. Actually, Mr. Green was the supervising team leader, at the Montego Bay office responsible for providing permission for our visitation. I hoped that once I physically returned to the island I could coral the three of them all together.

On Friday, just before the CDA closed for the weekend, I finally reached Ms. Wilton by phone. She said, "We need to lay things out on the table. Ashley is not available for adoption." We made a two o'clock appointment for the following Tuesday when I would be in Jamaica.

"Ashley is not available *right now*. We are her 'special friends' who only want to spend time with her," I reminded Ms. Wilton.

"Yea mon," she replied. "That is good. See you Tuesday to talk to Mr. Green." I hung up the phone, remembering how Sid and I failed to connect with Mr. Green when we were in Jamaica together.

Maryam wrote me that Friday evening;

> *We MUST meet/talk. My Jamaican number is 876-XXX-XXXX. We will be in Kingston Monday, and Daniel has his medical exam on Tuesday morning, but we will figure out a time/place to meet.*
>
> *We have to do things together. Have a good weekend, safe trip, and I look forward to seeing you next week.*
>
> *You will get Ashley. I will do everything in my little power to help you. I love that girl.*
>
> *Soon.*
> *Love, Maryam.*

The night before I returned to Jamaica, Maryam emailed me again, expressing how much frustration she'd endured over the past nine months. She also provided insight about what she thought of the people who worked for the CDA in Jamaica.

> *Erika, EVERYONE told me I wouldn't get Daniel. He is my son now. The last thing we need is the medical for his US visa. Stupid, frustrating process! If you know Ashley is your daughter, then you will bring her home.*
>
> *I don't know Ms. Wilton. Mr. Green is her supervisor and he is USELESS. Be nice to him, but don't expect anything from him. Mrs. O'Connor was our caseworker. Nothing good to say.*
>
> *The KEY person is Ms. Marjorie Tumming, the Adoption Coordinator in Kingston. She is out of the country for the next ten days, but she will make the final decision on your adoption.*
>
> *The other key person is Mr. Winston Bowen, the Director of Family Programs, also in Kingston. Bowen is actually the one you want to go to, because he is in charge of the children's files, so if Ashley's advertisement needs to be placed, or her parents need to sign her off, or you need her passport, he is the guy to push. He is nice, but he doesn't care. You can get their address and phone number from the CDA site.*
>
> *Please keep this all between us, yes? Doc's cave, by the way, sounds great. Daniel and I love it there.*
>
> *Maryam.*

The Jamaican process, despite my effort, continued to move at a snail's pace. I did not understand that Ashley's life was in legal limbo. Her birth mother allegedly abused and abandoned her, but there was still a *process* that needed to be meticulously followed, "ensuring that the adoption is in the best interest of the child, the biological parents, and the adoptive parents," according to the Hague Convention.

Ms. Wilton, her blessed soul, worked relentlessly for the benefit of the child, particularly my child, although I could not see it happening at the time. She remained responsibly ethical throughout the process. I have since learned to appreciate her unwavering dedication. Ms. Wilton wanted to insure that once Ashley was declared 'free for adoption,' no one could come back claiming a step was missed, thereby leaving Ashley unavailable. Our angel, Ms. Wilton, knew all along that we were waiting in the wings to give Ashley a better life, but she had to make sure to tie up the loose ends in the old life first. Months down the road, I complained about how inefficient the process was. "Yes it is," said Ms. Wilton, "But it is the only one we have."

The Lord knew what He was doing even if I didn't see the bigger picture. He is never doing nothing. I was being processed, ironically through the adoption *process,* He was making my path straight, but I had to learn to be the follower before I could see clearly.

I sat on a precarious precipice. I'd been accustomed to getting what I wanted having propelled through forty-eight years of life driven by sheer will and determination towards an intended goal. I focused on objectives, believing that the final aim of the situation was so important that any way of achieving my desired result was acceptable in the end. I bore the consequences like battle scars.

Something had always been missing in my life. No matter what I did, or didn't do, I felt empty and unfulfilled. It seemed as if an intricate error had been made when I was formed in my mother's womb making me deficient in some way; As if I'd been born with a nature to do wrong. I pondered these thoughts a full year before finding Psalm fifty-one in the Bible. "Surely I was sinful at birth. Sinful from the time my mother conceived me." How long did I wander aimlessly in such close proximity to the truth?

I hear his word more clearly now. "Yet, you desired faithfulness even in the womb; you taught me wisdom in that secret place."

There was no moral ambiguity in the quest to adopt Ashley. My objective was not self-serving. I began concentrating more on the focus of my character than on the nature of my purpose. I started looking outside of self for answers. Eventually, I began praying earnestly, learning that He always answers prayers.

The answer to the problem became brilliantly clear once I opened my eyes and turned from the darkness of Satan to the power of God. I'd begun to realize that the method by which any specific desire was obtained was as important as the result in terms of value and ethicality.

Oh how the enemy fought for me, knowing I how incredibly close I was to inviting the Lord to be my saviour, choosing eternal life. I wasn't aware of the raging battle between God and the subordinate evil spirit for my soul. Satan used every trick in the book trying to assault me through spiritual corruption. I was, however, still dominated and controlled by my willfulness.

SEVEN

BREAKING TRUST

That September, I couldn't ignore the burning desire to push our adoption through, taking on the Jamaican authorities with the determination of a Marvel superhero. The ground beneath my feet was soft as silt. The only strength I possessed dwelt in the confidence of my own will.

My vision has improved with hindsight. I'd greatly underestimated that red-suited, pitchfork carrying cartoon character residing on my shoulder who constantly whispered suggestions into my ear, purposefully leading me astray. I no longer think of the enemy so lightly. I see, now, that God's omnipotent power and grace has released me from the dark powers of worldly bonds.

I left home in a sneaky underhanded way when I lied to my husband. I said I'd accidentally picked up work that started in Toronto early Monday morning, feeding him a tale about needing to take the red-eye flight Sunday night in order to make my check in early the next morning. "Oh, what a tangled web we weave."

I left a premeditated trail behind me, perhaps unconsciously hoping to force the issue. Sid never said a word before the trip, presumably waiting to see if I would leave our home under false pretenses. I left my new blackberry charging on the kitchen counter sending a string of texts to Angie about going to the fruit market the following day. The facsimile record log also listed a neat path of faxes to the CDA stating my intentions. Obviously, I'd planned on returning to Jamaica.

The day before my escapade, the family spent the entire Sunday afternoon at Calgary Park, an amusement centre on the outskirts of

Calgary. We shared quality time on that crisp fall afternoon. We rode the roller coaster, enjoyed ice cream, French fries and frozen lemonade. Everyone, except Sidney who cleverly ducked behind my back, got wet when we hit the bottom of the imitation splash mountain. We ended the picture perfect day picnicking on the tailgate of our Hybrid Tahoe truck.

Later that night, I kissed my children's foreheads before settling down in front off my new laptop, documenting my true intentions for the coming week:

> *Maryam, I am so close to being back in Jamaica I can taste and smell it. My mind has been there all day. I made a few last minute preparations, by picking up a pink toothbrush for Ashley, and a Spiderman ball for Daniel. The items are frivolous, but chosen with care.*
>
> *At church today, the message was find you worth. Why are you on the earth? My answer was clear…I am here to take care of children, His and mine. I can't wait to feel the swarm of little bodies so deserving of love. I've packed books and markers to amuse them. I included a special drawing book for Ashley, hoping I can encourage her to share her feelings with me. She loves to draw.*
>
> *Maryam I can't wait to meet you! We are mothers who share a similar path. Perhaps ours will be parallel for a time. Am I prepared? What will the week in Jamaica bring? What will I learn? Will Ashley be closer to coming home, or maybe reuniting with her birth family? She needs a family who cares and loves her always-smiling face. My Ashley. She is in my heart. I will always care for her as a mother.*

I made my way to Jamaica that night paying little regard to the loved ones I'd left behind. The next afternoon I met with Ms. Wilton as planned. She handed me a letter allowing me to spend time with Ashley, but only "at the compound." I'd been doing that for five months already! I quietly accepted the letter seeing it as an admission that they were, at least, willing to work with me.

Ms. Wilton then leaned back and explained where Ashley's case stood in the process. Ashley Parkinson had arrived at Blossom Gardens in January of 2009 after being removed from her home due to emotional abuse. "Is there any indication of physical abuse?" I asked.

"Yes, beatings," Ms. Wilton answered. I hesitated before deciding to save questions concerning sexual abuse for another time. We expected issues. We would deal with them with professionals as needed.

Ms. Wilton held the open Ashley file in her hand, motivating me to probe further. I hoped to learn as much as possible about little 'Ashley Parkinson.' "What do you know about her?" I asked. Ms. Wilton, who maintained a poker face.

I slid an old Christmas photo of my brood of children surrounding Santa Clause across the social worker's battered desk. It was one of the few printed memories I had of all of them together. "These are my children, I explained, "before Sidney and Kaiden were born, of course."

"You look good for having all these kids."

"I spend a lot of time chasing them." I pointed out my eldest Erica. "We look alike, except that she has fair skin and blond hair."

Ms. Wilton looked down at Ashley's file. "Ashley is a child that needs a lot of love."

"That's the one thing I have to give," I said. "Ashley has bright eyes and a deep soul. She is very lovable."

Ms. Wilton then explained how she had done an assessment on Ashley in June, resulting in the determination that she should be placed up for adoption rather than be returned to the home. I also learned that Mr. Green, Ms. Wilton's supervisor, had informed her that he thought Ashley "had relatives around, who would have first right of refusal on the child."

My understanding was that both of the biological parents were deceased. I'd asked Ashley, and her answer was, "Mi mama be dye-ee-d."

"Is this true?" I asked. "Are both of Ashley's parents dead?"

"Both of her parents are alive," stated Ms. Wilton. "No, the next step is to place an advertisement in the paper looking for her relatives. I thought I'd done that, but there are so many children, I must have been wrong."

I quietly remembered sending three facsimiles to Jamaica over the past month inquiring about the advertisement."Do I need to call Mr. Bowen in Kingston to have the advertisement placed?

"No mon. I will do it." Commitment? I wondered, as I scribbled down the phone number for the house in Coral Cliff where I'd rented a room. Ms.Wilton promised to call me once Mr. Green arrived at the office. She called the orphanage notifying them that I would arrive within the hour to visit with Ashley. I glanced down and my watch, aware that it was already half past four. Sid and I had been turned away *before* five o'clock. Oh, how changing rules perplexed me.

I practically skipped down the concrete stairwell, finding Mr. Dixon parked on the side of the busy road, resting his eyes. "We can go straight to the orphanage. I get to see Ashley now!" I chanted.

Mr. Dixon's van rattled through the maze of downtown streets. And then, we headed up to the top of Brandon Hill where Ashley and sixty-one other orphans lived in 'a place of safety.' I rang the doorbell again at the gates of the orphanage. "Mrs. B is expecting me," I said to another unfamiliar face, who opened the gate and allowed me to entry. I made my way inside the building towards Mrs. Brown's office."

The kind, firm, woman gave me a warm, welcoming smile. "You are becoming Jamaican mon."

"I know that Ashley is not yet available for adoption..."

"Yes, yes, yes," she nodded. "You are a friend working with her. Ashley is in the yard."

I'd never seen the children dressed in school uniforms before. They all looked as if they might be attending a prestigious private school. The girls were wearing red-and-white-checkered gingham dresses, while the boys sported formal brown shirts and pleated khaki pants.

Ms. Matthews made an announcement when she saw me walking towards the kids, "Ashley's mother is here. Ashley it's your *mother*." I cringed because the plan was to introduce me to Ashley as her 'special friend.' I didn't want to be the cause of more heartache, if the system didn't approve this adoption.

"Hello Ashley, it's good to see you again. How are you?" I asked on bended knee. Ashley just barely smiled. Do you remember me? Do you know who I am?" A light flickered behind those dark chocolate M&M eyes. She nodded.

We sat together on that rickety picnic bench. I clutched what I thought of as my big red 'Mary Poppins' bag, packed to the brim with small games to ignite her imagination. I pulled out the striped zebra photo album. "Do you remember this?" I asked. Ashley's head bobbed more assertively. She took the album from my hand, and searched through the pocket inserts for the pictures she had seen before. I noticed a new pink scar on the back of her left hand, reminding me about the 'beatings' Ms. Wilton has described. "How did that happen?" I asked. Ashley quickly covered her hand hiding the fresh wound. She riffled through the album until she found a picture of herself wearing the white tie-dyed dress I'd given her on our last visit. "Do you remember that dress?"

"I remember the frock. What is your name?"

"My name is Erika."

"Are you my mother?"

"I am your special friend for now," I lied, betraying my own heart. "I am here to spend time playing with you. Would you like to do that?" Ashley nodded. "I like your hair." I told her. "It's gotten longer since I last saw you."

"Auntie Joy did it."

I've learned that children in Jamaica respectfully address adults as 'Auntie,' or 'Uncle,' without any implied relation. Jamaicans embrace the philosophy, 'it takes a village,' to raise a child. I hoped that Auntie Joy was someone that Ashley was able to build a relationship with, so that one day she might be capable of attaching to our family.

Attachment disorder was my biggest concern in adopting an older child. Children who haven't learned how to love, and be loved, by experiencing nurturing from biological parents, have a hard time bonding to a new parent who wants a healthy connection with them. In order for adoption to be truly successful, the adoptee must be able to transfer an emotional attachment from a primary caregiver to the adoptive parent. The existence of any prior relationship is always more important that the length and quality of it.

Suddenly, a gathering of little girls circled around us at the picnic table. Gingham dresses swarmed all around my head and feet like bees. I recognized Julieanne, the healthy twin, who once read me a library book that had travelled with me from Canada. Sabrina Williams, the girl who snatched the polaroid picture from Ashley's hand, pillaged through the red bag in search of a hairbrush. All of the girls were fascinated by the texture of my Caucasian hair, and fought to be the next to brush it. "Be soft," I said, more than once.

Then, I pulled out the Barrel of Monkeys game and explained how to make a long string of primates, each hanging off the next. The girls all reeled with laughter as they competed to make the longest strand. Ashley produced a genuine smile, not the picture perfect one she'd practiced for the camera.

I wondered how they played in the Jamaican sun without copious amounts of water as sweat beaded down my back beneath my linen shirt. I'd already drained my water bottle and felt dehydration creeping in. No wonder the whites of their eyes were yellowed.

At six o'clock, well past visiting hours, the children lined up to go inside for diner. I followed them into the cafeteria intending on staying until somebody asked me to leave. Forty kids sat noiselessly as they waited for their supper. "Close your eyes and shut up!" barked Ms. Matthews. (I noticed no one ever called her 'Auntie.') The children who dared to smile up at me were swiftly reprimanded with a stick on the back of their heads. I covered my eyelids with the palms of my hands hoping to get them to pray because I didn't want to be responsible for Ms. Matthews' wrath. The children recited the Lord's Prayer in perfect unison before Ms. Matthews retrieved the big silver trays of food from the kitchen.

I handed out the unevenly distributed bowls saving bigger portions for Ashley and the older boys. Ms. Mathews noticed and demanded that I "give the little ones their food first." We gave the children spoons, but they ate wildly with their hands like carrion birds. They shoveled the rice, kidney beans, and chicken into their mouths washing it down with less that a quarter cup of water.

To my recollection, the children never drank anything other than water, I never saw the older kids drinking milk, but I did see infants sucking down sweet fruit punch from their bottles.

That day, I assisted by handing out the small allotment of water after the evening meal. I arbitrarily gave a blue cup with a handle on it to a child who had finished his supper. The children all cried out in unison, "No! That is Alex's cup!" Immediately I corrected my mistake, taking the special cup from the nameless child, and presenting it to Alex, who was sitting alone at one end of the table. I wondered how Alex had staked a claim to a personal item when no child seemed to own anything in particular. Later, I learned that Alex received special consideration because he had AIDS. Despite the fact that sharing liquid from a cup does not transfer the disease, they were taking precautions so as not to spread the virus.

My innocuous visit continued, even after dinner when I followed the girls downstairs to a part of the orphanage that was new to me. In the laundry room, I walked past several washing machines and dryers that busily churned through mounds of dirty clothing. The girls stepped out of a back door to a concrete area and simultaneously began taking off their gingham dresses. I tried to hide the look of surprise on my face, not wanting the girls to feel uncomfortable around me in their nakedness. I realized how different each girl was beneath her school uniform. The gingham dresses hid the various sizes of booties and belly buttons that surrounded me. Ashley's body was long and lean, much like the girls in my own family. I wondered about Sabrina Williams' enlarged belly button. Was it normal? Did it indicate malnutrition? Dehydration? Our Jamaican cook told me, in earnest, that if babies were left to cry they got big belly buttons.

Ms. Mathews instructed the girls to wash their own panties with blue bar cake soap and a hose, which they did without hesitation. I stifled more surprise when each girl squatted to pee near a hole in the concrete that trickled down the hillside. An Auntie with kind eyes noticed my reaction. "They take their showers here in the hose because it is nice outside."

"Of course!" I said, recalling a time period when I could not afford to pay the gas bill to heat water in our California apartment. I had to take a bar of Dove soap poolside for Jonathan and Erica to take warm showers outside.

The girls then each grabbed a toothbrush out of a bucket to clean their teeth. Afterwards, they all put their used toothbrushes in a different bucket filled with water. A caregiver I did not recognize hovered behind me. She was a thinker who asked, "How long are you supposed to be here?"

"I do not know," I answered honestly. "I have a letter. I am allowed to visit Ashley."

"Visiting time is usually over now," the unnamed woman informed me.

"If you want me to leave I will," wondering if I might be jeopardizing future visits with Ashley if I pressed the issue.

The kind caregiver called Ashley over to pick out nightclothes from a Tupperware bib. "Let her help dress the child, and then she can go," she said. I gave her a grateful smile when she handed me a faded shirt with sparkling pink decals on it. "They wear the older clothes at night." I scanned the bins for the Ashley's white tie-dyed dress, but it was nowhere to be seen.

Ms. Matthews used a sickeningly sweet tone of authority to tell the girls how important it was to keep their bodies clean. "You must scrub your faces and in between your legs, and then rinse well under the hose." The innocent girls obeyed compliantly.

I noticed the little girl named Kimeysha whom I'd seriously considered when looking for my wild-haired child. She was well aware that I was watching her. I wonder if she knows about the nightmares she gave me for leaving her behind.

Ms. Matthews had taken a liking to a new girl named 'Abby' whom I did not recognize. She was the tiniest of the bunch, and Ms. Matthews treated her small sweetness gently. Abby cried when the cold hose water rinsed the soap off her small body. I fumbled for a piece of clothing little enough to fit her, and then dressed her for bed, softly, hoping she would somehow remember a mother's loving touch.

The boys came from the playground to begin their bedtime washing ritual when the girls moved up the stairs leading to the orphanage foyer. Eventually, they all sat together on the long bench in the main hallway, again uncommonly quiet. I walked down the bench touching each hand, praying each child would dream sweet dreams. And then, I had to turn my back on them and go.

I climbed into Mr. Dixon's van without saying a word. The van bumped down Brandon Hill, through the hip strip, and then over the unpaved road to the beautiful colonial home where I would rest my weary head. The proprietors, Jeremy and Clarissa were relieved to set eyes on me, their wayward guest.

I made my way down through the gated walkway to the hip strip for barbequed food at the Pork Pit, satisfying myself with a quarter of a jerked chicken before returning to the lovely yellow room beside the pool, and falling asleep before my head hit the pillow.

I woke up before the sun rose the next morning, not knowing what the new day would bring. I drank the Blue Mountain coffee that Angelica unexpectedly delivered to my door on a silver tray. Later, I moved to the veranda to eat ackee and saltfish. My taste buds had become accustomed to the distinct flavors that characterize Jamaican cuisine. I particularly liked the fried dumplings and plantains. I *was* turning Jamaican mon.

My patience waned shortly after breakfast. I called the general number to the CDA from my room, hoping Mr. Grant would let me take Ashley to the beach for the day. Surprisingly, Ms. Wilton answered the phone. "Ms. Isnor? I have been trying to reach you, but all I get is the voicemail. I need you to come into the office to sign a paper saying you will pick up Ashley Parkinson today and return her on Friday."

My heart nearly stopped. I'd been a mother for almost forty years, yet I found it daunting to be solely responsible for a little orphan girl for a few days. What if? *What if?* Did this mean that they trusted me? Would they do this with just anyone? Were we closer? Would Canada approve the home study? Was I crazy? How did one hand over a child to a virtual stranger for four days? How did one *return* a child they had taken care of for four days? *Of course I will be right there to sign the letter!"*

I called Mr. Dixon at nine-thirty asking for a ride down to the CDA. He said "he was doing something, but could get me at eleven-thirty."

"Eleven-thirty? Half the day was already slipping away!" Mr. Dixon sympathetically arrived within the hour. He took me to the CDA where he waited in the van below the offices.

I sat anticipating the conversation I would have with Ms. Wilton as I waited, silently rehearsing the script in my head, intending on pressing her to place the advertisement.

"Yea mon, I will do it," she promised after finally inviting me inside her cubicle. It seemed to take any eternity to make any progress at all in the process. It took the entire morning to complete the simple task of writing a letter allowing Ashley to leave the orphanage.

Ms. Wilton systematically composed the message in long hand, typed it out on the CDA letterhead, made a copy on an old Xerox machine, manually attached it to Ashley's manila file, and finally handed me the letter inside a sealed envelope addressed to "Ms. Geneva Brown ~ Blossom Gardens." I tucked it inside the red bag and bolted back to Mr. Dixon.

Ms. Oliver, a small brittle woman, opened the gates when we arrived at Blossom Gardens. She led me inside to the office where I recognized the woman sitting behind Mrs. Brown's desk. Carmellina was the smartly dressed woman who first opened the gates for us. "Good morning Ms. Isnor, please have a seat. They are preparing Ashley for you. They packed a bag of clothing for her."

"I have everything I think Ashley might need. I have clothes, sandals, jammies, and a toothbrush," trying to minimize the amount of time it would take to get her out of there. I continued sitting for an ungodly amount of time before Carmellina finally checked on Ashley.

"They are doing her hair. Soon come."

Ashley walked into the office, at long last, looking quiet and shy. They'd dressed her in a nice pair of pressed khaki trousers with brightly embroidered flowers on them. She wore a peach-coloured shirt laced with rhinestone trim and white Disney princess sandals. I'd never seen shoes on her feet before. Understandably, Ashley did not appear to be excited to leave with me. I was still a stranger to her. Eventually, she took my hand and we headed towards the gates together, leaving Blossom Gardens behind shortly before noon.

I wanted Ashley to immediately shed everything she'd worn at the orphanage when we got to the hotel. I opened the door to our room, excited to show her the buttery yellow walls I found so comforting. I asked Ashley to place the orphanage clothes on a chair, but she disrobed and dropped her clothes on the floor in front of me. I handed her the one-piece swimming suit I'd found on the summer clearance rack at our Winners Department Store in Calgary. When I put it on her, she looked like she was playing dress up in her mama's clothes.

We dipped into the beautiful turquoise water on that first afternoon. I thought, like Tejah she might fear the water, but soon discovered her respect for it, when I showed her where the shallow end of the pool sloped into deepness.

After swimming, we realized that we'd left the hotel key inside our room and that we were locked out. We had to go searching for the maid to open the door for us. I noticed how acutely observant Ashley was of her surroundings. I'd assumed I'd found an exceptionally bright young girl, using advanced cognitive skills, because she attached the turquoise elastic band to her tiny wrist, and kept an eye on it like a hawk the entire time she was with me.

I would learn that due to "emotional abuse and beatings," Ashley's brain development was delayed. Ashley's brain was wired for survival to help her stay safe. She often acted from instinct instead of reason, perpetually scanning the environment for sights, sounds, people, behaviors, smells, or anything reminiscent of threat. It must have been exhausting for her to remain in a perpetual state of hypervigilance.

Once inside our room, we changed out of our swimsuits before walking down the hill to the Pork Pit where we shared a meal together. I'd brought Ashley a pair of pink shorts, an adorable pink and green plaid cotton shirt, and a set of matching green sandals for her to wear on our first excursion.

The new clothes looked like they'd already been through the wringer at the very first meal. Ashley shoveled every morsel of chicken, and rice and peas into her mouth with her hands. I decided not to provide a second portion because I didn't know how her tummy would react to being filled. Grape soda dripped down the front of her plaid shirt. I hoped there would be plenty of time to work on manners later. We certainly had a lot of hard work ahead of us.

Ashley took my hand and we walked back to our room. She easily climbed inside the tub for a warm bubble bath, thrilled by the novelty, but it took some coaxing and a promise of a story to get her out. She dried off with a soft towel, brushed her teeth with her personal pink toothbrush, and then climbed into our double bed. Ashley was unaccustomed to sleeping with a pillow, or even a top sheet at the orphanage, so I was happy to see her take pleasure in the comfortable bedding. We fell asleep nesteling together underneath those sweet smelling linens. My last thought before drifting off, was that according to the schedule I saw posted at the orphanage, Ashley would be awake by five-thirty in the morning.

Her internal alarm clock worked well, because she opened her eyes right on time the next day. "Good morning sunshine," I cooed. Ashley smiled. I searched her face looking for any trace of concern or confusion about being with a stranger. There was none, so we snuggled together in bed, reading the storybooks I'd brought from Calgary until the sun came up.

Later that morning, we traversed the wraparound porch exploring the beautiful grounds of the colonial style house. I snapped photographs of Ashley surrounded by fuchsia bougainvillea with the turquoise pool behind her. Ashley's stunning profile reminded me of Iman, the high fashion model born in Somalia, who ironically also had a sister named Nadia.

I wanted to get a feel for where Ashley stood academically. I'd learned from her teacher, Ms. Cambell, that Ashley had never attended school before her arrival at Blossom Gardens. The day that Sid and I tried to visit the orphanage, Mr. Dixon offered two women a ride down Brandon Hill to Sam Sharpe Square. I recognized one of the women as Ashley's teacher. Mr. Dixon introduced me to Ms. Cambell who'd said, "Ashley has a willingness to learn. The girl catches on quickly. If she were in regular school right now, she would be in grade one."

I'd learned it was a privilege, not a right, to receive an education in Jamaica where school fees, book fees, uniforms, and 'polishable' brown shoes made an education prohibitively expensive.

I pulled out some washable Crayola markers and a math workbook from the red bag. The first worksheet showed a mirrored image line drawing of a girl. The picture on one side looked like a colouring book waiting for attention, while the other side appeared finished. The instructions read, "Colour the girl so that they both look the same."

Methodically, Ashley picked up the yellow marker and filled in half the stripes on the girl's top. Then, she chose the red marker finishing the shirt. I sat back watching, as she carefully coloured within the lines, making the shorts blue, shoes brown, and purple socks. Ashley's tongue stuck out the side of her mouth as she worked.

We filled the hours before breakfast getting to know each other. I wanted to discover what made Ashley tick. What games could we play together that would capture Ashley's attention, allow natural communication, and form a lasting bond of connection between us? The first five years of a child's life are the most formative, and Ashley was already six. That day, I set an unreal expectation that this goal could be accomplished in four days, ignoring the tick-tocking sound of the metronome in my head, warning me that it was already to late.

In time, we put away the school work and moved towards the veranda to share a meal. Our breakfast settings included a bread plate, water glass, china cup and saucer, folded serviette, and formidable cutlery. I picked up my napkin intending on introducing a new game. "Every time we sit down for a meal I want you to pick this up and place it in your lap." I showed Ashley the crease at the fold of my serviette. "This fold belongs at your tummy. This is what you use when some food accidentally gets on your face." I dramatically dabbed the corner of my mouth.

Ashley impulsively popped up from the table and pointed at the ships she'd noticed in the bay. Her serviette dropped helplessly to the floor. "Come back here young lady," I said with mocked sternness. "When you get up from the table during a meal, you are to leave the serviette on your chair, showing others that you are not finished eating." Ashley politely returned to her chair, and placed the fold of her napkin at her waist as I'd requested.

During breakfast, I encouraged Ashley to use her spoon and fork instead of her fingers. She instinctively shovelled as much food into her mouth as quickly as possible. I'd cut the flour dumplings in half showing her how to use the bread as a 'pusher' towards her fork. The soupy combination of fish, gravy, vegetables, and ackee garnished Ashley's brand new clothes, and Clarissa's beautiful table linens.

Ashley devoured every morsel on her plate before reaching for mine. I quickly scooted my plate out of her reach, remembering another girl, named Helen Keller, who had once blindly taken food off others plates, before her teacher, Annie Sullivan, taught the child social graces. I noticed scrapings of food scattered all over the floor when we left the table.

We returned to our yellow room answering a call from my Internet friend Maryam. Their adoption had been finalized, yet they remained in Jamaica waiting for Daniel's visa from the United States embassy in Kingston. I picked up the receiver, but all I heard was static.

"Erika?" I distinctly noted a New York accent.

"Yes, Maryam, it's me Erika," the annoying static continued, but Maryam spoke through it.

"Daniel and I really need to get out of the city, we were thinking of going up to Negril. Daniel loves Negril, and I know of a small cheap hotel where we could all stay. The kids could swim at the beach…"

I'd already paid for the beautiful yellow room. Also, I remembered the expensive chartered taxi ride we'd hired when we went to Negril to see the cliff diving at Rick's Café.

"It's only six dollars if you don't mind going local. The children are free, at least Daniel is as he can sit on my lap. The hotel would cost us thirty dollars US, each."

I hesitated about thirty seconds. "Yes, we'll go," I answered.

"Meet me at the bakery downtown."

"The bakery downtown?"

"Yes, it's easy to find, just follow Bottom Road into town. You'll run into the bakery. It's where all of the local taxis pick up people going out of Mobay. We might have to share with others."

"Sounds good," I said, wondering what the heck I was getting myself into. I packed a small overnight bag with jammies, toothbrushes, a spare set of clothes, and fresh underwear for each of us, and we were already wearing our swimming suits beneath our clothing. Our room key dangled from the elastic band on Ashley's wrist as we left our hotel room headed towards the bakery.

Maryam said it "wasn't too far." We walked along the ocean side of the street, well past Margaritaville, and the concrete inlet where the presumably safe JUTA taxi drivers waited in their vans. I recognized the Pelican restaurant, owned by our hotel proprietors. Further down the street was the two-story Burger King. I wouldn't dream of eating American fast food when the Pork Pit stood less than a hundred feet away. Still, we kept walking in the heat, towards Aqua Sol. It looked like a run down theme park with an ancient go-cart track and rusty bumper cars. Ashley began to complain.

"Pick mi up!"

"Yeah right. You pick *me* up!" I said hoping to keep the mood light. It was *stinking* hot and we still had a long way to go. I was more concerned about the 'what ifs' than Ashley's actual behaviour. *What if* Ashley threw a fully-fledged tantrum? We were only beginning to know each other. *What if* she freaked out and ran in to the street in front of a car? *What if* I ended up in a Jamaican jail cell charged with the death of a child? Ashley continued walking beside me sulking and dragging along just like any normal six-and-a-half-year-old child. I thought she looked like dark chocolate melting in the Jamaican sun.

"Maybe we can find a taxi..." I said out loud, but more to myself than to Ashley. Immediately, her long arm shot straight up into the air. Obviously Ashley knew how to flag down a taxi. She must have done it before. When and with whom? I wondered.

We moved to the other side of the street, like we were entering the water at the inside of a river bend where the water is shallow. The intersection where the road narrowed forced the cars to pile up like converging currents. "Hold my hand," I ordered. "When I say run....run! Ashley looked up at me with those beautiful brown eyes. We locked hands. "Run!" I shouted, imagining animals in the Serengeti defying Mara River crocs, and any notion of logic, but making it safely to the other side.

We followed the road with uncertainty; Ashley held my hand with certainty. The closer we got to the city, the more populated the streets became. A Rasta man held out his hand asking me for money. I ignored him, and kept walking until we spotted the corner of Harbour Street where the taxis lined up. Maryam and Daniel were waiting inside the corner bakery. Ashley started jumping up and down when she recognized the two of them, unafraid of displaying her joy.

Maryam turned out to be a tiny specimen of a woman, who by sheer determination could have slain Goliath; for she had David's courage and huge heart. I never guessed she would have been so small and dainty looking, but no one who knew Maryam would have described her as either gentle or motherly. Maryam and I embraced as if we were lifelong friends. Maryam, was yet another diamond set in my path to teach me about the ways of the island, and the Jamaican adoption process. We didn't know each other, but we *knew* each other. Our parallel paths seemed destined to cross.

We all climbed into the vehicle driving north bound up the beautiful Jamaican coast to Negril. Car rides have always made me drowsy, especially when the road rocks back and forth like a lullaby. Our two little ones fell fast asleep, and I struggled to keep my eyes open, afraid of what I might miss should I too give in to sleep. We passed a country club resort featuring exclusive executive villas, and private pristine beaches. The highway weaved through several small fishing villages, where docked boats rested, after their early morning trips to sea, and uninhibited naked children played in the water. The dichotomy between rich and poor boggled my mind.

Two hours later, our driver signaled left, turning into the rocky driveway of a hotel named New Moon Cottages, where there were no large protective gates. When Maryam and I split the thirty-dollar cab fare, she asked for the driver's business card to add to her arsenal of Jamaican contacts. That day, following Mayam's lead, I accepted the first card beginning my own collection.

David, the owner of New Moon, emerged from his private residence located in the main house, a separate building situated close to the highway. He and Maryam engaged in a lengthy discussion about whether we wanted to be in the back, or front of the rental house, and whether we wanted twin or double beds. Apparently, there had been some trouble with people looking into the windows in the back of the house.

"Daniel will sleep with me in a double bed. What about you and Ashley?" I couldn't help but think of the beautiful yellow room waiting for us in Coral Cliffs.

"We can sleep together too." I wanted to be in the *front* sharing a connecting porch with Maryam.

The children were running around the large yard playing tag when I heard a ferocious dog barking. I dropped my backpack on the porch and ran towards the noise, expecting to protect them from great gnashing teeth. Thankfully, the mad dog was chained, but we clearly needed to establish boundaries. "You are not to cross this concrete sidewalk. Do not go on that side of the property." I said, sounding exactly like Sandra Bullock in The Bird Box. "Do you understand?" Both children nodded.

I realized that Maryam frequented New Moon when I watched her retrieve a backpack from behind the bushes next to the main house. "These are my summer things. Hopefully this will be the last time I need them here."

"Mi hungry! Mi thirsty!" sang our children.

"If you tend the children, I'll walk down to the little store around the corner to get us some water," Maryam offered.

I watched the kids resume running around the yard, tinkering with the idea of just spending a couple of hours in Negril before hiring a driver to take Ashley and me back to Montego Bay. I toyed with the business card hiding in my pocket.

Maryam returned shortly with four bottles of water, which we all quickly drained. Note to self, *never go anywhere in Jamaica without water!* We decided to grab another cab ride up to Rick's Café for an early dinner. We walked down the driveway to the busy main highway, where cars were ripping past us from both directions at breakneck speeds. I held Ashley's hand tightly as Maryam negotiated $200 JMD for the two-minute ride to the infamous tourist spot. We were soon delivered safely at the entrance, where Maryam instigated an argument with the two hundred pound bouncer who noticed the bottle of water in her hand.

"No outside drinks," he said firmly.

"I'm not going to drink it inside. *See,* I put it in my bag. I promise I'm not going to drink it inside."

I believed Maryam's promise, but apparently the bouncer didn't. "Everybody says that," he said, as Maryam tucked the bottled water deeper into her backpack before walking past him. Maryam had balls.

I'd come to Rick's before, when we'd all jumped off the cliffs into the water below, but I didn't expect to be doing that with Ashley. We headed directly for the pool hoping to find one of the tables set up inside its shallow end. I pointed out the diving platform hovering seventy-five feet above our heads.

The divers were men of steel with bodies shaped like the letter 'Y.' They worked the crowd with a tin bucket, collecting tips, before taking a death-defying plunge into the sea below. I couldn't believe that the weight of those men didn't snap the skinny trees. Once over our heads, they stood on an edge so small, that their toes dangled over the end of it. "Ashley, Daniel look up," I said, just in time for the kids to see a man swan dive into the water.

Our kids splashed and played, scooting themselves around crocodile style, in the pool beneath our feet. There was another table not five feet away where a foursome of leathered retirees sat sipping cocktails. They complained that our children were getting them wet. I could tell by the expression on their faces that they looked down on our beautiful black children. "You are *in* a pool," I reminded the grouchy foursome."

I ordered chicken wings and beer for Maryam and me, hamburgers, coke, and fries for the kids. I never found a great burger in Jamaica. The meat tastes different, and you don't see many cows grazing there. I remembered our first driver, Easten, chuckling behind the steering wheel at the sight of a truckload of cows being pulled over by the police."They probably stole the cows. There's a big fine for that," he'd said.

I decided we would stay the night, and return to Montego Bay the next morning. It had been a long and exciting day for all of us. I finished Ashley's half-eaten hamburger and paid the tab. The sun set, making the entire trip to Negril worth every extra cent. I supposed that Maryam would have probably chosen a less expensive place to eat, because her finances had been depleted by their elongated stay waiting for Daniel's traveling visa.

We were exhausted when we opened the door to our simple room at New Moon. I helped Ashley pull a yellow nightgown over her wiry hair and brush her teeth. And then, she jumped into my arms under the scratchy covers. "Goodnight mommy," Ashley said quietly, stealing my breath away.

Ashley fell asleep quickly nestled against me.

"You will always be safe with me," I whispered kissing her forehead before joining Maryam on our shared porch.

That night Maryam filled me in on what life was really like at the orphanage for our children. She told me that the kids didn't have pillows, or covers, because the workers would take anything nice home for themselves. The little ones slept on just a fitted sheet covering a cheap mattresses.

Kristy B., another adoptive mother, later verified that 'Embracing Orphans' had once remodeled the children's bedrooms providing curtains, pillows, sheets and comforters. The next time she'd visited everything they'd brought before had disappeared. How do you steal from orphans?

Maryam voiced her concern about the use of medication to calm some children down. She told me that Daniel never said a word the entire three years he'd been at the orphanage, because of the medication. It dawned on me, that the day I'd identified Ashley, Maryam's Daniel was the boy sleeping on the desk next to her.

Maryam and I talked about the child abuse running rampant through the orphanage sharing stories about Ms. Matthews. Authorities higher than Mrs. Brown believed she was an asset to the compound because she kept the children in line. There was a distinct cultural difference between what was considered abuse in the Caribbean and North America. In the Caribbean, discipline was taught through authority rather than with reasoning and choices.

We sat together on the little porch between our rooms, talking late into the night. I shared my experience of seeing a five-year-old boy tied to an iron headboard with a bed sheet at Blossom Gardens. The bed sheet had been twisted to resemble a rope. His two hands were bound together at the wrist. In Canada, that constituted abuse. In Jamaica, it did not. We thanked God that Ashley and Daniel would be leaving such a place.

The next morning we all woke up starving. We carefully walked down the shoulder of the road to eat breakfast at Jenny's. I ordered my coffee with sugar and cream, but Maryam wisely suggested I taste it first, because Jamaicans use sweetened condensed milk in the beverage. We filled our stomachs with ackee and saltfish, fried plantains, broiled dumplings, and bammy; a pancake-shaped deep-fried cassava bread. Ashley piled the sugar-sweetened guava jam on top of everything. Man, that kid could eat!

Afterwards, we took a cab into downtown Negril...*we was goin' swimming!* The driver dropped us off at the craft market near a stretch of free beaches. When I asked if he might be available to make a trip to Montego Bay at 1:30, I learned that drivers drove specific licensed routes identified by a sign painted on the side of the taxi door marking the legal perimeters."Yea mon, I can do it."

We kicked off our flip-flops, dropped our outer clothing in the sand, and raced to the sea. The calm, bright, clean water soothed the body and soul by gently toning down the mid-morning heat. "Let us draw near with a true heart in full assurance of faith, having our hearts sprinkled from an evil conscience, and our bodies washed pure with water." (Hebrews 10:22)

Horses pacing up and down the beach carrying tourists on their backs mesmerized Daniel. Back and forth they went, back and forth, with Daniel sitting in the sand patiently watching their parade. I wondered what was going on in his mind, as the large animals seemed to have him in a trance.

At long last, the guide stopped to let Daniel touch the horse's chest and head. "How much for him to get on?" Maryam asked.

"Twenty-five dollars mon."

"Twenty-five dollars just for the boy to sit on your horses' back for a minute? That's *robbery!*" Maryam stormed. The guide simply shrugged and walked away.

I taught Ashley and Daniel a game my brother, sister, and I played when we were small. We called it 'monster.' Our monster was the foam on the edge of the waves that couldn't touch your toes. You had to run back and forth on the sand evading the unpredictable movement of the sea. If the monster touched your toes, the monster won.

We are all running from evil monsters in the world.

The glorious water renewed my awareness of God's presence. I'd arrived on this majestic beach, showing a stubborn determination to do exactly as I pleased, acting on emotions, regardless of the consequences or effects. But, God was the Lord of a million second chances, one from whom I could ask and receive forgiveness.

Learning obedience is a lifelong process, and I continued struggling to understanding it. I've learned God wants us to trust and obey him, but then, the word *obey* only held negative connotations for me, as if it was something I had to do against my will.

That's not the kind of obedience that's in God's word. God wants us to see obedience to him as a relationship of love. Obedience comes from knowing that God loves you, and you love him in return. Only one, Jesus Christ, could walk in perfect obedience.

About that time, a Rasta man and this two-year-old son arrived on our beach. If the Rasta man had shown up alone, I'm certain my reception towards him would not have been a warm one. A man with a child seemed to be much less intimidating than a lone, black, tall, muscled, nearly naked, dreadlocked man.

The Rasta man shared his belief that Africa was the birthplace of mankind, where paradise would be created in the end of times. He was of the opinion that Jesus Christ was a black man, and that the western white society had been "deceiving us for centuries, maintaining superiority over all people." The Rasta man explained how he'd found faith and inspiration within himself.

The Rasta man honored me by asking me to hold his young son, so that he might take a swim in the turquoise water. His son, a powerful being, was firmly bonded to his father. The entire twenty minutes I held the boy, he *willed* himself toward the man who swam on the horizon. The Rasta man took long, purposeful, rhythmic strokes with his arms, swimming back and forth looking like a man at peace with himself attuned with the water.

I wanted that kind of relationship with my Father.

When Jesus said, "difficult is the way which leads to life," he was explaining how hard being a Christian really is. I believed the only way to the heavenly kingdom was through Jesus, but I was only taking baby steps getting to the Lord.

"I am the LORD your God, who teaches you what is good for you and leads you along the paths you should follow. Oh, that you had listened to my commands! Then you would have had peace flowing like a gentle river and righteousness rolling over you like waves in the sea."

That day, during my experience on the beach, a hunger seeded. I began to perceive that I was experiencing an internal transformation. I contemplated the simultaneous sanctification that was occuring. I began realizing that I needed more than a superficial cleansing. I desired something that would purify my soul, ease my thoughts, scrub my motives, and clear my conscience. I knew I could not keep lying to myself and the ones I loved. I could never go to another turquoise beach under false pretenses again. My soul desired a purging, but needed something to replace what would be expelled. Somehow, water seemed to be an essential element that would relieve me of my sin, guilt, and rebellious nature. I would learn that sanctification is an addition, whereas cleansing is a subtraction. In new life, what is added is Christ. What is subtracted is old patterns.

"Mi hungry, mi thirsty" Ashley yelled from the seashore. Her stomach demanded immediate attention or else we would probably still be on that beach.

We circled back through the seaside craft market into the town centre of Negril. Maryam suggested that we feed the kids lunch at The Lavish Chicken, where they drank Ting, and ordered curry chicken, and rice and peas. "Ting is da best," sang Daniel through a big white smile. Maryam recommended the curry goat, so I tried it. It has its own unique flavor, and a tougher texture than beef. I had a hard time getting used to the idea of eating an animal that roamed their island streets like a stray dog.

After lunch we wandered into a small Internet roadside café, where Maryam received an email from the Adoption's Coordinator, Ms. Marjorie Tumming, in Kingston, requesting the final piece of required paperwork to process Daniel's visa. Maryam ecstatically suggested we all celebrate the event by eating double-decker ice cream cones.

And then, we carried the kids piggyback style to New Moon, where our morning driver sat waiting, in hope of transporting us back to Montego Bay. Maryam suddenly decided to leave Negril with us, earlier than expected, to make final preparations for their eminent trip to New York. She asked the driver to allow us a half-an-hour to settle our accounts with David, and pack our belongings. Then, the four of us climbed into the taxi south bound back to Mobay, all falling asleep to the sound of rain beating on the top of the van.

It was nearing suppertime when Ashley took the plastic elastic coil off her wrist, and handed me the room key. I pushed the door open, and entered our comfortable yellow sanctuary. It had stopped raining, and the sun was shining brightly, so we decided to go swimming in the pristine pool before another early dinner at the Pork Pit.

Clarissa stopped by our breakfast table in the morning. We discussed our plans to visit the CDA that day, hoping to learn where we needed to go to get Ashley's birth certificate, a critical piece of the jigsaw puzzle, required before Ashley could apply for a visa. I assumed I knew Ashley Parkinson's full name, but had very little else to go on.

The first time I saw the remnants of Ashley's dark past was when I asked her about her birth mother. "We need to get some papers so that you can have a home and a mommy like Daniel. Will you tell me your mother's name?" Ashley's normally bright eyes darkened as if a storm cloud had passed over them. She shook her head slowly from side to side.

"Do you know your birthday? Or where you were born? She looked down at the floor and shook her head again. "I think it is critical to know when and where you were born. Do you want to know your birthday?" The light returned to her eyes, as her head bobbed up and down in an affirmative action. "Make sure you have the keys to the room, put your sandals on, and let's go!" Ashley raised her arm high in the air, she shook her thin wrist to show me she had the keys. And then, we went in search of her birthday.

We grabbed a cab down to the Digicel shop in Sam Sharpe Square. People were crammed in the store, so we had to wait in line at least a half an hour before buying the least expensive prepaid phone available. Ashley couldn't seem to stand still despite being asked to do so several times. A woman behind me was watching both my frustration and Ashley's mischievousness grow. She was one of those grandmotherly women wearing church clothes, and a quiet dignity. "We don't parent our children,' she said with a trace of condemnation coloring her words.

When we left store with a new Nokia flip phone, I scanned the street for a taxi with a red Rose Hill sign on its door. Maryam had reminded me to negotiate and agree on a fare *before* getting into a cab. "One hundred Jamaican dollars to go to the CDA on Kerr Crescent?" I asked the cabbie. He nodded, and we joined a continuous flow of people coming and going through his car. The fare was decidedly better that the twenty US dollars I'd been spending every other time I'd made the trip using charter drivers.

I wanted Ms. Wilton to see Ashley in person, so that she would have a face to attach to the manila file on her desk. I never knew what to expect upon arriving at the CDA. Surprisingly, Ms. Wilton ushered us into her cubicle right away. "We just wanted to stop in to say hello," I said, hoping Ms. Wilton would see how well we fit together.

"I can't believe how much this child can eat!"

"You need to be careful with food. They do tend to overeat and then get sick," said Ms. Wilton. I nodded, pretending that the possibility of overeating hadn't occurred to me. "Have you spent some time at the beach?" Ms. Wilton asked.

"We did. Ashley is a bundle of energy. I think she is having a fine time," I said. Ashley, bored with the adult conversation, inserted her pointer finger into a small round hole in the top of Ms. Wilton's desk, and twisted it around getting her finger stuck. I could see a look of panic growing on her face, very nearly causing me to laugh at the audacity of the situation.

Ms. Bradford, another social worker whose desk sat next to Ms. Wilton's, arrived in the cubicle with a lubricant that would gently ease Ashley's finger out of the hole. We didn't have any difficulties together until we were right under the noses of two social workers! I silently prayed that they would be as efficient in processing Ashley's paperwork, as they had been at extracting her finger from Ms. Wilton's desk. Ashley sat quietly by my side for the remainder of the time we were in the cubicle.

"When we were having breakfast, I asked Ashley when her birthday was, but she didn't know. I was wondering if you might be able to tell us." Ms. Wilton swivelled her chair around, so that she could reach the file cabinet behind her. She opened the middle drawer, reached back to the '*P's*,' pulled out a legal-size manila envelope, and then turned back to face us. Ms. Wilton flipped through the pages in the Ashley's file. "Ashley Parkinson was born on the 13th of October."

"What year?"

"2002." *Victory!* Ashley had her birthday.

"When we went to the beach, Ashley told me she was from Westmoreland Parish. Is that true?" Ms. Wilton glanced at the file.

"No mon. Ashley was born here in Montego Bay, at the Cornwall Regional hospital." *Thank you God! Another sign!* My mother's maiden name was Cornwall.

I took another deep breath. "Has Ashley's advertisement been placed?"

Ms. Wilton was a smart woman. I wondered what sort of education she required to be responsible for all of those children's files in her cabinet. I learned months later, that she first taught high school, before moving into "a more challenging career" in children's services. "Ms. Isnor, I told you I will not fold my hands, the advertisement will be placed." Ms. Wilton leaned back in her chair before asking, "Do you have a driver waiting for you?"

I puffed up my chest before speaking. "No mon. We are using local taxis now! They are much less expensive."

I called Maryam on my new Jamaican cell phone, arranging to meet back at the Butterflake Bakery. Maryam needed to pick up Daniel's medical clearance for his US visa at the Half Moon Medical Center in Rose Hall. She expected to return to Kingston the next day, and hopefully be headed home to New York the day after that. Ashley and I decided to tag along with them, and then stop by Angie's villa so that I could introduce her to my Jamaican friends.

I found Maryam's reluctance to share details about where she and Daniel had been living over the summer odd, because the conversations we held into the wee hours of the morning were without reservation. I would soon learn why. We left Rose Hall, sharing a cab back to Ironshore where Ashley and I got out at the villa. We hugged each other tightly, knowing it would be the last time we would be together before they left Jamaica.

Ashley and I walked through the iron gates up the steep familiar driveway. Predictably, we found Angie, Avion, Charnell, Rej and Duj all sitting under the mango tree, as if they knew we were coming. That night, I tried to explain to Angie why I wasn't staying at the villa any longer. "It was a matter of logistics and finances." I didn't admit that I felt a self-imposed obligation to feed Angie's family. Money ran out of my pocketbook like water through a sieve, if I planned on continuing to return to Jamaica, I needed to be better at managing money.

Later that evening, back at the Polkerris, Ashley and I lounged around in our yellow room. She soaked in another bubble bath, we read stories under the bed covers together, and we sang our bedtime prayer praising God for the gift of knowing Ashley's birthday. And then, she fell asleep in my arms, just as Kaiden would after a busy exciting day.

The next morning we ate French toast for breakfast, hoping the meal would be easier for Ashley to manage with a fork than ackee and saltfish had been. Our time together was quickly coming to a close. We swam in the pool while reality descended, upon which time Clarissa arrived poolside, wanting to know what time I should leave for the airport. I suggested that Mr. Dixon pick us up at noon.

We came out of the water at eleven o'clock, showered, and packed our suitcases. I folded Ashley's clothes lovingly, knowing I would wash them at home. Clarissa knocked on our door, giving Ashley a book of Bible stories that we placed on the top of her clothes, "I'll keep this safe for you and bring it back when I come back to see you." We rolled our bags into the grand foyer, where we stacked them up, with forty-five minutes to spare.

We decided to take one last walk down the unpaved road to the hip strip, passing all the closed souvenir shops. Montego Bay was not an early riser like us. Ashley looked birdlike hopping along beside me, making me think of the Dr. Seuss book *Are You My Mother?* A little bird dropped, "down, down, down, out of the tree…" The bird went on a quest to find his mother before being return to the nest by the giant Snort. That baby bird ran into scads of trouble looking for his mother.

"When are you coming back?" Ashley asked.

"On your birthday Ashley. Do you know when your birthday is?"

"My birthday is October 13," she said with a smile. Man, that kid was smart.

"Yes, it is Ashley and I promise I will be here for your birthday." My God, what had I just done? I'd made a *promise.*

Shopkeepers began emptying buckets of water out onto the sidewalks, mopping the filth of the night into the streets. We allowed one woman to entice us towards her, even though I wasn't interested in taking anything but Ashley home. "Are you adopting her?" the shopkeeper asked.

Ashley and I looked at each other.

"Yes," was all I said.

"Will you be taking her home today?" I looked down.

"No not today, we still have some paperwork to finish. She has to go back to the orphanage today."

"Blossom Gardens?" asked the shopkeeper. "Come in...come in," she beckoned. Oh great, now I had been lured into a shop, and would have to endure the vendor pushiness I'd thus far so artfully escaped. Ashley touched a little wooden bracelet. "Pick one out," said the shopkeeper, obligating me to pay for whatever Ashley chose. "Not that one, its too big for a little girl like you. Do you like this one?" Ashley nodded. "It's yours," said the shopkeeper, putting the multicolored, beaded bracelet on Ashley's wrist.

I felt so ashamed that I chose a wooden fish carving, I didn't need, or want. "How much for this?" I asked.

"You can have it for twenty-five US dollars."

"I have twenty." She nodded, and wrapped it up in brown paper for the flight home.

"When you come back, let me braid her hair properly," she said.

We expressed our appreciation for the shopkeeper's generosity before climbing back up the hill to our hotel. I held the package tightly under one arm, and Ashley's palm gently with my other hand. Mr. Dixon stood on the outside curb, with our bags already stowed in his van, when we returned.

Ashley slumped against my shoulder when we pulled up in front of Blossom Gardens. "Mi gonna ball," she said softly.

"Mi gonna ball too," I said, not believing how quickly our four days together had disappeared. Everything had changed, and I had so much explaining to do when I got home.

We both got out of the van. I let Ashley ring the bell, knowing how much pleasure it gave Sidney and Kaiden to push buttons. When I noticed the bead bracelet the shopkeeper gave Ashley dangling on her skinny wrist, I thought about the white tie-dyed dress, that she'd only ever worn once. "Ashley, do you want me to put your bracelet in your suitcase until I come back for you?" She didn't hesitate an instant, before taking it off her arm, and putting it on mine.

I turned around to face Mr. Dixon. "I won't be long," I didn't see any reason for prolonging our goodbye.I wanted to make the transition for Ashley as smooth as possible.

Auntie Joy opened the gate for us. We walked down the main corridor to the office where I hugged Ashley, and she hugged me back tightly. "I'll see you soon Sweety."

"On mi birthday, October 13," she said quickly, before turning to run towards other children in the yard.

Mr. Dixon left me at the airport well before my departure time. "Next time you're in Jamaica, call me and I'll make sure to get some Blue Mountain coffee for you. I can get it cheaper."

I checked in at the airline counter before passing through the immigration line. I wondered how hard it would be to smuggle Ashley home with me. They all looked alike, didn't they? If I could just get someone else's black child's passport, I could weave through this line with her, hold Ashley up for inspection when the immigration officer asks me to, like I did with Kaiden and Sidney. I could take her home, lose my job, be arrested, and possibly remain in jail for the rest of my life. I felt numb. I knew smuggling Ashley home was not an option.

I returned to Canada blinded by my conviction to change Ashley's life. I felt as though I had everything perfectly under control. Sid picked me up at the airport at 2 o'clock in the morning. I'd been traveling for fourteen hours, so I was physically and emotionally drained. He packed my luggage in the back of the Tahoe Hybrid, never uttering a word until we were home, and I'd lay on the bed.

"I know you went to Jamaica," was all he said.

I didn't want to answer to anybody. I'd been self-sufficient for nearly half a century, and refused to start asking someone else's permission for anything. My marriage seemed to be crumbling, like a city whose walls are broken through, because I lacked any sense of self-control. My most meaningful relationships were suffering, and I felt like an animal caught in a snare, strangling myself. I was broken.

Sid and I were miles apart. We cared very much about each other, but we were lousy at communicating. I learned, through the process, that it's impossible to love someone else before you love yourself. I still needed to learn how to forgive myself for my human weaknesses. It was only by God's grace, that our marriage had survived almost ten years, without my understanding the true meaning of love.

EIGHT

TURNING SEVEN

Eight weeks had gone by since Sid and I made our intentions clear about adopting Ashley, yet nothing seemed to have happened. *God's timing is perfect, not mine. I am not in control, but I am deeply loved by the one that is.*

There was little I could do from so far away, except to move words through emails and faxes, like rhetorical questions. I kept expecting instant replies, not realizing that Ms. Wilton's Internet was sporadic at best. Ms. Wilton's polite professional responses to my emotional inquiries always seemed to arrive by snail mail.

> *Ms. Isnor,*
>
> *We wish to express appreciation for the interest you have in sharing your heart and loving hands to one of our wards, namely Ashley Parkinson. I see where you have requested to be notified as soon as the advertisement is placed in the Daily Gleaner.*
>
> *Please bear in mind that the opportunity given to you to socialize with Ashley was on the basis that this child was not matched to you for adoption. Subsequently, there is no need for a constant update with regards to the advertisement.*

I have also noted your request in spending time with Ashley,
on her birthday, in October. A permission letter will be sent
to Ms. Brown's office.

My best regards,
Marcia Wilton

"What kind of stupid game was this?" I screamed at my laptop. I couldn't figure out the mixed signals I was getting. I didn't understand, at the time, how often Ms. Wilton protected our interests. In this case, she recognized our predicament, where we would not be allowed to form a relationship with a child for the purpose of an adoption, nor would would we be allowed to adopt a child unless there was already an established relationship. There seemed to be no escape from the dilemma, due to the conflicting, dependant conditions. Now I see how Ms. Wilton furnished opportunities for us to 'become special friends,' to build the necessary attachment, without revealing the nature of our true objective.

Ms. Wilton,

I have been looking in the Daily Gleaner everyday. I did not
see any advertisements for wards of the CDA. Perhaps I am
looking in the wrong place?

Ms. O'Connor referred us to you, as Ashley's social worker.
We have come to Jamaica six times in as many months. In this
time, we have not made any progress in identifying whether
or not Ashley is available for adoption.

Ashley will always be in our hearts. IF she is claimed,
fantastic, we will have been instrumental in finding her
Jamaican home. IF she is placed on the waiting list, we will
have a chance to be matched to her. It is in the best interest
of the child to move forward. You will find a home for one
child and free the spot for another in need.

We have a loving home available, ready and waiting, for Ashley. She has been in Blossom Gardens since January 9, 2007, yet no family member has claimed her. It is my understanding that Ashley is one of the oldest in a home for children up to age seven, which she will turn in two weeks. Where will she go from there?

I know I am only a special friend of Ashley's, but in my heart I am her mother. A mother will go to the ends of the earth for her child. Ashley needs a lot of love, and we have that to give.

Ashley is in your hands. We know that you have many children in your care. God never gives us more than we can handle. We are a comfortable, but not a wealthy family. We cannot continue the expense of monthly trips to Jamaica. Please help us economize by placing the advertisement so that we might start the process to bring Ashley home.

Kind regards,
Erika Isnor

I called the CDA in Montego Bay, hoping to speak with Ms. O'Connor, impatiently waiting for the Adoptions Officer to answer. The digital clock on the microwave displayed exactly how many expensive international minutes had already ticked away before she finally picked up the phone to listen to my concerns.

"Ms. Wilton is doing her job. Things take time," she replied.

"Is this a dead end?" I asked boldly.

"There is no getting past the process."

"What happens to Ashley once she turns seven and is too old to stay at Blossom Gardens?"

"When does the child turn seven?" Ashley was in Government care, how could she not know her age?

"She turns seven October the thirteenth," I replied politely.

"Then the child still has a year at Blossom Gardens." Ashley would be allowed to remain in an orphanage for another year, without a pillow, blanket, or anyone to kiss her eyes goodnight.

"Would it help if I called Mr. Bowen in Kingston to facilitate the process?" I asked.

"No sense in calling Kingston," she replied.

The conversation seemed fruitless.

I dialed Maryam's New York phone number, never expecting her to answer on the second ring. "Erika, I was just thinking about you, this is God's work!" Funny, how much my faith had been faltering before making the call.

"Maryam, you are home with your son!" The accomplishment was amazing!

"Yes, we are home and he is doing well. He is cold." They had begun an ordinary family life.

Maryam described Ashley as looking "lethargic and unresponsive," during their final trip to Blossom Gardens, before leaving the island. "She'd drastically lost weight."

I couldn't conjure up an image of Ashley looking any more skinny than she was wearing her purple swimming suit. I closed my eyes, picturing Maryam whispering words of comfort into Ashley's ear. I envisioned my friend wrapping her arms around my weeping child, under the mango tree in the schoolyard. Ashley listened attentively. The scene unfolded peacefully in my mind, as a moment of serenity passed between the two of them, Maryam mothering my daughter in my absence. A moment later, in my daydream, Ashley suddenly jumped out of Maryam's lap to join a game of keep away with the other girls in the yard.

I snapped back into reality. "Maryam, how did you get Daniel's ad placed?

"I hounded Mr. Bowen. *Simply hounded him.* I emailed him, and called his cell phone every single day," she confessed. I could do that! I decided to begin my own hounding of Mr. Bowen, after being fuelled by my conversation with Maryam.

I immediately called Kingston, and was transferred to a male assistant. "When might Mr. Bowen be available?" I inquired.

"Try back in twenty minutes or so," he advised. I set the timer on the microwave to be alerted as to when the time had passed, and then redialed the Kingston number when it buzzed.

"Hello, Mr. Bowen. This is Erika Isnor from Calgary, Canada. I spoke with you in September, regarding the placement of an advertisement of a ward of yours. Ashley Parkinson, in Montego Bay, who is currently living in Blossom Gardens. It is my understanding that a request to place the ad was sent to you by her social worker, Ms. Wilton, but she didn't give me any specific information." I waited.

"The request is in Kingston, and we are going through with the process," said Mr. Bowen, stunning me into silence. Mr. Bowen then suggested that I "file an application for adoption in Montego Bay."

"The application to adopt has been filed with Mrs. O'Connor, who is waiting for the child to be identified as 'free for adoption,' before matching her to us. We will be returning October ninth, and I hope the ad will have been run by then." He made no promises, only giving me his word that the process was in motion.

I disconnected with Kingston, and called Blossom Gardens. Carmelina put Ashley on the phone immediately and her smile radiated through the line. "Do you know who you are talking to? I asked, imagining Ashley's little head bobbing up and down in response. "Do you know how much I love and miss you?" Silence. I needed to ask a question that did not require a simple yes or no answer. "What did you have for lunch today?

"Chicken."

"Oh I know you *love* chicken! Who are you playing with today? Sabrina Williams? Julieanne?"

"Yes."

"I'm coming back on your birthday. Do you know when that is?"

"October thirteen."

"Yes, my darling, your birthday is October thirteen. I will see you then."

I hung up the phone feeling uplifted after speaking with Ashley. And then, I decided to forge forward in my quest with tenacity, planning on saving Ashley from all of the earthly entities that were failing her.

In time, I sat down in front of the Macintosh I'd screamed at to compose emails of a more grateful nature:

Ms. Wilton,

It appears as if I owe you an apology. You gave me your word that you would work on Ashley's file. Although I never doubted you, apparently I was impatient, in my faith. I am working on patience. Please understand that my pushiness is in good faith. Thank you so much for working with us and taking such good care of Ashley.

Erika Isnor

The Internet enabled me to keep tabs on Ashley through a variety of different sources. I contacted Ashley's teacher, Ms. Campbell, by email, asking for her assistance in caring for Ashley while I was so far away:

Ms. Campbell,

Thank you for always being so loving and kind to all the children in your care. We are truly blessed to have you as Ashley's first teacher. She sings me your counting songs, and is so very willing to learn. We would love to hear about what is going in her life anytime.

Kind regards,
Erika Isnor

Ms. Campbell soon responded to my email:

Ms. Isnor,

Ashley is doing fine showing lots of interest in school, as usual. She remembers her birthday, October thirteen, and keeps reminding me also. I am so happy for her, and do hope this process will not be as long as we all think. I will surely watch over Ashley for you, and I hope and pray that all will be well soon…God Bless.

P. Campbell

Thanksgiving is traditionally a time to express gratitude in our home, but my state of being that year was clearly more willful than grateful. We have a very real enemy who thrives on destroying unity in every relationship. The cunning enemy is quick to launch a spiritual assault when a fault line surfaces in a marriage. The attacker wants us to look to the world for answers.

Our marital relationship experienced uncomfortable growing pains, particularly in the early stages of the adoption process when we weren't seeing eye to eye on important issues. It seemed easier to avoid conversations in our deadlocked state, than to risk getting feelings hurt, and drawn into uncomfortable confrontations.

We are not sent down righteous paths, we are led, sheep don't know where to go without a shepherd, and I was the black sheep gone astray. We both believed in the sanctity of marriage, and the solid foundation of our life together was based on our shared value system, but maintaining a blissful matrimonial home while in the midst of a disagreement threatened the entire families stability. I was anything but submissive.

I suspected rebuilding Sid's trust in me might be difficult after my lie, so I compromised by promising to be truthful when our aspirations were not perfectly aligned. I agreed to communicate, but not to change my course of action. Our most ineffective discussions took place through email, rather than face to face, because we were both lousy at conveying ideas and feelings. My written words were blunt and to the point. In one email, I asked Sid if the family could go to Jamaica for the Thanksgiving break, but felt shot down with his curt reply. "I have a work commitment on the thirteenth," he answered.

"Is it something that could change with enough notice?" I asked hopefully.

"No." Sid's work always came first and it frustrated me to no end. Sid's loyalty to his job made me feel like he was married to it instead of me.

"Fine. I'll take the girls then," I decided settling the matter. There. I'd communicated.

I felt like a caged canary with clipped wings. At the time, I was afraid of surrendering my independence, unaware that by entrusting my vulnerabilities to someone I deeply loved, it would liberate my soul, and create a strong bond of unity between us. It took me a long time to learn that the Lord did not create a hierarchy in marriage, He wants us to love each other equally.

The girls and I took the red-eye from Calgary, Sunday night, arriving in Montego Bay at two o'clock the next day. It was Nadia's first trip to Jamaica, Alyssa's third, and my fifth in eight months. Mr. Dixon picked us up at the airport and drove us directly to the CDA, where we anticipated receiving written permission to take Ashley to Negril for her birthday, as promised in an email from Ms. Wilton.

Apparently, "in the best interest if the child," Mr.Green retracted his permission allowing Ashley to go to the beach with us on her birthday. He cited concerns that we were "becoming too attached to a child not declared free for adoption." Ms. Wilton handed me an unsealed letter containing the sad news, already printed on official CDA stationary, explicitly stating our visit's boundaries:

> *Kindly allow Mrs. Erika Isnor, and her daughters, to interact with Ashley Parkinson, at Blossom Gardens Care Facility, during your visiting hours. Visits should commence October twelve through October fifteen 2009.*
>
> *Thank you,*
>
> *Signed*
> *Marcia Wilton*
> *Children's Officer*
>
> *Signed*
> *Oliver Green*
> *Team Leader*
> *St. James/Trelawny*

I tried asking Ms. Wilton about the advertisement, but she cast me a look more serious than a vehicle warning light flashing on my dashboard. "Ms. Isnor!" I closed my mouth.

We left the CDA with Mr. Dixon, who dropped us off at Blossom Gardens, where we planned on staying until they kicked us out. The orphans were playing in the dusty yard. Alyssa grinned when she heard

Ashley calling out her name, *"E-L-Y-EEEE C-A!!!"* using a very long e vowel sound. Ashley threw herself upon the girls, demanding hugs from each of them. It occurred to me that Ashley displayed indiscriminate affection, taking to Nadia like peanut butter does to jelly, a single minute after being introduced.

I lent Ashley my portable CD player to listen to a Beanie Man recording. She sat cross-legged on the ground, next to Sabrina Williams, sharing a single set of earbuds. Their adorable heads were bobbing, in sync, to the beat of the Grammy award winning Jamaican reggae artist. "What other singers do you like?" I asked the girls.

"Michael Jackson," they screamed in unison.

I watched Jodieanne, the twin with cerebral palsy, playing musical chairs around the picnic table with the others. Her limbs moved awkwardly, seemingly without purpose. Her legs crossed, in a scissor-like motion, becoming more exaggerated the faster she ran. One leg appeared to be shorter than the other, her pelvic bone tilted, and her spine curved. An aide promptly insisted that Jodieanne sit down, so that she would not slip and fall running around the benches. A beautiful smile fell from her face, as she sat beside me. I wrapped my arm around her shaking shoulders. "I know you could do it," I said hoping to restore her confidence. Jodieanne leaned against my side, while the other children continued cavorting merrily.

I'd learned that Jodieanne's father placed his twins in care because he could not afford the medical bills. Jodieanne and Julieanne were resilient, beautiful girls. When I inquired about their availability, Ms. Wilton flatly stated, "Their father will never sign off those girls."

Kimeysha followed Nadia around incessantly, like a curious puppy. Like Ashley, she had a quick smile. Her laugh resonated from the depths of her round belly. She was barely five-years-old, but had wise eyes. I appreciated those mischievous eyes, always following my every move, completely aware of the individual attention Ashley received from our family.

Alyssa's Arabic father blessed her with thick, dark hair. She sat on the bench under the mango tree letting the girls play with her long locks, which looked like ribbons attached to her head. When the smaller girls tugged and danced around Alyssa, pulling her hair from fifteen different directions, she said she felt like a maypole.

At five-thirty the children lined up for supper. We followed them into the dining area, where once again they ate chicken and rice, out of plastic bowls served from the aluminum tray. I sat beside Ashley who was devouring her food as usual. She looked up at me, and then picked up a spoon demonstrating her understanding of manners. I put my arm around those tiny shoulders, and gave her a squeeze of approval. "Are you going to take me to the beach?" Ashley asked.

"No baby, not this time. I couldn't get permission, but do you know what day tomorrow is? It is a very special day."

"Mi birthday?"

"Yes, tomorrow you will be turning seven."

"Tomorrow is October thirteen?"

"Tomorrow is October thirteen, and we will be here to celebrate with you."

According to Ms. Wilton's letter, we were only authorized to be at Blossom Gardens during visiting hours. Official visiting hours started at two o'clock, and ended at four.

Eventually, the children were all given their ration of water, before being scooted out the back door of the cafeteria. I knew the girls were going to take their showers in the hose, while the boys played in the yard. I blew a kiss to Ashley as she descended the back stairwell. And then, we called Mr. Dixon for a return trip to the Polkerris.

That night, we ate our Canadian Thanksgiving dinner at the Pork Pit, and then climbed up the concrete stairs, to sleep in a garden level room at the hotel. I would share a double bed with Nadia, knowing how Alyssa moved like a fish out of water when she slept. I declined the offer of joining the girls for a night swim, and curled up underneath my covers hoping to catch up on my sleep. I teased Nadia, as she slipped out the door, "Keep out of Jeremy's waterfall, it's for decoration only."

Mr. Dixon picked us up after a late breakfast, and drove us to Mega Mart to buy a birthday cake. Mega mart was a humongous Costco warehouse style store with a bakery tucked into one corner. I went looking for something pink.

"I'd like to order a birthday cake."

"It will take twenty-four hours to fill an order."

"What about all these cakes in the case?"

"They were ordered yesterday."

"Do you have anything for a seven-year-old girl? She is in an orphanage and we would like to take her a cake."

"Let me see what might be available." The clerk left me standing at the counter to see what she could find in the refrigerator. She returned with a round cake covered in white buttercream icing.

"How many people would that feed?" I asked.

"It depends how small you cut the pieces. Twenty to forty I would think." I tried figuring out how many children would fit in the cafeteria at the same time. "Is that the biggest cake you have?"

"Yea mon. This is the biggest."

Sold. "I'd like you to put some pink flowers on it, and write 'Happy 7th Birthday Ashley, please."

"Yea mon." The clerk passed me a pad of paper and a pen, to write down the message I wanted on the cake, "You can collect the cake in fifteen minutes."

We left Mega Mart, with the beautiful pink cake, and three colorful plastic blow up rafts, for the girls to float on at the pool. It rained cats and dogs while we were shopping, flooding the parking lot with at least a foot of water. Mr. Dixon was waiting in a parking stall just outside the door, watching for us when we came out. He suggested we stand on the curb while he brought the van around, and then held a large umbrella over our heads to keep us dry. He got soaked.

It was close to two-thirty in the afternoon by the time we maneuvered through the wet city. Our visiting hours were ticking away. We would only have an hour-and-a-half with Ashley on her birthday.

The children were all very excited about the treat. Ashley had gained a sort of celebrity status with the other orphans because of her white family. The other children had stopped picking on her, and I no longer discovered new cuts or bruises on her body. I leaned down to whisper in her ear. "I promised you I would be here for your birthday, and I am here."

"Are you going to be here on my next birthday?"

I honestly couldn't answer that question, especially now that I knew her birthday landed smack dab in the middle of the Canadian Thanksgiving long weekend. Travelling standby on any weekend was a crap shoot at best.

94

Besides, I hoped she would be in Canada by the time her eighth birthday rolled around.

The cake fed seventy-two people, including staff, at Ashley's birthday party. Everyone in attendance received a sliver of sweetness. I took great pride in providing cake for orphans, forgetting to even acknowledge another who once fed five thousand with only two fish and five loaves of bread.

The only photograph that survived Ashley's seventh birthday shows Ashley's resilient spirit, despite being out of focus. Ashley owned a piece of information that no one could ever take away from her. The only gift she received was the knowledge of the day she was born. I gently kissed her forehead when the clock struck four. Nadia and Alyssa gave the seven-year-old great big old bear hugs, and then we left, again, in Mr. Dixon's van.

We ate appetizers at Jamaican Bobsled restaurant for dinner. The girls each ordered a Ting, and we shared an order of fried coconut chicken. I paid the bill and we returned to the garden room where I promptly retired. My girls watched the late night TV movie until the wee hours. I noticed remnants of peanut butter and jelly sandwiches in the morning, but I'd never heard a peep during the night. I slept like a dog all night.

The next morning, I had to shake my nocturnal girls to wake them up for brunch. I slipped a cover-up on over my swimming suit, and set out for the table before them, needing my morning coffee. The girls eventually joined me on the veranda, just as I was finishing my second cup, where we ate outside under a cloudless sky. Nadia surprised me when she ordered ackee and saltfish, while my less food adventurous daughter chose French toast.

After breakfast, I suggested that the girls get their swimming suits on and bring up the Mega Mart floaties. They ran like schoolgirls downstairs to retrieve their toys. It took me longer than thirty minutes to blow up each raft. Yes, I did it, despite my refusal in Mega Mart. We shared some quality girl time floating the remainder of the morning away.

Finally, I suggested we check out Margaritaville. I looked forward to introducing Nadia to the yellow banana bridge floating between two trampolines, but the restaurant was overrun with tourists that morning. The cruise ship had already docked, and released its passengers. Nadia wisely took a single plunge down the two story slide to cool off, knowing we would be retracing yesterday's steps into the hot city.

We'd arranged to meet Charnelle, Angie's daughter, near the bronzed freedom fighters statues, in the middle of Sam Sharpe Square. We intended on visiting the children at Blossom Gardens together, but first stopped for take out chicken at Juici Patties on Union Street. Once fed, we all jumped into a Mount Salem taxi that took us all up Brandon Hill for $500 JMD. I was glad I didn't have to fork out another twenty for a private chartered driver.

The three teenage visitors went outside to play with the youngsters at the orphanage. Ms. Brown invited me to sit on the hallway bench to wait for my first official visit with Ashley. A small-framed Rasta woman, who was well into the second trimester of her pregnancy sat next to me. We remained together for several minutes before Irishun and Ashley, the only two children expecting visitors that day, came down out of their classroom. The pregnant lady turned out to be Irishun's birth mother, and I had to fight very hard not to be judgmental as I listened to her reading to her son. I had difficulty grasping her reality. I'd heard Irishun's mother described as 'brilliant,' but if she already had one son living in an orphanage, why was she pregnant? Everybody and their brother who were looking to adopt inquired about Irishun. He was the exceedingly charming Rasta boy I'd met on our first visit.

Ashley and I eventually moved outside, where we played games out of my red bag until they kicked us all out at four o'clock. I couldn't tell Ashley exactly when I would be coming back. How does a child grasp the concept, "I'm coming back for you, but I don't know when?"

I didn't need to be concerned about how we'd get back down the hill without Mr. Dixon. We quickly caught a cab just outside the orphanage. I learned that drivers worked specific routes on the hillside randomly picking up passengers for the fare of one dollar per passenger. We all ended up in the heart of the city as the bustling five o'clock hour approached.

Charnelle led us through the side streets back to Butterfield Bakery where taxi's lined up to take people out of the city. Charnelle stopped to buy a phone card from a vendor standing on the street corner wearing a bright green and yellow apron. She paid $200 JMD, adding minutes to her prepaid Digicel phone. I had no idea how much credit remained on my own phone, so I bought a card as well, activating the time by first dialing 331, and then the inserting nine digit code from the back of the card.

Charnelle climbed into a waiting taxi expecting the girls and me to follow."We can't get in," I protested. "The taxi doesn't have a *red license plate!*" I'd read all the warnings in the guidebooks, about how important it was to only get into cars that are specifically identified as legitimate transportation.

It's alright I know him." Charnelle said in a soft-spoken manner not unlike her mother's. Angie had instructed her daughter to only get inside a vehicle when the driver was familiar to her. Sometimes Charnelle waited an hour before finding someone she knew to take her home. I trusted Charnelle, so we got in.

We left the city center, driving towards Ironshore to spend our last night on the island with our Jamaican family. The taxi dropped us off at the Blue Diamond shopping center, where Charnelle phoned Angie for a ride up the hill. We picked up a few luxury snack items to share at the villa while we were waiting for Angie. I noticed a huge difference in the convenience store pricing compared to what we paid at Mega Mart. Angie already had jerk chicken sizzling on the grill when we arrived a the villa. I swear, Angie would give away the last morsel of food in her pantry without ever worrying about how she would get her next meal.

The girls swam together until their fingers wrinkled, before Suan drove us back into Mobay for a good night's rest. I struggled to get to sleep that night, worrying about when I would be able to return to the island. Our trips always came at a significant cost. My two teenage girls needed to concentrate on their High School marks, because no matter how valuable the time was we shared together, time away from school took a toll on their grades. I'd been using every dollar I made flying to finance my frequent trips to Jamaica.

My bank account had been depleted and needed replenishing. The only way I could stop mulling over troubles beyond my control, was to change my focus and begin praying. The Bible says "do not worry about tomorrow, for tomorrow will worry about itself. Each day has enough trouble of its own."

The next morning we left Jamaica. Daniel, the customer service agent at the check-in counter gave us a bit of a tongue lashing for not having our Canadian Permanent Residence cards in our possession. We rode the Boeing 737-700 series plane to Toronto, making the transfer to our Calgary connection. We arrived home just before midnight, twelve hours after leaving Jamaica. Travelling had ceased to be an adventure. It had become tedious. No wonder more than three months would pass before we mustered the courage to return to Jamaica.

NINE

NEGRIL

It had been three months and thirteen days, give or take an hour, since we left Jamaica; the longest time ever between visits. The dust had settled a bit since Ashley's birthday.

Sid and I agreed that the kids and I would make another trip to Jamaica only after we received confirmation that Ashley could spend a few days with us in Negril. I'd tried a couple of times since October, without success, to get permission to take Ashley out of the orphanage. Mr. Green even gave me the verbal go-ahead once in late January, and I tried to get him to fax me the confirmation letter, but apparently faxes only went into Jamaica. I'd phoned him at the CDA, where according to the receptionist his belongings remained at his desk, although she was unable to locate him. Suspecting he was avoiding my calls, I warned the receptionist that I would continue calling until he picked up. Ms. Wilton finally answered the phone on my fifth attempt, informing me that Mr. Green had gone to the hospital.

Neither Ms. Wilton, nor Mrs. O'Connor would grant permission for a private visit with Ashley, each stating the reason for their refusal as not being "familiar with the circumstances of the case." Bull crap! I didn't wish Mr. Green great harm, but if he were in a hospital, he'd better be dying!

A week after Mr. Green's hospital adventure I called the CDA and connected with him on the first try. "Good afternoon," said Mr. Green.

"Good afternoon. This is Erika Isnor from Calgary, Canada. How are you today Mr. Green?"

"I am fine."

"I'm glad to hear of it. I heard you were in the hospital and I was worried about you," I lied.

"No mon. I am well. It is not long lasting. I was in hospital, but all is well now mon."

"The reason for my call is that I am seeking permission to take Ashley out of the orphanage for the weekend. We have not come to Jamaica because we have not been able to get a letter from you."

"Yea mon. I felt bad for that."

"No worries. Your health is most important. Is it possible for you to fax a letter to my home before we leave this evening?"

"Yea mon. I will do it right now."

"Bless you, Mr. Green."

"No mon, I am only doing my job." I waited three hours before confirming that Mr. Green was unable to send out an international fax. I'd asked him to direct the letter to Mrs. Brown at Blossom Gardens, and resisted making our standby reservations until I confirmed that Carmelina had, in fact, received the letter.

I dialled the number to the orphanage, "Good afternoon, Blossom Gardens."

I recognized the voice immediately. "Good afternoon Carmelina, this is Erika Isnor from Calgary, Canada."

"I know who you are," she said.

"We are finally coming back to Jamaica tomorrow, and I have received permission from Mr. Green to spend time with Ashley away from the orphanage."

"Yea mon. I have the letter."

"You *have* the letter?"

"Yea mon, it just came."

"Wonderful! We will be there tomorrow. Our plane arrives at one-thirty, so by the time we clear customs, we should get to Blossom Gardens by three.

"Do you need any clothes for Ashley?"

I'd long since repacked Ashley's Disney Princess suitcase with a swimming suit, jammies, underwear and frocks. It stood in wakeful readiness for its return to Jamaica. "No mon, I have everything she needs thank you. Thank you so very much. We will see you tomorrow."

I hung up the phone and began preparing for our trip. I'd kept our summer clothing packed in suitcases nesting in the corner of the spare room. Nadia's midterm tests were finished, meaning she could join the boys and me for five glorious days in the sun. Once I had everything organized, I phoned Sid letting him know, as promised, that I'd received permission to take Ashley to the beach.

One way or another, we *always* left for Jamaica on somebody's birthday. The family splurged on a gourmet meal at the Keg Steakhouse celebrating my husband's fortieth. Kaiden led us into fits of laughter when he reminded us that we wouldn't be eating steak anytime soon, because there weren't very many cows on the island. We devoured medium rare tenderloins, and shared a decadent warmed chocolate cake dripping with rich ganache, before Sid dropped our full bellies off at the airport.

We'd perfected the art of travelling light, having each child pull their own carry on rollie bag behind them. I learned from Maryam to carry a backpack filled with a change of summer clothes to take onboard the plane. In Toronto, we'd go into the washroom to shed our winter sweaters and long pants. In Jamaica, we used the sac to carry our towels and sundries to and from the beach.

Sid always stocked a checked snack bag with peanut butter, jam, bread, juice boxes, Doritos, and Pringles for us, because in Jamaica those sorts of treats were all imported, and prohibitively expensive. When we emptied the backpack, I'd refill the bag with Blue Mountain coffee and a bottle of twelve-year-old Appleton Rum reserve to bring home for Sid.

Thankfully, our arrival into Montego Bay was uneventful. We breezed through immigration, and out the airport doors finding Mr. Dixon standing on the curb with open arms. We waited as he ran for the Scooby Doo van, and then drove directly up the hill to get Ashley.

I promised Mr. Dixon we would not drag our feet when we arrived at the orphanage, wanting to make the long trip to Negril as soon as possible. We recognized the brittle woman, Mrs. B. who shuffled out to open the gate for us, and then found Ashley sitting alone inside on the hallway bench, wearing a turquoise and white short set shined and ready to go for the weekend. Great care had been taken to prepare Ashley for her time with us. Auntie Joy had combed out her hair, and decorated it with some classic plastic dime store barrettes. The clock above her head read two-fifty.

I suspected that Ashley had been sitting alone on the bench, waiting for us for the better part of an hour.

Carmelina came from the kitchen escorting two well-dressed black ladies who were touring the facility. She introduced me as "Ms. Isnor." I shook their hands, "Pleased to meet you. We are 'working' with Ashley. We come down here a lot."

"A lot," Carmelina nodded in agreement. She asked Auntie Joy to sign Ashley out in the book. "Have her back Sunday evening," she said.

"I believe I am allowed to have Ashley until the first of February." That was my understanding, according to Mr. Green's letter. Everything needed to remain clean.

Carmelina checked Mr. Green's letter. "You are right, she is to be returned on the first," she said before continuing on with her tour.

"Where are you taking Ashley?" asked Auntie Joy.

"Negril," I answered, as I filled out the required information in the book. "We are going to spend time at the beach." Auntie Joy smiled as big as if she were hiding a red silk petticoat.

We left Blossom Gardens heading straight for Negril, with absolutely no idea were we were going to lay our heads for the night. I pulled out the hand-cut New Moon Cottages business card I'd been carrying, from the arsenal of Jamaican contacts I'd accumulated since meeting Maryam.

The hotel, used by locals, was owned and operated by David. His business card read, *"It's a Home Away From Home Atmosphere."* I dialled the number noted on the flimsy card, using my prepaid Digicel flip phone. "Hello, this is Erika Isnor, from Calgary Canada. I am a friend of Maryam."

Jennifer, David's assistant, answered the call. "Yea mon. I know who you are."

"I am wondering if you have a room available for me, and my kids. We have Ashley."

"Yea mon. We have rooms. When will you get here?"

"We are just leaving Mobay now."

"Yea mon, see you when you get here." I hung up the phone feeling incredibly relieved.

Mr. Dixon didn't like not knowing exactly where he was going, but I was fairly confident that I would recognize the spot along the two-lane highway. "Is the hotel before, or after the bridge?" asked Mr. Dixon.

"I'm not entirely sure. I only know that it is about five minutes this side of Rick's Cafe," I answered. 'The bridge,' separated two distinctly geographically different areas of Negril, in the Parish of Westmoreland, on the south side of the island. We passed the famous seven-mile sandy beach, before crossing into downtown Negril.

I remembered using a Scotiabank ATM in Negril, with Maryam, and asked Mr. Dixon to stop so I could get Jamaican money. I needed the cash to pay him for the trip. The kids all waited in the car with him, while I tried to make a withdrawal inside a private banking enclosure. The ATM machine provided either American, or Jamaican dollars. Initially, it seemed like an enormous amount taking out twenty-thousand JMD, but that was only a mere two hundred thirty, Canadian dollars. No matter how well I budgeted, I spent an average of a hundred dollars a day. My bank charged me five dollars for each ATM transaction, so I tried minimizing how many times I used bank machines, without carrying too much cash.

The bank screen read 'not working at present, try again later.' *Crap!* I had to pay Mr. Dixon for our transportation. A line of people formed behind me. "It's not working, do you know where there is another machine?" The lady at the head of the line pointed towards a convenience store, about a half block away.

I ducked inside the grocery store. Thankfully, the second ATM worked. I decided to pick up a six-pack of Red Stripe, using the handful of Jamaican dollars I had leftover from our last trip. When I paid for my beer, I asked the girl at the checkout stand what the exchange was for eighty US dollars.

She used a calculator, deciphering, "eighty American dollars comes to six thousand seven hundred Jamaican dollars.

"Thank you very much." Maryam and I paid thirty-five US dollars for the van from New Moon to Montego Bay. I figured that since Mr. Dixon had picked us up from the airport, and collected Ashley from the orphanage, I owed him more. Sixty-seven hundred JMD seemed fair.

Mr. Dixon had asked locals for directions to New Moon Cottages, while I was inside getting cash. He'd learned that the hotel was about ten minutes up the road, just past the hardware store.

I climbed back into the van, exhausted, after all we'd been traveling for nearly eighteen hours. I looked forward to getting settled in a room where we would stay put for the next three nights. The kids spilt out of the van like milk out of a jug, once we pulled into the driveway of the hotel. They'd been extremely well behaved travellers.

I'd already warned everyone about the mean dog tethered to the tree behind David's residence. There was now a second dog chained at the front of the property. "Is this dog mean?" I asked.

"No mon. This one is friendly. Only the other one is mean. I bought him that way. He has bad blood. His parents were mean too." I wondered how long it would take for the friendly one to turn mean, if he was kept chained to a tree. My wavering about whether the boys were safe, or not, around the new dog departed when the little guy rolled over on his back for a tummy rub.

When Mr. Dixon pulled our luggage out of his van, he asked me if I would require a ride back into Montego Bay. I sensed he had reservations about leaving us at New Moon. I said we were uncertain as to when we would leave, but that I had to get Ashley back to the orphanage before bedtime on Monday.

"Yea mon, you have my number. Call me if you need me." Mr. Dixon pounded my hand, moving our thumbs from side to side in respect. I placed the folded money in his palm, and then he got back into the van to return to Mobay. I was happy that he'd brought his daughter along with him to keep him company on the way home.

David carried our luggage to the back of the house. He offered us a room with two double beds for forty-five US dollars a night, giving us three nights at New Moon for the cost of a single day at Polkerris. Granted there was a world of difference in what we received for the money. The Polkerris Bed and Breakfast oozed comfort. New Moon Cottages only provided the basic necessities of a shower, a toilet, and beds, but we had no intention of being cooped up in the room. We would use it only for sleeping and bathing. The best part about the arrangement was that there were kitchen privileges. The accommodations enabled me to shop at the local grocery store for supplies, such as boxed milk for cereal, and eggs for breakfast. I hoped to conserve more money by not eating every meal out.

David helped us get settled. He offered transportation to anywhere we needed to go. I said that I used local taxis, because I needed to watch my pocketbook and couldn't afford more chartered drivers.

"Yea mon, I will take care of you because you are staying here."

"How much to take us to the beach?"

"Don't worry mon, I will take care of you." *All the guidebooks warned foreigners to agree on a price for transportation before climbing into a taxi.*

We walked in single file about a hundred yards, on the shoulder of the road, to get to Chicken Lavish for dinner. "Hold Sidney's hand firmly, and watch out for oncoming traffic," I reminded Nadia.

Ashley wore the pink flip-flops that I'd purchased for her in Maui. Kaiden walked directly behind her, and kept stepping on the heel of her flip-flops. She'd frequently stop short, let go of my hand, and reach down to put the shoe back on her foot. I scolded her again, and again, until I finally understood why she kept letting go of my hand. We walked very close together like a human chain, stopping and starting, until we reached our destination.

The outdoor setting at Chicken Lavish was informal and inviting. Peter, the owner, recognized Ashley and me. He handed us laminated menus while taking our drink orders, and asked if I'd heard any news about Daniel.

Nadia and I ordered a plate of curry chicken and a plate of jerk chicken to share. The kids each ordered a two-piece fried chicken meal, with French fries, coleslaw, and rice and peas. Ashley chewed the chicken bones down, until they were ground into a fine dust, always looking like a little scavenger not knowing where the next meal would come from. I was determined not to let her overeat, thinking she might eat herself silly.

Five of us shared two double beds in the cheap room. We intended on putting the boys together in the smaller bed, but I fell asleep cuddling with Kaiden. I woke up in the middle of the night nearly frozen to death. I turned off the noisy overhead fan, and went scrounging through the boys' luggage looking for the two fleece travel blankets we used on airplanes. I covered both boys with one, and Ashley and Nadia with the other.

Ashley peed the bed that night. I must have fallen back to sleep, because I never heard Nadia get up with her. The girls were lying on the top of their fleece blanket covering a wet spot on the mattress in the morning. I spied a pile of wet clothes on the floor. "When I woke up, Ashley was hiding in the bathroom. I took off her clothes and dried her off with a towel," Nadia explained through sleepy eyes. I wondered what Ms. Matthews did to Ashley when she wet the bed.

We all took quick warmish showers before getting dressed for breakfast. I usually had to coax Kaiden out of the shower, so I was surprised when he jumped out so quickly, soaking wet. Apparently, he hadn't been alone. I spied a three-inch long cockroach when I pulled back the plastic curtain. I quickly grabbed a handful of toilet paper, picked it up, and flushed the unwanted guest down the toilet, explaining to Kaiden that cockroaches have been around since before the dinosaurs, so the little bugger would survive.

We wore our swimming suits underneath our clothing when we walked down to Jenny's restaurant for breakfast, planning on going to the beach after eating. Ashley finally put on the purple polka dot two-piece swimsuit I'd gotten her at the International Market in Honolulu, wearing a lavender t-shirt, and a short white skirt with hand painted purple flowers over it. She loved the color purple. I'd always find her digging through her Disney princess suitcase, flinging clothes over her shoulder looking for something purple to wear.

"No Ashley, you can't do that," I reprimanded, as I repacked her belongings. And then, she her scolded her baby doll. "Bad baby! Bad Baby!" Ashley snarled, pointing her index finger into the dolls face.

Prior abuse was something I expected to deal with, eventually. I calmly took the baby doll from Ashley's grip, and held it close to my breast. I lovingly patted it on its back. "We don't ever hit babies, Ash. We love babies." I gave the doll back to Ashley, wondering what she would do with it. Once again, I felt like Annie Sullivan with the wild untamed Helen Keller. She snatched it, immediately slapping its face. I suspected I had witnessed either something that Ashley had seen, or something that actually happened to her. I took the doll and placed it on the top shelf of the closet where she couldn't reach it. She cried, throwing a full-fledged tantrum. And then, when I landed an open handed swat, on the small of her clothed backside, she curled up in a fetal position on the bed and wailed.

The boys each sat on the end of a bed with wide opened eyes. "I don't spank very often, but if one of my children asks for a swat with that kind of behavior, I am obligated to give them what they need. Kaiden, when was the last time you got a swat?"

"I can't remember."

"Sidney, when is the last time you got a spanking?

"I don't remember," Sidney answered.

I don't believe in corporal punishment. I used an open hand on a clothed rear end for the purpose of getting her attention, and I got it. Again, I wondered what sort of abuse Ashley had suffered. I hoped we were working towards trust and healthy discipline. "Ashley, you will always be safe with me. We will always treat each other with respect," I promised.

I thought I should parent an adopted child the same way as I had done with my biological children. An orphaned and abused child, from a different country, might as well have been an alien from a different planet. I learned, much later, that using an incentive or reward worked better than using a consequence, especially a physical one.

Ashley climbed off the bed and wrapped herself around me. She acted as good as gold for the rest of the morning. I left the doll on the top of the closet for a 'try again' later.

"Who knows where the room key is?" I asked hoping to redirect her attention. Ashley frantically scrounged through everything on the dresser in search of the single key, attached to a thin wooden disk, without a trace of a tear on her face.

"Mi found da key."

"Yes you did Ashley, thank you very much." I said while picking up the pile of wet sheets and clothes, and then locking the door on our way out. Jennifer, David's house lady greeted us through the screen door of the front house. "Good morning Jennifer."

I handed her the pile of wet clothes. "Ashley peed the bed last night."

Jennifer gave Ashley a stern motherly look. "Give me the key to the room so that I can take care of the mattress." Ashley relinquished the key reluctantly.

We walked past the friendly dog still chained to the front tree. Nearby, David sat on his front porch. "Going to Jenny's for breakfast?

"Yes. And afterwards to the beach."

"I'll be ready to take you."

"Sounds good," I said in passing, feeling pressured, but figuring it might be worth eliminating the hassle of getting a cab.

We formed our single file line holding hands, walking along the road, past Chicken Lavish towards Jenny's Café, grateful for the safety of daylight. There were two four tops inside the restaurant, pushed together, that seemed to be waiting for us. All of the other tables inside the bustling hot spot were occupied.

The boys both asked for two easy over eggs, they called 'dippin eggs,' toast, hashed browns, and bacon. The girls both ordered ackee and saltfish plates. I doubted Ashley had eaten any fish since I'd seen her in September. I chose callaloo and saltfish, with coffee and condensed milk. The delicious breakfast marked the beginning of a glorious day in paradise.

I kept track of our expenses for the trip in a small writing journal. The breakfast bill came to just over $2,100 JMD, including tip, converting to approximately twenty-five US dollars. I'd budgeted a hundred dollars a day including transportation, accommodations and food for the six of us.

We paid for our meal at the cash register where the glass cabinet displayed baked goods and fried chicken. The hand written menu noted that a slice of cake cost $100 JMD. The price for a piece of chicken was $80 JMD for dark meat, or $100 JMD for white meat. We soon learned that Jenny's fried chicken disappeared pretty darn early in the morning, so we'd have to buy it at breakfast if we ever wanted to pack it up for lunch because picnicking for the midday meals seemed like a pretty good idea. I'd brought a loaf of bread, a jar of peanut butter, and some strawberry jam, for lunches, from Canada. That day I purchased only two large slices of the lemon cake to share that the cashier wrapped in waxed paper and put inside a brown paper bag. "Let them eat cake."

We retraced our path back to New Moon where David waited with his keys in his hand to take us to the beach. Jennifer had already hung Ashley's freshly cleaned clothes out on the line. She'd dragged the mattress out into the yard, scrubbed it down, and suggested that we restrict Ashley's fluid intake before bedtime.

We all climbed into David's truck excited to visit the famous seven-mile beach. "Trust me I know where to take you," David said driving down through Negril, past Scotiabank, over the bridge. When we turned left into the driveway of privately owned villas, an attendant came out of the small hut to raise a barrier allowing us access to the parking lot. David spoke briefly with the him in Patois.

I read the sign over the hut, 'Beach House Villas,' intending on looking it up on the Internet, to see what the rates to stay so close to the beach would be. We climbed out of David's truck and followed him down a path leading to the beach. "You can buy food and drink there if you want. I will be back to pick you up at one-thirty." I thought our white skin would be a nicely toasted shade of brown after three hours in the Jamaican sun.

The tropical garden path opened out into a white sandy beach, lined with thatched umbrellas situated between the water and a lazy patio restaurant. The sky and sea blended together in various shades of blue, looking quite like a scene from Fantasy Island. The open-air eatery sat twenty feet from the ocean, separated from the sand by a tier of two stairs wrapped around its perimeter.

The boys threw their towels on a lounge chair, kicked off their flip-flops and charged into the water. I religiously slathered their faces, shoulders, and calves with sun block throughout the day, but they still ended up with pink cotton candy faces.

Eventually, I blew air into the two remaining Mega Mart rafts we'd bought on Ashley's birthday. The boys turned them into pirate ships, until one got a hole in it and sunk. Then, Nadia, Ashley, and me strolled down the long narrow beach, while the boys followed in the water, looking like dolphins leaping and jumping alongside us.

The water on the seven-mile beach looked remarkably beautiful, but there were dilapidated structures in disrepair, and buildings in various stages of stagnant construction intermediately placed between the operating hotels and restaurants. The tin fencing separating those areas from the beach was a constant reminder of the island's financial struggles.

Even though we set a specific time for a pick up, I never expected David to come for us before we called him. Time was the farthest thing on my mind as we sauntered the blissful beach. We didn't return to the Beach House Villas, until nearly two o'clock that afternoon. The bartender said David had been there pacing the beach looking for us, so I borrowed the house phone at the bar to call him back. The boys stayed in the water until David reappeared, and then we rinsed the sand off our feet in a plastic bucket set at the bottom of the white tile stairs. After four hours in the sun, we put on our flip flops and walked back down the garden path to David's waiting truck, brown as toasted coconut.

David stopped at the grocery store on the way back to New Moon so that I could pick up some essential supplies. I bought Easispice chicken seasoning, rice and peas, nutmeg, boxed milk for the cereal, and a pint of rum for David. I learned that peas are not peas at all, but a red kidney bean. We dropped the groceries off at the hotel, putting the perishables in the dormitory sized fridge, before continuing on to Rick's Café. I was already five dollars over budget for the day.

We arrived at Rick's at three-thirty that afternoon. We ate at a table half immersed in the shallow end of the swimming pool, hovering over the cliffs of Negril. Ashley splashed around in the shallow water assimilating well within our pack. I was relieved that she appeared more comfortable in water than Tejah had been, but I would soon discover she was by no means a swimmer. With the kids playing at my feet, I basked in the sun. "Life is Good," I thought.

"Look up into the trees," I said, after I'd noticing that one of the cliff divers had scurried up the flimsy tree trunk, fifty feet above our heads. He milked the crowd for *oohhs, and ahhhs,* before performing a beautifully executed swan dive into the water below. I leaped out of my chair. "Who wants to jump off the cliffs?" Ashley looked at me with a cock-eyed expression we would all come to know well. Nadia and the boys sang, "We do! We do!" in unison.

We journeyed down the stone stairway to the lowest level of the three cliffs where the boys hit the water before I got to the platform. When Nadia jumped off, Ashley peered below seemingly afraid of going too close to the edge. Nadia resurfaced, then returned to stay with Ashley, allowing me to take the plunge. Surprisingly, Sidney challenged the higher tiers, while our daredevil Kaiden remained in his own comfort zone.

We asked Ashley if she would like to jump, promising that Nadia and I would both go in first to be there to catch her. I never thought she would follow us, but she did! That's when I learned the kid couldn't swim! She wrapped her arms around my neck, and held on tightly as I doggie-paddled back to the ladder. "Not too tight Ashley or you'll choke me." That kid had guts. Yes, she belonged in our pack.

Once again David arrived precisely when he said he would. We gathered our towels, and piled into his truck for the short ride back to New Moon, where the kids all shed their swimming suits like snake skins in our room. I picked them up off the floor to hang them up to dry.

I dressed Ashley for dinner in her white skirt with the lavender collared shirt, and the boys each changed into golf shirts with shorts. The air was warm, but I expected a cool breeze once the sun set, so we grabbed our hoodies to go out for dinner. David dropped us off at a place called On The Rocks, agreeing to come back for us in an hour-and-a-half.

We never actually ate at On The Rocks. The restaurant was completely empty when we first arrived, so we were able to sit at a table directly overlooking the gorgeous cliffs of Negril. Our waitress delivered our drinks relatively quickly, and nothing seemed out of the ordinary when she took our food order; Nadia and I each chose the evening special of curry goat, and the kids all wanted fried chicken. But, our order never came. The empty tables soon filled with more people, all various shades of black. It seemed a bit unusual for a restaurant, in the resort town of Negril, not to have *any* other white people eating there. Locals only. We suddenly realized that the lack of service was decidedly intentional. I wondered how many black people had experienced that same moment of awareness in the deep south where my ancestors were born. We never got a bill, so finally we left without even paying for our drinks.

David's headlights came up behind us just as we entered the New Moon driveway. He'd passed us on the road, but had to travel a bit farther down the narrow two lane highway before he could turn his truck around. David's impeccable timing meant that we'd waited an hour-and-a-half for our food. Thank God Sid had packed peanut butter and jelly! Nadia made everyone sandwiches for my hungry brood.

We were careful not to give Ashley anything to drink before bed. The next day, Ashley woke up dry. We used the boxed milk and ate the individual cereal packages that I'd brought from Canada. I cut the center of the cardboard, folding back the slits to use the containers as bowls. My four kids ate the entire package of twelve cereal boxes, the sugar kind I would never allow at home, taking turns diplomatically choosing between Captain Crunch, Cookie Crisps, Fruit Loops, Corn Pops, and Rice Krispies.

I repacked the Bob Marley day bag with Pringles and as many juice boxes as it would hold. We reloaded the last surviving fluorescent pink floater back into the truck and headed back to the beach. David invited us for a backyard dinner, informing us that Jennifer had already begun to prepare a jerk chicken feast. I promised to give him a call when we were ready to leave the beach.

The boys weren't in the ocean water five minutes before Kaiden complained that his pee pee stung. I got apprehensive when he sat motionless on the lounge chair for a long time looking a bit pale. I wondered if he had a urinary tract infection. My panic rose when I realized that all of the medical facilities were closed because it was Sunday.

I remembered a sign posted on the inside door of our room at New Moon listing emergency phone numbers, including a 'Doctor.' I pulled out my Jamaican cell phone from the Bob Marley bag, but it was dead. I'd forgotten to charge it. I asked the bartender if there might be a hotel Doctor on the premises after explaining Kaiden's uncomfortable predicament.

The first time we went to the island Kaiden had developed a fever. Angie drove me down to the pharmacy at the Blue Diamond to get him some Children's Tylenol. I'd learned to carry a small emergency medical kit including Ibuprofen, a plastic bottle of Pedialyte, Pepto-Bismol, and ear drops...just in case. In my haste to get back to Jamaica, I'd left the medical kit behind. Jamaica was not a place you wanted your child to get sick.

Luckily, Kaiden recuperated quickly. I decided it had probably been the salty seawater irritating him. He'd scooted around in the sand on his underbelly quite a bit the day before. It relieved me when he got back into the water without further incident. I thanked God for taking care of Kaiden's vulnerability.

We stayed at the beach until well after four o'clock wandering aimlessly along the seven-mile shoreline looking for shells. We made our largest Jamaican souvenir purchase ever on the beach that day. We'd been dragging our hotel bathroom towels through the sand for two days, and I didn't have a place to do laundry, so I bought four practical beach towels.

Sometime in the mid-afternoon we stopped at a patio restaurant hoping to take the edge off our growing hunger. The boys were thrilled to find familiar grilled cheese sandwiches on the menu. Nadia, Ashley, and I shared a barbeque platter of jerk chicken and ribs.

I spent the rest of the afternoon reading on the fluorescent floater with the children circling the shallow water beneath me like sharks. They got out only after their fingerprints had shriveled beyond recognition. I'd let them swim as long as they'd wanted not knowing when we'd get back to another beach, because we were obligated to return Ashley to Blossom Gardens before bedtime the next day.

David suggested that the boys jump into the outside shower to get the sand off their bodies at New Moon. They cleaned themselves inside a freestanding concrete block enclosure, with a shower head attached to the top of vertical piece of PVC piping. The door was made out of rippled tin, haphazardly nailed to the structure. It scratched like nails on a chalkboard whenever someone opened or closed the door. Kaiden happily obliged, having convinced himself that Mr. Cockroach might still be lurking inside our room shower. I hung the boy's swimsuits, towels and clothes on the line hoping they would be dry by morning. I brought their jammies to the outside shower where they dressed for bed after sharing a clean room towel to dry off.

After the boys, Ashley climbed into the shower where we failed miserably trying to get the beach sand out of her coarse hair. I virtually had no experience with a coloured girls hair. I couldn't figure out the best way to comb through it, so I made a mental note to research hair products when I got home. Ashley passed her swimsuit to me through the tin door, and I hung it on a branch in the tree next to the shower. And then, I handed her the freshly cleaned yellow nightgown that Jennifer had washed and hung on the clothesline.

Nadia and I showered inside.

David treated us to supper. The chicken smoked slowly in a metal barrel out in the yard all day. I was glad that the boys had filled their tummies with grilled cheese at the beach because Jennifer's chicken tasted like fire. Nadia and I loved it, and Ashley devoured her pieces beyond recognition. We sat in the folding chairs in semi-circle around the campfire after Kaiden fell fast asleep in my arms at the picnic table. I sipped on the

Red Stripe I'd placed inside the shoebox-sized freezer of our kitchenette when the boys were showering. The perfectly frosted beer cooled the hot spices on my tongue. Then, I excused myself and carried my youngest son to bed, with Sidney and Ashley trailing behind us. I decided we would return to Montego Bay early the next day, so as not to risk getting Ashley back any later than I'd promised. Soon we were all sleeping beneath the noisy rickety fan.

Ashley wet the bed again, and Jennifer was not happy about it. She said "a seven-year-old was too old to wet up the mattress." Clearly, there were extenuating circumstances beyond Ashley's control. Only God knew what sort of physical and emotional punishments she had endured. I recalled the record of beatings in her file, or perhaps there was a physical problem that we were not aware of yet. I made another mental note to pack a rubber bed sheet for Ash for subsequent trips.

We polished off an entire dozen eggs for breakfast that morning. I scrambled them in a heavy deep iron frying pan. Then, the kids played in the yard as I packed up our belongings. I was collecting laundry off the clothesline, when David asked me to come to his office to settle my bill with him. The towels were still damp, but I folded them anyway, putting them in the designated dirty clothes bag before meeting David in the front house.

David's desk sat beneath a window facing the tree of the chained up dog. He sat there preparing my bill when I arrived. We'd agreed on forty-five US dollars per night for the room. I figured I owed one hundred thirty-five US dollars for the accommodations. That was the easy part. I'd felt uncomfortable running a tab for our transportation, preferring on paying as I went rather than racking up debt. I suspected David wanted charter rates, but I'd taken local cabs and knew what they cost. We finally agreed I'd pay twelve dollars a day for three days of transportation. And then, he asked how much I'd paid for the ride to get to Negril. I told him I paid fifty dollars when I'd given Mr. Dixon eighty.

"That's cheap," he said. "How about eighty dollars" he countered.

"How about sixty?"

I paid David two hundred forty dollars US for our three day holiday, including the ride back to Montego Bay, both of us considering it to be a fair deal. David agreed to stop at the Scotiabank on the way back to

Montego Bay to refresh my funds. I gave Jennifer my last two thousand JMD for her kindness before we left.

Jamaican women became quite direct with me once they got to know me, often giving me instructions on how to take care of my black child. Jennifer said that Ashley needed her hair combed out. She sat Ashley down between her legs and started picking at the fuzzy braids on her head for the better part of an hour. Ashley's resigned patience for the task surprised me, so did the auburn colour I noticed in her beautiful hair. When I touched it, it felt both coarse and soft. It sure looked like I'd found my wild-haired beach child.

I'd brought twenty t-shirts to Jamaica with the words, 'All We Need Is Love' embroidered on the front of them. I bought the shirts at our Canadian Superstores in Calgary, scouring through all the stores in the city collecting them. I hoped to get a picture of all of the older children wearing them at Blossom Gardens, but I never got to do that. Instead, each time I returned Ashley to her 'place of safety,' I dressed her in one of them. I suspected that the shirts would be taken home to the children of the employees, just as the white tie-dyed dress had, but it didn't matter because I was leaving an important message on the island.

Jennifer asked Ashley, in Patois, where she lived before going to Blossom Gardens. Ashley always maintained that she'd lived in Westmoreland, "in a park." Ashley told Jennifer she was from "Sav-la-Mar," as she got her hair brushed out.

"Is it a rough area?" I asked.

"No mon, but you don't want to go there alone," Jennifer replied.

"Is it far?"

"No mon." Jennifer and another boarder, who occupied the front room, spoke in more Patois together. I listened as the young man made a call on his Digicel phone. It was hard for me to understand, but I picked out an intermingled English word every now and then; Blossom Gardens, child, girl, and Parkinson. Soon, I figured out that the conversation was about Ashley.

"Someone will know something about the child," Jennifer comforted me. I gave her my contact information before leaving, should she ever track down anyone that might know anything about 'Ashley Parkinson.' I gave her all the cash I had left. "I wish I could give you more," I said before we drove away.

David's truck required a new starter. I think the money I paid for our stay provided the necessary car part. A mechanic showed up, and put it in before we could leave for Montego Bay. When we finally left Negril around ten o'clock, David said he preferred stopping at the Scotiabank in Negril, "I don't like Montego Bay. It is very dangerous. The people there are unfriendly."

I hadn't yet found anyone unfriendly in Montego Bay. Certainly there were places I wouldn't venture on my own, but there were places like that in every city.

It didn't matter to me where we got the money. I would actually be relieved to have the money in my hands, because I found bank machines unpredictable in Jamaica. Kaiden thought that whenever I needed money I just had to stop at the bank to get it. He didn't yet understand that someone had to put money into the bank before I could take it out. Everyone waited in the car when I went into the ATM to get another three hundred dollars. When I left the enclosure I put what I owed David inside a Scotiabank deposit envelope, tucking the remainder of the cash in my wallet, before crossing the street to get back in David's truck.

"All is good," I said handing David his envelope.

"Take out $200 JMD for me," he said. I did what he requested as we drove over the bridge, past the Beach House Villas, in the direction of Mobay.

"How far is it to Sav-la-Mar?" I asked.

"Not very far. I can take you through there on the way back. We will not stop. I do not want to get mixed up with these people. The mother must be unfriendly," David said.

I had no intention of stopping either, I only wanted to see Ashley's birthplace. I remembered the time that Duj had gone into Montego Bay to see his mother with our first driver, Easten, who stated that it was not a place for me to go. I'd watched the boy slip behind a piece of tin fencing, into an area where many one room houses were made of wood, and tin, built by squatters. I sat with Easten, waiting in the van for Duj to return.

"Do people live there?" I'd asked Easten.

"Yea mon," was all he said. Mr. Doug, the owner of the villa, told me that Easten lived in a similar kind of shantytown close to the airport that was ruled by a Juan. The leader of the community known as 'the Juan' led with brawn and brains. I imagined guns and shootings and all kinds of Hollywood drama.

"How long has the child been at the orphanage?" David asked.

"Ashley's been in Blossom Gardens since last January, so it's been just over a year now." I wondered what Ashley thought as we talked about her as if she weren't sitting in the back seat of the truck.

"She hasn't seen her mother for the whole year?"

"No mon." I replied.

"Then the woman is unfriendly. Do you know what I mean by that? David asked. I shook my head from side to side. "There must be a reason for a mother to stay away from her child for a whole year. She is unfriendly. She doesn't care. You don't know what she is like, what she might do if you just show up."

"I would never just show up on her mother's doorstep, especially with Ashley."

"You need someone to go there that knows the area and the people. You never know what she has told people about why the child is gone." I hadn't thought about that. I knew that Ashley was taken away for 'emotional abuse and beatings,' but I didn't know who committed the abuse. I imagined two very different scenarios surrounding the deception that Ashley's mother might have woven when she explained her missing child.

In my gentle version, I pictured a woman sick with grief that suffered considerable abuse at the hand of a man who drank and stole her hard earned money. This woman used her body to shield Ashley from harsh drunken blows. She dropped Ashley off at the CDA, on an intake day, hoping to save her child from the beatings that had grown more frequent and severe in the last couple of years.

Ashley's gentle mother held her head high as she told the curious neighbours that Ashley had gone to Miami, Florida to live with a distant Auntie. She believed that Ashley lived in a pink stucco house with green grass in front of it. Ashley went to school, and had learned to read. She was loved, and spoken to softly. Ashley's Auntie read her stories every night, kissed her forehead, and told her how much her mother loved her even though she were so far away.

Ashley didn't have to worry about making too much noise, laughing too loudly, or not having enough to eat. Ashley's gentle mother was proud that her daughter had moved out and on. I hoped we would become friends who might somehow share in the bringing up of our daughter.

The other woman in my mind did not suffer in Ashley's absence. I'm confident she felt relieved of the burden of Ashley. Never once did she regret the moment the social worker came to pick Ashley up from her home. Ashley didn't cry when she left. The only feeling Ashley had was one of guilt for leaving her big brother and little sister behind.

This woman felt the incorrigible child had it coming when she slapped Ashley's face for back talking. She'd split Ashley's eye leaving it closed and blue. She'd sliced the edge of her ear with a knife leaving it deeply scarred when the child asked for more fruit to eat.

This woman took great pride in her appearance. She adorned herself with gold jewelry that shone brightly against the darkness of her skin. Ashley had the same deep dark chocolate colouring of her birth mother. This woman manicured her long purple fingernails. It surprised me they were real not acrylic. She wore tight clothes around an ample body. I doubted she could sit down in her designer labelled jeans. She double processed her hair; straightened and dyed it. An asymmetrical cut swept down over one alluring eye. I would not trust this woman. I believe she would have expected a return on Ashley. I wanted Ashley to be as far away as possible from this woman.

"No, we need not stop." I said quietly.

We drove into the town of Savannah La Mar, a coastal village which replaced the city of Banbury as the capital of Westmoreland in 1730. The villagers there descended largely from the indentured laborers who came from Jamaica after slavery from India. They were known locally as "Indie Royals," because of their mixed East Indian and African heritage. I smiled, imagining my Ashley as an Indian princess.

The town of Sav-la-Mar didn't look dangerous or forbidding. It resembled many a small town USA. We braked on the highway at a four corner stop sign before making a right hand turn. I glanced back at Ashley to see if I might find any semblance of recognition in her face. David then made a left turn. We passed the Savanna La Mar Hospital on my right side. I wondered if Ashley had been born there instead of Cornwall Regional Hospital. "Poor people stayed put," said Ms. Wilton. "They didn't have money to move around from place to place." Ashley stood up in the back seat behind me. She leaned over my shoulder and looked out the window.

"Do you know where you are?" I asked.

"Sav-la-Mar," she said quietly.

"I know where she lived," said David. There are apartments over there behind the hospital."

"Did you live in those apartments?" I asked. Ashley nodded.

David took another right hand turn. He travelled down the street a block or so, where there was a row of three-story apartment buildings on our left. We stopped at a small intersection. "Did you live in those apartments there?" David asked Ashley. Once again, she nodded.

I looked to the left, and wondered if Ashley's mother might be behind one of those apartment doors. Was she preparing rice and peas for the remaining children in her home? Did she ever think of Ashley? Did she miss her? Feel remorse? Regret? According to Ashley's file she had no siblings, but that's not what Ashley told me. She said she had a bigger brother named 'Jim' and a smaller sister named 'Kimeysha.' Was Ashley's mother lounging on a couch there, puffing through a pack of cigarettes?

We passed through the intersection, veering to the right into the Petcom gas station to fill up. In Jamaica, pump attendants fill the gas tanks, moving the cars in and out of the stations quicker than a ball bearing in a pinball machine. My eyes remained glued on the apartment building across the street.

I wondered what the seven-year-old in the back seat of David's car thought. How did it feel to be so close to her birth mother after all of this time? I looked over to see if I could find answers in Ashley's beautiful face, but she seemed not to have a care in the world. We pulled out of the gas station leaving both the imagined birth mothers behind.

David made a second quick stop at a small Digicel outlet to purchase minutes for his pay as you go cell phone. I gave him money to buy me some minutes as well, needing to make some calls to find a place to stay in Montego Bay.

I tried phoning Polkerris first, but the Bed and Breakfast had no vacancies. I called Angie, but there were guests at the villa. I decided that the best plan was to stop by the Caribic House where Carl, from Embracing Orphans, usually stayed. I hoped they would have a room.

We followed the road through Westmoreland Parish that weaved down the coastline precariously through the mountainous terrain. The dense vegetation required that houses be built on stilts nestled into steep slopes. I listened as David questioned Ashley about her previous family. "Is your mother a drinker or a smoker?" Ashley bobbed her head up and down.

"Yes," said Ashley.

"Which one?" asked David.

"Smoke," said Ashley. I did not doubt her memory.

We traveled on. "Are we going into St. James Parish now?" I asked David.

"How do you know?" he asked.

"We just went through a place called 'Border Town,' I knew that St. James Parish was next to Westmoreland." He smiled. The scenery changed. Crops in the fields soon lined the roads. We drove through farming country, seeing mostly sugarcane, but other agricultural products were growing too, including bananas, coffee, ginger, cocoa, rice and breadfruit.

I'd eaten boiled breadfruit before, not in Jamaica, but at Oistins Bay in Barbados. It grew in a tree like a coconut, and had a firm, potato type texture inside. I had trouble thinking of it as a fruit; just like I thought of a tomato as a vegetable. My thoughts wandered as we passed through the serene countryside.

David was not familiar, or comfortable driving through Montego Bay. I gave him directions to Bottom Road, and asked him to stop at the Caribic House. When we got there I told the children to stay in the truck while I checked to see if we could rent a room.

"Hello," I said to the receptionist. "I am a friend of Carl's. I can't remember his last name."

"Carl R.?" the receptionist asked.

"Yes, that's him. He volunteers at the Blossom Gardens orphanage. He recommended your hotel. Do you have a room for the night?"

"How many in your party."

"I have two boys and my daughter." I did not include Ashley in the count because she would be sleeping at the orphanage.

"How old is your daughter?"

"She is seventeen."

"I will have to charge her as an adult. The children are free. The room will be fifty-five US dollars for the night."

SOLD! "Thank you very much."

We unpacked the suitcases, thanking David profusely for his kindnesses, and then climbed the steps to room #9 on the second floor. I opened the door expecting to find a room similar to the one we had rented from David, but was pleasantly surprised by its cleanliness. There were three single beds; one straight in front of us, and two on the sidewall. The kids immediately claimed which bed they wanted. Ashley asked for the bed closest to the door leading out to a small balcony, expecting to sleep with Nadia. It felt so very natural for her to think she would remain with us. I sighed knowing we would soon be returning her to Blossom Gardens.

We still had the rest of the afternoon to spend at Doctor's Cave. "Last one into their swimming suit is a rotten egg!" Ashley tore into her Disney case in search of her polka dot swimsuit. "Mi no fine mine," Ashley whined. I too ruffled through the clothes looking for the purple two-piece, but it wasn't there. I realized that it was still hanging in David's tree at New Moon. Luckily, I'd also packed the one-piece suit she'd worn with me the first time I took her out of the orphanage. I brought two, because swimming suits always get sandy. Thank God for the back up plan.

I gave Ashley the one-piece suit and instructed her to go into the washroom to change. Little did I know that she would eat the vanilla cream cookies out of the garbage can that I had thrown away because they had crumbled up inside the Bob Marley snack bag! "Ashley we don't eat out of the garbage can. When you are hungry tell me and I will get you food."

"Mi hungry Mommy," she said looking at me with those big dark eyes, like a child on the Save the Children infomercials.

"Let's get a snack before we go to the beach," I said. We picked up our towels, locked the hotel room door, and headed down the stairs. We crossed the street, stopping to buy some chips and four bottles of Ting at The Weekender souvenir shop.

It cost twelve US dollars to spend the afternoon on one of the most beautiful beaches in the world. The boys swam back and forth between the shore and the trampolines, while Ashley played in the sand, near Nadia and me. A black woman next to me asked me if Ashley was my daughter.

"Not yet. We are working on it though."

"It's a good thing you are doing," she said.

"We are getting ever so much more than we are giving," I replied.

I met many interesting people sitting on those beaches as I watched over my children. Some were Jamaican women returning to visit their homeland, who often confessed that their hearts belonged in Jamaica, no matter where else they lived. I sensed the ocean soothed their souls.

"Mi hungry mommy." Ashley's stomach required a proper meal before going back to Blossom Gardens. I waved the other kids into shore, providing clean towels for each of them. We were all ready for what we call a sit-down dinner. We returned to the room to shower and change into dry clothes before walking to the Pork Pit to fill our bellies. That night we ordered our food with extra drinks because the food turned out to be more spicy than usual. We ate family style at the picnic tables in the open air.

It was already after six. I'd stalled as long as I dared before calling Mr. Dixon to ask for ride to take Ash to the orphanage. "Yea mon, I can do it. Where are you?" Mr. Dixon asked.

"We are at the Pork Pit," I said.

"You are in Montego Bay already?"

"Yea mon." I realized he'd been willing to drive to Negril to pick us up. Bless you Mr. Dixon.

"When do you want to go?" He asked.

"Whenever you are able. We are ready now."

"I will be right there." He must have been just around the corner, because it was no more that five minutes before Mr. Dixon walked up to our picnic table. We threw away our garbage, put a couple of hundred Jamaican dollars in the large glass pickle jar 'for the boys' at the grill, and climbed into Mr. Dixon's Scooby Doo van. It had been a great day.

Sidney fell asleep on the back seat in the van on the way up to Brandon Hill. I had to wake him up when we got there so that he could go inside with us to say goodbye to Ashley. We rang the bell and were let in quickly, finding many familiar faces sitting on the hallway bench in front of us.

Ashley suddenly realized we planned on dropping her off and leaving without her. She clung tight to my lower body. "No mommy. No!" She'd never called me mommy in front of anyone at the orphanage before. Tears streamed down her precious face.

"Ashley, I will come back to get you," I promised. "I have always come back for you." My eyes filled with tears too. I couldn't look down at her or they would spill. I heard Ms. Matthews chuckle when she saw our pain.

Auntie Joy stood beside us. Bless you, bless you Auntie Joy for always being there. She pried Ashley from my body, and held her with firm kind hands. Sidney dropped his head, as Auntie Joy whisked Ashley away. I heard Auntie Joy asking, "Did you spend time at the beach?" Bless you, Auntie Joy. Bless you.

Mr. Dixon returned us to the Caribic House after committing to take us to the airport the following day. I did not yet know where this journey would end. I was only just learning to trust that God planted the desires of our hearts, and would that He would take care of our hearts desires.

Mr. Dixon picked us up in the morning, promptly as usual. He never asked for a specific amount of money, and was always generous with his time. I took a few extra of his business cards, should I ever have the opportunity to recommend him as a trusted driver. He unloaded our suitcases at the airport, putting the bags on the curb. That day, he worried about our standby status. He wanted me to call him if we didn't get seats on the plane. I never found Jamaican people to be demonstratively affectionate. It might have caught him off guard initially, but Mr. Dixon always accepted a hug from me whenever we were coming or going. He understood how hard it was leaving the island without Ashley. "You have to leave to be able to come back to Jamaica mon," he said. I hugged him leaving his fare in the palm of his hand, always wishing I could give him more.

The people at the airline check in counter were all becoming familiar to us. Douglas, our customer service agent, asked for all out passports. He also requested Permanent Residence cards for Nadia and me, because we were Americans living in Canada. The PR card, as defined on the Canadian Immigration Services website "is a status document that provides secure proof of permanent residence status." The PR card had become a compulsory document for all residents since our last trip to

Jamaica. "Moreover, any permanent resident who leaves Canada and then wishes to return to Canada will not be granted entry unless they produce their PR card."

Nadia and I did not have the cards in our possession because I'd sent them in for renewal. I didn't have the expired cards because we were required to include them with that request. According to the government website, it took approximately 233 days to process each application. I'd travelled for well over a year, as a flight attendant, without carrying my PR card. I'd never before encountered an issue.

"You may not travel without the required documents," Douglas advised me.

"We come here a lot; I've never had a problem before."

Most of the customer service agents around us knew who we were. "Yea mon," confirmed Natalie at the next counter. "I've checked you in twice before." Douglas obtained special permission from his supervisor to let us through security.

We always allotted extra time to pass through immigration when we left Jamaica. That day, it pleased me to see unusually short lines ahead of us. I expected to pass through quickly, enabling me to pick up a bottle of Appleton Reserve Rum for Sid's birthday.

"Next," called a green-eyed female immigration officer, with Sabrina William's cream coloured complexion, at the thirteenth stall. We handed over our passports, one at a time. Each passport contained the required Jamaican immigration exit card that we got on the way into the country. I had to pick Kaiden up so that he could be seen for inspection. "Where are the permanent residence cards for you and Nadia?" *uhhh ohh busted!*

"Well we don't have the cards," I tried to explain. "We sent them in for renewal. I have the receipts." I had been advised to carry the receipts with me as documentation by a Canadian immigration officer.

The green-eyed woman locked a look on me in a way that only people of colour are able to do. The look meant, *"Are you serious? You can't pull that one over on me."* Usually, I'd only have to endure the look, for a moment, before being allowed to pass. "You cannot leave the country without proper documentation." We were at her mercy. She picked up our passports and landing papers, and took them to her supervisor for a more thorough inspection.

We stood in front of her empty customs booth. Nadia pointed out that the landing papers read 'not to be used for travel.' I shot her one of my own very best mom looks. "Please don't say that in front of the officer." Why had I taught her that she could say anything she needed to, as long as she spoke in a respectful manner? Nadia also pointed out the digital clock ticking out the minutes as we stood waiting. We still had lots of time.

The male officer in the fourteenth stall wasn't busy. "Is she going to let you pass?" I shrugged, wondering for the first time if we might be refused re-entry into Canada. Would it have been so bad to stay in Jamaica? How long would my bank account hold out?

Kaiden stuck his head around the empty booth to look at the immigration officer's computer screen. I suspected the screen displayed our entire travel history. "She's playing Pac-Man," Kaiden noted. I scolded him and pulled him back to stand beside me.

Our officer returned briefly to inform us that her supervisor "would be calling Canada to see if they would accept us," before allowing us to clear security. The digital wall clock kept moving. When she returned she said, "Do not come back to Jamaica without the required documents." I wondered if she'd made notes on our file, or simply returned to the Pac-Man game once we passed.

We learned that we still had lots of time when we got to the top of the escalator. Our flight showed 'delayed' on the departure screen. I'd promised to buy individual pizzas at the Dominos in the airport before the four-hour flight to Toronto. I paid more money for the kids meals than I did for Sid's Jamaican rum at the duty free shop.

The flight home went smoothly until Sidney complained about his ears hurting on landing. I wondered if jumping off the cliffs at Negril, or our excessive swimming, had caused an ear infection. Thank God we could go to a medic center once we reached home.

I wondered if someone in the orphanage would address or even notice that Ashley was coughing when she returned. I suspected that she'd had a cold for a while because I remembered Carl mentioning it when he was there over the New Year. The volunteers from Embracing Orphans had scheduled an outing to the beach, but Ashley was on a list to stay behind because of her ear. Carl promised to get her earplugs, and a swim cap, so that she could go with them. I talked to Carl the morning of the beach trip; he'd promised to watch over Ashley while he was in Jamaica and I was not.

We arrived at the Canadian Customs counter to find another rigid female immigration officer. I'd figured upon landing on Canadian soil, our homeland for the past decade, we would pass through customs quickly. *Wrong again.* We received a great big red slash across our Canadian Customs form. No PR card? Do not pass go, and head straight the immigration line on the left. The secondary booth in Toronto was not numbered. A big brother Orson Welles like voice summoned us to the counter, "next."

I automatically handed over our four passports. "What is your status in Canada?" I explained that Nadia and I were landed immigrants and the reason for not having the required documents. He quickly typed something into his computer that pulled up our records on his screen. "How long have you been in our country?"

We'd moved to Canada in August of 2000. I'd married a Canadian born citizen almost ten years ago. *For GOD's sake! My seven and nine-year-old sons were children of this country; I was their mother and married to their father!* I refrained from using the angry inside voice that screamed in my head.

"You first arrived in Kouts, Montana, August 19, 2000." Kaiden didn't have to go behind his stall to tell me he was not playing Pac Man!

"Yes, I spent the entire summer of 2000 in Calgary with Sid gathering immigration information on the toll free call line. I'd been instructed to turn in the 'intent to immigrate' documents in when I arrived at the border. I followed the instructions as given. When we got to the border I honestly announced our intent to remain in Canada."

The officer scrolled over our immigration history.

"I *do* have two Canadian sons and we have been living in Canada legally for almost ten years," I stated, probably looking a bit miffed.

"That doesn't matter at all," he explained. "People come over here *illegally* all the time and have children here. Their children are considered Canadian citizens and can stay, and the parents get deported. I believe you. I am going to allow you entry, but I *could* let the boys stay and make you and your daughter go back."

I bit my tongue to keep my inside voice quiet. *How, exactly...*
logistically... would that work? Where would they have taken my boys? Where
would 'back' have been? Jamaica? The United States of America?

"The refusal at Kouts sends up red flags that permanently tags you.
If you are a Canadian Citizen, this all goes away," said the officer. He'd
finally given me a piece of useful information. I intended upon applying
for Citizenship immediately.

"I guess I'd better learn the song."

It took four-and-a-half more years for me to become a Canadian
Citizen to make those red flags go away. We'd spent twice as much time
in front of the Canadian immigration officer that we had in Jamaica. We
missed the last flight that connected to Calgary, by four minutes, so we
had to spend the night in Toronto hotel.

I had crossed the Rubicon. We came to a point of no return within the
course of action. Turning back now became impossible considering our
developing attachment to Ashley. How could we join the long chain of
people who had abandoned her? The distance and effort behind me seemed
far greater than the remainder of the journey and task yet undertaken.

I yearned for peace and needed to eliminate the chaos I'd stirred
up in our lives. I vowed not to return to Jamaica until I'd received the
proper identification documents, deciding to ask to work domestically,
and refused to subject myself to the ridiculous degradation of dignity at
the hands of another customs agent.

Once home, I checked on the status of the PR renewal package I'd
sent to Mississauga, Ontario via Federal Express for processing. The
representative I spoke with assured me that if I'd included documentation
of eminent travel, the application would receive priority status and be
processed quickly. The next day a letter arrived summoning me to pick up
the PR card at the Harry Hays building in Calgary, in three weeks time. I
checked my work schedule, and noticed that the appointment conflicted
with a scheduled work flight to Cancun, Mexico. I decided to make a trip
downtown to see if I might be able to get the documents earlier.

I stood in line at the Canada Immigration Services processing center,
hoping to show proof of my work schedule to a person who would
respond as a human being. The woman at the intake window asked for
my identification and reason for my visit. When I gave her everything in

my possession, she asked me to wait a moment, while she checked to see if the PR card had arrived. Soon, the officer returned, wearing a pleasant smile and handed me my Canadian Government issued proof of residency card. "We love your airline. We always try to do our very best for the people who work there." I thanked the woman profusely, tucking the card safely inside my leather travel folder. *Yes! There are angels among us, even some employed by the Government.*

Ashley wore a pink rayon skirt and a simple yellow cotton t-shirt. She climbed up on the bench, posed, and gave me a perfectly practiced smile under the mango tree. This is the picture that hung on our refrigerator in Calgary during the entire adoption process. This was our first trip to Jamaica.

Kaiden, me, Sidney, and Alyssa at Margaritaville, the day before we officially met Ashley.

Ashley sat next to Alyssa and leaned on her, wrapping those long, svelte, dark arms around Alyssa. They both looked up and smiled at the camera capturing what would become our 'ahh haa moment.' Later, in Canada, I realized that what we had hoped to find had been right in front of our faces all along.

Ashley and me under the mango tree together. This was our trip of perfect serenity when Sid met Ashley. I knew that when he saw the circumstances of her life, he would change them.

Ashley smiled, looking confused at the unexpected attention she was receiving. Sid took pictures of both of us wearing white dresses together. I could only imagine what that dress would look like after thirty minutes in the dirt. I wanted Ashley to know that someone in the world cared about her.

I shared the Barrel of Monkeys game, explaining how to make a long string of primates, each hanging off the next. The girls all reeled with laughter as they competed to make the longest strand. Ashley produced a genuine smile, not the picture perfect one she'd practiced for the camera.

Gingham dresses swarmed all around my head and feet like bees. All of
the girls were fascinated by the texture of my Caucasian hair, and fought
to be the next to brush it.

Our first morning together. After swimming, we realized that we'd left the hotel key inside our room and that we were locked out. We had to go searching for the maid to open the door for us. I noticed how acutely observant Ashley was of her surroundings. I'd assumed I'd found an exceptionally bright young girl using advanced cognitive skills, because she attached the turquoise elastic wrist band to her tiny wrist, and kept an eye on it like a hawk the entire time she was with me.

I'd learned it was a privilege, not a right, to receive an education in Jamaica where school fees, book fees, uniforms, and 'polishable' brown shoes made an education prohibitively expensive. I'd learned from her teacher Ms. Campbell, that Ashley had never attended school before her arrival at Blossom Gardens.

Colours are more vibrant in Jamaica than anywhere else in the world. Ashley sat beside Jeremy's pristine pool at the Polkerris Bed and Breakfast overlooking Montego Bay.

Ashley and Nadia; chocolate and vanilla.

The only photograph that survived Ashley's seventh birthday shows Ashley's resilient spirit despite being out of focus. The only gift she received was knowing the day she was born. Ashley owned a piece of information no one could ever take away from her. The pink Mega Mart cake fed seventy-two people at Ashley's birthday party.

Nearly fifteen hours of traveling behind us, I was weary, yet content to have my salt and pepper twins, Kaiden and Ashley, beside me.

My pink cotton candy boys on the seven-mile beach in Negril. Kaiden standing to the left of his big brother Sidney.

Sidney Smiles

Ashley lets loose in the pool at Rick's Café in Negril.

Ashley smiles, playing crocodile in shallow pool at Rick's Café.

Sidney, Kaiden, Nadia, and Ashley exploring Jamaica's white sandy seven-mile beach. The water was remarkably beautiful, but there were dilapidated structures in disrepair, and buildings in various stages of stagnant construction intermediately placed between the operating hotels and restaurants. The tin fencing that separated those areas from the beach was a constant reminder of the financial struggles of the local people.

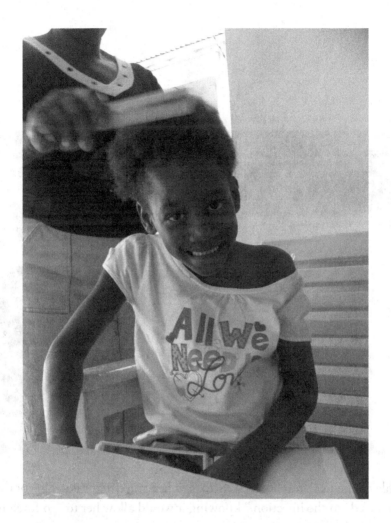

"All We Need Is Love!" I picked up twenty of these shirts for the girls at the orphanage. I dressed Ashley in one each time I had to return her to a 'place of safety.' I suspected that the shirts would be taken home to the children of the employees, just as the white tie-dyed dress had, but it didn't matter because I left a message on the island.

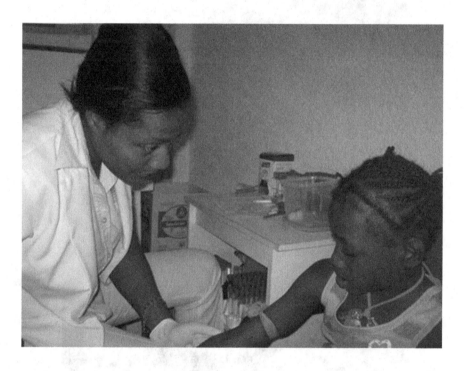

Ashley's medical test for AIDS to get her traveling Visa. She bravely submitted "to the injection," knowing it would allow her to "go foreign."

Our driver, Mr. Dixon, with Ashley the day she left Jamaica. "You've got gold in your hands."

Ashley's first plane ride to Calgary, Canada. We sat across to each other, in aisle seats, leaving Jamaica. Her eyes got as big as wagon wheels, and she took the hand of the nice lady sitting next to her.

Ashley meeting her Dad at arrivals in the Calgary airport. March 2, 2011.

Ashley's first night at home, in the family bed.

Ashley, me, Kaiden, and Sidney exploring hot exotic destinations. The Grand Cayman Islands in 2015.

Sid and me, celebrating our 9th anniversary.

This picture is our adoption announcement of our 8th child...who was black.

TEN

'FREE FOR ADOPTION'

I spoke with Ms. Wilton on the phone who advised me, "Things are moving along."

'Has Ashley been declared 'free for adoption?'

"You will have to talk with the Adoption Coordinator next Wednesday," she said. *Funny*, Ms. Wilton never redirected me before.

"If she is, I will be down on the next plane."

March 16, 2010, Ashley Parkinson was moved from a 'place of safety.' at Blossom Gardens, to a permanent residence institution in Anchovy, Jamaica called Garland Hall. According to Angie, Ashley's new home sat directly across the road from Charnelle's High School. I'd made the trip up the narrow 'Long Road' one morning with Easten to drop Charnell off for classes. He'd said that the high school students occasionally had to walk up that steep embankment in inclement weather, or when traffic stalled, to get to school.

I found Anchovy on my computer using a now obsolete program called Earth Viewer 3D, mapping Earth by the superimposition of images obtained from satellite imagery and aerial photography. The detail of the virtualization showed some wooden huts that I recognized, where students would purchase snacks across from Charnelle's school.

I wondered how my child fared. She'd left Blossom Gardens less than a week after the new playground equipment Embracing Orphans had donated was installed. Just another irony. They'd finally disposed of the rusted swing set, and replaced it with state of the art equipment, and then Ashley moved. Time and time again, her resiliency was tested, with one more placement added to her resume. It had to end. I sent her a letter hoping to encourage her.

Dearest Ashley Parkinson,

Today I have learned you have moved. I hope you like your new home. I thought you might enjoy seeing some pictures of the time we spent in Negril. We all send our love, and hope to see you again very soon. Work hard in school and say your prayers.

Love and kisses,
Auntie Erika

I emailed David thanking him for all he'd one for us, especially for driving us back to Mobay through Sav-la-Mar. I asked about Ashley's swimming suit that I'd left hanging in the tree next to the shower. I hoped he would keep it safe until we returned.

On April 20, 2010, I called Mr. Bowen. Months had passed since I'd last spoken to him. "Hello Mr. Bowen, this is Erika Isnor from Calgary, Canada."

"Good afternoon Ms. Isnor."

"I am calling about Ashley Parkinson. I have heard that her paperwork has been sent to you and I am wondering what the next step in the process is."

"What paperwork do I have, and where did you get this information?"

In my phone conversation with Ms. Wilton, she advised me that she made the recommendation for adoption, and then forwarded it to Mr. Bowen, requesting that he "initiate the process."

"I do not know what paperwork has been sent to me so I cannot make a comment. I will call Ms. Wilton. Can you call me back?"

"Of course I can," I said. "I will call you tomorrow."

"Very well then."

I called the CDA in Montego Bay again, asking to speak to Ms. Wilton, who told me to hold the line. She kept her hand over the mouthpiece while she spoke with Mrs. O'Connor.

Mrs. O'Connor eventually picked up the phone to inform me that Ashley's file had finally been officially transferred from Ms. Wilton's desk, a whole ten feet, to the Adoption Coordinator's desk. Ashley's file had gone to court and been declared 'free for adoption.' "I must now review your file and see if there is anything missing from it, or not, before we can proceed. I will prepare a list of any outstanding items to give to you on your next visit here."

"Does that mean that Ashley Parkinson is matched to us?" I inquired.

"Yea mon. The child is matched to you."

Hallelujah! My heart soared, like it was on its way up to heaven.

"Have you completed the home study?" asked Mrs. O'Connor.

My heart dropped right back down to earth. "We're working on it," I said. The phone went dead. I replaced the receiver in its cradle while lowering my head. So many thoughts and feelings surged through my body. Do I act emotionally or respond intentionally? Do I fix my eyes on Jesus and follow Him, or give into my feelings of anger, fear, and self-doubt? We had waited so long for this moment, when Ashley was declared *free,* but the home study hadn't even been started. The grim reality was that we were not yet associated with an adoption agency. Moving forward required faith.

I bowed my head and prayed for direction. "Lord, you know my heart. I know that you have been here leading me through these unchartered waters. Lord, show me your will, whatever it may be, take my hand and have me follow you. I honestly want to do what is best for Ashley and our family. Open my eyes and guide me."

I lifted my head and opened my eyes, instantly understanding that I needed to contact Christian Adoption Services. I looked for the phone number in the yellow pages before dialling, and then glanced at the clock. It wasn't even eight o'clock in the morning. No business would answer the phone that early. It rang four times.

"Good Morning, Christian Adoptions."

"Good morning." I inhaled deeply. "My name is Erika Isnor. I'm calling because my family has been visiting Jamaica for over a year now, hoping to adopt a little girl named Ashley. She was living at an orphanage, Blossom Gardens, and has recently moved to a permanent residence called Garland Hall. Ashley has been declared 'free for adoption.' We are matched to her, but as yet have been unable to complete our home study." I continued describing the extenuating circumstances of our intervention by social services. And then, caught my breath and waited.

I'd been speaking with Wendy Robinson, the Director of Christian Adoptions. She'd had the business phone forwarded to her home, in case a birth mother needed to contact her. She shared her personal experience of Jamaica, specifically how she had volunteered at Blossom Gardens many years earlier, confessing that she'd left Jamaica, needing to focus her energies more effectively.

Wendy Robinson told me she was familiar with both Mr. Winston Bowen, and Ms. Marjorie Tumming. Mr. Bowen was "brilliant and truly cared" about the children. Ms. Tumming, on the other hand, was "a woman ruled by greed."

Wendy relayed her memory of an incident that had occurred a very long time ago. Once, when Wendy placed a package containing a birth certificate on the desk in front of Ms. Tumming, the Adoption's Director had stated, "Now we're talking." She was expecting cash to be inside the envelope.

"Garland Hall is a terrible place, we have to get Ashley out of there," said Wendy. I think I heard the sound of angel wings applauding. I heaved a huge sigh of relief. Thank God someone was willing to help.

"You'll need to apply to the Alberta Government for an Application of International Adoption," said Wendy.

"Done," I said.

"You'll need documents notarized, and referenced," said Wendy.

"Also done. I think I have the entire dossier composed," I said hopefully.

"Why don't you bring everything you have to me, and I'll take a look," suggested Wendy.

"Gladly. When are you available?" I asked.

"Give me some time to get to the office. How does eleven o'clock sound?" she asked.

"It sounds perfect," I said, hanging up the phone, and dancing around the room in praise of God.

I called Adoption Options, giving the requested courtesy call, advising the receptionist of my plans to pick up all of the paperwork. The receptionist, Vivien, treated me in a respectful and dignified manner when she turned over the package of documents for me to transfer to Christian Adoptions.

Nadia and Alyssa came with me to the initial meeting with Wendy Robinson. They provided moral support, wanting to give their perspective on adopting Ashley. I'd left Christian Adoption Services as a last resort, avoiding calling the agency because I didn't feel worthy. The enemy wants us to feel guilt and shame. Wendy never sugar-coated the probability of success, or encouraged a fool's paradise. What she did was offer grace, showing us compassion in a judgmental world, when she committed to overseeing our home study. No one else would touch us with a ten-foot pole.

We returned to Jamaica in a euphoric state, engrossed in the belief that the process was finally moving along, gaining momentum like a freight train speeding downhill. Sidney, Kaiden, and I took the Calgary red-eye back through Toronto, before landing in Mobay an unprecedented thirty-minutes early. I'd called Mr. Dixon, from Toronto, asking him to collect us after we'd gone through immigration.

I'd noted on the immigration card that I'd visited Mexico, within the last sixty days, so I was sent to the Minister of Health desk to obtain medical clearance before entering Jamaica. The boys waited, in the slow as molasses in January line, while I spoke to a nurse. "When did you visit Mexico and how long were you there," the nurse asked.

"Last week for twenty-four hours," I answered honestly. The nurse raised her eyes to meet mine with direct contact. "I am a flight attendant. We had a short layover in Cancun on April ninth. I was working." The nurse stamped my immigration card, allowing me to return to my place in line with the boys.

Mr. Dixon drove us straight to the CDA for a printed letter enabling us to take Ashley out of Garland Hall for the weekend. The boys and I soon sat in the front room, where the fan stirred, because Ms. Wilton had left the office shortly before we arrived. Our plan was to get the letter, and then put in some afternoon beach time, when the sun was at its hottest. Sidney's young patience waned with the heat, but I sat resigned to wait as long as necessary, so that we could pick up Ashley first thing the next morning.

Two other people sat in the area with us, a middle-aged black woman, and a small, disheveled, obviously distressed, Jamaican man. He spoke to the woman across from me in Patois, but I had difficulty understanding what he was saying through his sagnent sobs. Protection Services had apparently taken his daughter away from him. The mother was gone and the child had been left alone. He said she had plenty to eat and he wanted his daughter back. He asked the other woman in the room to make a phone call for him. He tried to reach someone named 'Wendy,' but she was not available. The woman asked if he wanted her to call anyone else. He shook his head back and forth.

I saw Ms. Wilton pass by the glass door headed in the direction of Mr. Sidney Grant's office. And then, the distressed man was called into a cubicle. "That was very kind of you to make the call for him," I told her.

"He was upset," she said. The woman moved from the far side of the room to the chair beside me, in front of the fan.

"He's having a rough time," I said. "Will he get his daughter back?" I asked.

"He will have to prove that he can take care of her," the woman told me. We sat side by side for some time.

"Are you waiting for Ms. Wilton," I asked the woman.

"Yea mon." She'd been there before me, so that made my wait longer.

"Do you have a child here?" I asked brazenly.

"My daughter has been at Blossom Gardens."

I perked up. "Really? I know Blossom Gardens well. The girl we are working on is from Blossom Gardens. She has just been moved to Anchovy. What is your daughter's name?"

"Sabrina."

"I know Sabrina. Sabrina Williams. She is the lighter girl with the dark front tooth"

"Yes, Sabrina William's is my daughter. I am here to get a medical form signed for her. I am going to start to take her out on the weekends."

I imagined the possibility of sitting in the waiting room with Ashley's birth mother. I wondered what would happen if she wanted to take Ashley out for weekends. It would have changed everything.

"Is Sabrina's brother's name Orlando?" I knew one of the boys was her brother, but I couldn't remember which one.

"No," she said.

"What is his name?" I asked.

"Sabrina does not have a brother that I know of." We were both confused. I assumed she was the birth mother. It never occurred to me at the time that she might have been adopting.

Ms. Wilton returned to the office a half an hour after we arrived. She greeted Sabrina Williams' mother and me warmly. And then, Ms. Wilton took Sabrina Williams' mother to her cubicle. I hoped Ms. Wilton didn't have to write a letter. She'd said it had slipped her mind that I was coming, but it shouldn't be much longer. "No problem," I said as I prayed for patience. I've since learned not to do that anymore because I now know He will provide opportunities to test it.

We passed Ms. Wilton's previous cubicle, where Ashley's finger got stuck, walking towards the area where we met Tejah. "This used to be Mrs. O'Connor's office," I said.

"Oh yes, you remember that. Ms. O'Connor is only here on Wednesdays now. The rest of the week she works in Trelawny," said Ms. Wilton. We sat opposite each other while Ms. Wilton talked on the phone, arranging files on her desk. I wondered which one of those was the Ashley Parkinson file. "I will write the letter for you now for you to take Ashley out at noon tomorrow. She must be returned on Sunday night for school on Monday. I will collect her for you tomorrow."

"Thank you so very much."

"I have another matter to deal with now." Ms. Wilton picked up the phone and then hesitated. She was talking under her breath, trying to figure out the name of a child. "Samantha?"

"Is it Sabrina?" I asked. "Sabrina Williams?"

"Sabrina?" she questioned.

"Yes. Sabrina Williams. She is from Blossom Gardens, like Ashley."

"Do you have a driver who can take you to Anchovy to collect the child?" asked Ms. Williams.

"Yes, I do, but I don't know exactly how to get to Garland Hall." Mr. Dixon had already said he'd made a commitment to other houseguests to go to Negril the next day. I supposed I would hire a different charter driver.

Ms. Wilton picked up the phone to call Garland Hall. "Ms. Isnor would like to collect Ashley on Friday. If it would be possible to get the child at noon that would be the preference." I was ever so grateful for the extra half day. "Ms. Isnor will be bringing another envelope with the medical form for Sabrina Williams. Will you have the guidance counselor make certain that Sabrina Williams sees the Doctor? She will be having visitations on the weekends." I noticed the way that Ms. Wilton negotiated requests rather than demanding her own way.

I left the CDA with a letter in hand to collect Ashley Parkinson from her new 'place of residence,' Garland Hall. The letter was in an unsealed envelope with the name 'Mrs. Hardy' handwritten on the outside. I also agreed to courier a letter regarding one Sabrina Williams. That letter was inserted inside a second envelope with a single staple piercing its layers, insuring privacy. I had no intention of snooping at that letter, feeling honored that I was trusted to deliver it. We climbed in Mr. Dixon's van and he took us to the Caribic House, where we arrived shortly after four in the afternoon. It had been a prosperous first day.

It didn't take us long to shed our traveling clothes. We put on our swimsuits, grabbed the beach towels, and headed up the road to Margaritaville. The Dreamer catamaran was already temporarily docked at the landmark restaurant, and was stocking the waters with tourists. Sidney expressed his annoyance about how many people were in the water. My sons waited for the boat to leave before swimming out to their familiar yellow banana tube.

I ran upstairs to buy a Landshark beer for me, and a 'dirty banana' for Kaiden. The new bartender said he was unable to make Kaiden's drink without rum, so I settled on getting him a non-alcoholic banana daiquiri. When Kaiden questioned why his drink was white instead of brown, I answered, "They used clean bananas."

"I like the dirty ones better because they have chocolate in them," said Kaiden.

"Where would we find really good local food, beside the Pork Pit?" I asked the waitress.

"How far do you want to go?" she answered.

"We are meeting friends in Ironshore later tonight," I said. I'd left a message on Angie's voicemail hoping to get together later in the afternoon.

"There is a place just past Ironshore called Scotchies that has good Jamaican food; jerk chicken and pork." Perfect!

We left Margaritaville and stopped at the Scotiabank ATM for cash before heading back to the Carabic House for a quick shower. Angie called when the boys were soaping up, telling me that she was on her way, and would be in front of the hotel in five minutes. I prodded the boys with the prospect of a night swim to get them downstairs.

We poured out onto the street freshly scrubbed, just as Angie and Rej rolled up together in her Toyota. We all climbed in the backseat, did a quick U-turn in the Burger King parking lot, and then headed to Scotchies to pick up some takeout food to eat at the villa.

I paid a grand total of twenty-six dollars in US funds for a virtual feast. I ordered a whole chicken, a pound of pork, some festival bread, rice and peas, and a Red Stripe to drink while the food grilled.

Our meal was packaged in a combination of Styrofoam and foil, neatly stacked inside a plastic bag. I put two hundred JMD inside the empty industrial sized mayonnaise jar, for 'the boys.'

And then, Angie drove us up the hill to the villa to eat by the pool. Afterwards, Kaiden and Sidney circled its exterior like sharks, until Kaiden *accidently* fell into the water. "Let them swim," said Angie. Soon Sidney, and Rej and Duj were all splashing around together.

Angie suggested that I put the boys to bed in the living room on the black leather couches, but I declined, because I'd already paid for our hotel room, so Angie and Suan helped me pack my tired boys into her car, and drove us back down the hill. We had a big day coming. We planned on picking up Ashley at Garland Hall and spending the entire day at Doc's cave.

Mr. Dixon woke me in the morning, calling my Jamaican phone asking if we could make the trip for Ashley before noon, so that he'd be able to take his other clients to Negril as planned. "Absolutely, we can be ready anytime," I said. He arrived shortly after ten to take us up the Long Road.

We delivered Sabrina Williams' medical letter at Garland Hall, but Ashley had not yet returned from school for lunch. Ms. McLean, the house lady, suggested we go directly to the Anchovy Primary School to get Ashley. She instructed one of the older girls in the house to show us the way. "Is it far?" I asked wondering whether we should walk or take the van.

"No mon, it's not far," said the girl. I wondered why she was not dressed for school, for she couldn't have been older than fourteen. When she began walking down the road leading to the school, Mr. Dixon suggested driving there, because he needed to return to Montego Bay for his other clients. He veered off the main highway, onto a bumpy a dirt road going very slowly, because children of all sizes were walking in the center of the road towards us. Apparently, classes had just let out for the noon hour, and judging from the number of students in the street, it must have been a huge school. I scanned through the crowd searching for Ashley's familiar face.

We must have been quite a spectacle my two toe-headed boys and me, a white woman inside Mr. Dixon's van. He eventually pulled inside the schoolyard and parked the van under a shade tree. I asked Mr. Dixon to watch over the boys while I collected Ashley.

"No problem mon," said Mr. Dixon.

I got out of the van to walk towards the entrance of the school, and was immediately surrounded by all sorts of children. One nameless girl took my hand. "I'm looking for Ashley Parkinson. Do you know who she is?" I asked. A ripple of Patois spread through the children, as the news traveled, about who I was looking for.

"Are you Ashley's mother?" asked the children.

"Yes, I am Ashley's mother," I responded.

"I will take you to Ashley," said the girl holding my hand. We walked inside a rectangular courtyard, beyond the nurse's station, and past several classrooms. The girl poked her head inside each empty room looking for Ashley.

We found the grade one class where a teacher sat behind a heavy wooden desk. "Is Ashley Parkinson here," I asked.

"Yea mon, she is right over there," said the teacher. I looked around, but could not see Ashley.

"She is right there at her desk sleeping. She sleeps every day, all day long."

"*Ashley* sleeps? Every day?" I asked. I must have sounded surprised.

"Yea mon. Every day, all day long," said the teacher.

"How long has she been at this school?" I asked.

"One month now I think," said the teacher, "and she never says a word."

"This child talks my ear off!" I bellowed, as I bent down over her sleeping body to pull her upright. I put her tiny face into the palms of my hands, "Ashley, Ashley honey, are you awake? Ashley do you know who I am?" Her little eyes rolled into the back of her head, but she smiled, and recognized me. "Ashley its mommy. Wake up Ashley. I am going to take you with me." I got her to her feet. Ashley leaned against me, and we started walking out of the classroom.

"Don't forget her backpack," said the teacher. I looked inside it, expecting to find a lunch box or some sort of schoolwork. There was nothing except for a single wrinkled page of work, obviously recently printed on an old ditto machine. I recognized the purple ink and distinct odor from my childhood.

We walked back towards the van, stopping at the office to let them know I was taking Ashley out of school, and that she would not be returning for the rest of the day. The principle photocopied my driver's license and called Garland Hall to verify that I had their permission, before allowing me to leave with Ashley.

I bumped into Sabrina Williams, hardly recognizing the child, the mischievous girl who had snatched a photograph from Ashley, ran away, and taunted her with it. The child in front of me bore no resemblance to that impish girl, except that she had the same light skin, hair, and dark front tooth. I felt like I was walking through the set of The Village of the Damned.

The memory of the boy who slept in the classroom, the day I officially found Ashley, accosted me in my tracks. I remembered Maryam saying Daniel never spoke the entire time he lived at Blossom Gardens. Once removed, he talked incessantly. These repressed children had plenty to say. I later confronted both Mr. Green and Mr. Bowen, stating my concerns about the use of drugs that managed the children's behavior. No one has ever admitted to drugging the children.

Mr. Dixon remained with the boys at the van, and was shooing kids away when Ashley and I arrived. "You are different from them, your skin is lighter, they are curious," he said explaining why the children had surrounded the boys, poked, and prodded them.

I climbed into the van madder than a hornet. I wasn't angry with the children. I was livid at how the adults ran the system.

Ashley slumped over my shoulder with her ear oozing puss. I'd mentioned the possibility of an ear infection the last time we visited, two months ago. Obviously, Ashley's ear infection had gone untreated. I called the CDA, but Ms. Wilton was not available. I explained that Ashley was sick, and needed medical attention. "If the child is sick, return her to Garland Hall, the house mother will take care of her." *Fat chance of that happening!* I wasn't about to return Ashley to the negligent housemother like an unsatisfactory library book. I planned on taking Ashley to a doctor myself. I just had to figure out where and how.

Mr. Dixon listened to my ranting and raving about how poorly the Jamaicans cared for Ashley. I continued on about the screwy Jamaican health care system. He must have been thinking, "How can you say to your brother, 'Let me take the speck out of your eye,' and behold, the log is in your own eye.' He never said a single word and delivered us at the Caribic House before noon, just in time to pick up his other clients at the Polkerris. I thanked him for his continued kindness, and asked him to meet us at the Pork Pit Sunday evening in time to return Ashley to Garland Hall. "Call me if you need me," said Mr. Dixon before driving away.

We were indeed on our own. One white woman, two white boys, and a sick little black girl. A whole day passed before Ashley spoke a single word. I took the kids to Doc's cave beach, so the boys could swim, while I tried to figure out where to take Ashley for medical care. I called Angie. She advised me to either take her to Hope Medical Centre, near Rose Hall, or to the Hospital downtown; both options sounded expensive. We ate dinner next door at the Jamaican Bobsled restaurant. Ashley didn't have an appetite, but I had to feed the boys. We retired early hoping to find a doctor for her first thing in the morning.

Ashley and I walked to Miss Dolly's shop the next day, intending on grabbing a strong cup of morning coffee. Miss Dolly, an ancient black woman who hasn't yet learned that tact is the intelligence of the heart, asked Ashley, "How are you doing." Ashley did not answer. "Why do you not speak child, are you retarded?" Obviously, Miss Dolly did not know that Ashley had been given medicine to keep her quiet. I didn't care how ignorant Miss Dally was; I didn't need a cup of coffee that badly. I took Ashley's hand and we left the shop never to return.

We woke the boys and meandered into St James Place for breakfast, before heading off to the medical centre. We filled our bellies at a small open-sided hexagon shaped dwelling with a thatched roof made from dried palm leaves. Everyone liked the inexpensive locals only restaurant. The boys were able to get dippin' eggs, and Ashley ate her favorite, ackee and saltfish. I filled up on a fruit plate of fresh bananas, pineapple, papaya, mango, and two cups of Blue Mountain coffee. The waitress brought out a small pitcher of milk, but I for requested condensed milk to sweeten my cup.

I asked the waitress if she knew where there might be a church close by where we could worship the Lord to the sound of soulful music. "You can go with me to my church if you like," she offered. A substantial white smile crossed her face. I asked her to put her number into the contacts of my Digicel phone, so that I could call her in the morning.

After breakfast we went looking for someone to take us to a doctor. Several drivers stood outside Doc's Cave, waiting for a fare. One asked, "Do you need a taxi?"

"I need to take my daughter to a doctor, but I don't know where to go. Do you know where she can be seen? The driver gave us the once over.

"I can take you to the hospital on Orange Street downtown," he said.

"Is it open on Saturday? How much will it cost?" I asked.

"I think its open today. It is early. It's best to go early. I think it will cost you around thirty-five hundred JMD to see the doctor.

"How much will it cost for you to drive us?" I asked.

"Twenty dollars," he said.

"Will you do it for one thousand JMD?" I asked.

"Yea mon. I will do it for you."

"I need to get some money out of the bank machine before we go, I'll be right back."

"Yea mon, I will wait," he said.

I crossed the street, took out some Jamaican cash, and returned with kids in tow to climb into his meticulously clean car. The driver's name was Winston. He said he had a daughter about the same age as Ashley. He made sure that the hospital was open, and that we would be seen before dropping us off. He asked me if we would be alright by ourselves downtown.

I looked around to get my bearings. He left us at 15 Humber Avenue, only a block or two away from Sam Sharpe Square. "We'll be fine, thank you."

The Doctor was able to see Ashley immediately, once we'd signed her in. I described Ashley's symptoms, describing how she had been sick since our last visit. I hoped he'd see the need for antibiotics.

"What is your relationship to this child?" asked the Doctor.

"She is my daughter. We are in the process of adopting her," I answered.

The Doctor scribbled out two prescriptions; a liquid antibiotic that required refrigeration, and some cough syrup, both to be taken morning, noon, and night, with food. "Follow the yellow line down the hallway," said the Doctor dismissing us.

We followed that line to the closed door marked 'CASHIER,' where I wondered if I would find a note reading, 'drink me.' The cashier and the pharmacist turned out to be one in the same. I knocked, and waited for him to open the door. I paid the doctor's fee before receiving two amber colored bottles of medicine for Ashley's ailments.

It cost approximately thirty-five Canadian dollars for Ashley to be seen the doctor, and get her medicine, and we'd been at the hospital less than ten minutes before we were on our way. I couldn't get that kind of health care in Canada!

We stopped at a downtown grocery store to pick up a few items before finding a taxi to take us back to the hotel. We bought some orange plastic bowls, real cow's milk, and a box of Honey Nut Cheerios, so that we wouldn't have to go out for breakfast. The girl who bagged our groceries flagged down a cab for us establishing the cost of three hundred JMD to get us back to the hip strip. "Wow! Thanks," I said. "It cost us much more than that to get here."

"That's because of the color of your complexion," she said. I handed her two hundred JMD for her kindness.

We put the medicine in the small fridge in our room after giving Ashley her first dose. When I called Angie to let her know that Ashley had seen a doctor, she invited us to the villa for the evening for supper and to swim. "I'm makin' Sidney's favorite *fried chicken*," said Angie. I appreciated her offer.

And then, we decided to go the beach! The boys donned their suits and grabbed their towels, while Ashley and I put our bathing suits in the Bob Marley bag, because I didn't know if she felt well enough to swim, or not. We were staying at the Caribic House, directly across the street from the beach, so we could come and go as we pleased once we paid the daily admission.

I met Helen, an English woman who lived and worked in Jamaica since she graduated from Oxford University. She was a retired teacher who'd just published her first children's book. Helen promised to bring me a copy of her writing the next time she came to the beach. We sat and talked while Ashley played silently at my feet, and the boys jumped on the distant trampolines.

"Mi want to go swim," said Ashley. I looked down, surprised to hear her speak.

"Good idea. Let's get our suits on." I excused myself from Helen, and called out to to the boys. "BOYS...you need to get out of the water for a few minutes while Ashley and I get our suits on!" I waved my arms wildly, knowing they couldn't hear me on the trampolines, but they saw me, and started swimming towards to shore. "Stay on the sand please," I instructed once they reached us. "We won't take very long. We just need to get our suits on."

Ashley and I rinsed our feet in the foot shower before going into the woman's dressing room. We changed quickly, and then returned to find that the boys had gone back in the water.

"I guess it's time to leave the beach," I said. I was mad, and it took a lot to get me there. As far as I was concerned, this was a safety issue. It was not safe to swim without parental supervision, even if there was a lifeguard on duty.

I needed to cool down. I dove into the sea headfirst and swam to the trampoline, and then back to shore, fully intending on drying off and leaving the beach. The boys sat sulking in the sand, but Ashley bound into the water towards me. Mommy, give them one more chance *please*." Her words shocked me. She had barely spoken a single syllable since I'd picked her up, and here she was using an entire English sentence. I was flabbergasted.

"You *can* talk!" I lost all trace of the anger that had nearly overtaken me and changed the path of our day. There was no doubt in my mind that I was being manipulated, but I was relieved that Ashley was back. It had taken her most of a day to come down off of whatever it was she was on, and return to normal.

The boys were well aware that Ashley saved them. We stayed and played at the beach for the rest of the afternoon. The boys swam in the deeper water while Ashley remained at the shore, careful not to get her ears wet. We left in the late afternoon when the color of the sky changed, and the breeze chilled our tingling skin. We left to freshen up, because we had accepted Angie's invitation to dinner.

I stopped at the ATM for two hundred more US dollars. Angie agreed to take us to Mega Mart for supplies to make fried chicken at the villa. I spent one hundred and twenty of those dollars at Mega Mart, mostly on Blue Mountain Coffee, because it was cheaper there than at duty-free at the airport. I tucked the remaining eighty dollars cash inside my Coach wallet. I thought money seemed to flow out of it like water.

After dinner, I let the kids swim with the twins well into the night. They were all tired and ready for bed by the time I coaxed them out of the pool. Angie asked us to spend the night again, but guests were expected at the villa the next day. Angie needed a good night's sleep. All three of my babies fell asleep on the ride back to the hotel.

Our friend Nicolas, the Jamaican tourist officer, stood next to the 'Valet Parking Only,' sign in front of the Jamaican Bobsled Restaurant. He and the security guard for the Caribic House helped Duj and me carry my sleeping children upstairs to their beds. Angie waited in the Toyota curbside for Duj's return. I thanked everyone for their assistance, and gave Duj a good squeeze before locking the door behind them.

I tucked in each child, kissed their foreheads, and then checked the lock on the back door that led to the small balcony. We'd all had a long sun drenched day. Once again, I fell asleep before my head hit the pillow.

I woke up at about three o'clock in the morning, noticing that the bathroom light was on. I felt relieved because I knew the kids could make their way, if they needed to use the washroom. And then, I noticed that the balcony door was open. That seemed odd. I remembered locking it before climbing into bed.

Locking up the house was not included in my bedtime routine. Sid locked our house up at home, but I was in Jamaica where I knew there were safety concerns. There was no doubt in my mind that I'd closed and locked the balcony door. I wondered if perhaps Sidney had woken up, and opened the door for air, or to get a drink from the cooler we kept out on the porch. I shut and locked the door again, and went back to sleep.

I woke up that Sunday morning at about seven o'clock, looking forward to going to church with the waitress who worked as the St James Square restaurant. I searched for my Digicel phone to call her, remembering that I'd plugged it into the charger on the desk. There was only one electrical receptacle in the room, so it had to be there. It wasn't. I looked on the nightstand, but the phone was nowhere to be found.

The black and white Hawaiian print cooler bag was not on the desk either. Curious, I had not used the bag. It had been sitting on the desk ever since our arrival. I looked for my Canadian TELUS blackberry cell phone, that I'd *most definitely* left charging in the bathroom over the sink. It was gone too. I looked for the Coach wallet, that the boys called my 'C wallet.' I'd left it on the nightstand between the twin beds. It was empty. I knew I'd tucked eighty US dollars inside it at the Mega Mart check out stand.

The only place we'd gone after Mega Mart was Angie's. I actually suspected the pool boy, Avian, of taking the money. I panicked because I couldn't find either my red pass (RAIC), which was required for work, or my newly acquired permanent resident card. Our passports had all been tucked into the side of the Hawaiian cooler bag. I couldn't find the new iPOD Sid had given me for our ninth anniversary. What saddened me the most, was that the camera that had documented our entire journey with Ashley, thus far, was also missing. I thanked God that the disk in the camera was a new one. Sid had run out last minute to replace it before dropping us off at the airport. I'd taken the original disk out to print the pictures from our previous trips, neglecting to put it back in the camera.

Only then did I remember the balcony door being open at three o'clock in the morning. I walked outside. A couple of filthy dirty handprints were on the wall between our room and number eight. They hadn't been there the day before, I would have noticed.

The Hawaiian cooler bag sat on the round patio table. I grabbed it to check the pockets. The passports, my RAIC, and permanent resident card was still there, but no sign of the phones, or my new iPOD. Someone had tucked my black Ralph Lauren handbag inside the cooler bag, so clearly, we'd been robbed. I immediately felt guilty for suspecting Avian.

The kids continued sleeping. I closed and locked the door to our room, and walked down the steps to the front desk, to inform the hotel about the robbery. The hotel's reaction to the news dumbfounded me. They insinuated I was lying, insisting that the hotel had never been stung before, and that I must be mistaken. But, I remained steadfast in my claim, as I reported our missing items.

"It must have been someone you know," accused the security officer.

"It was not. Those people have been my friends for a long time," I maintained.

The security guard glared at me with the eyes of a dishonest teenager. He was either preoccupied at the time, or had a hand in it. He tried several tactics to deflect his responsibility, including saying I'd made the story up. His accusatory looks infuriated me.

The receptionist called the owner of the company that the hotel hired for security. He arrived shortly after eight in the morning to make a report about the incident. He too seemed skeptical when he asked if I was willing to talk to the police about the robbery.

"Absolutely," I answered. I was expected to wait for the police to arrive at the hotel. We waited, and waited. Meanwhile, I emailed Sid to have him disconnect my Canadian phone, hoping to stop anyone from causing international charges from the Caribbean.

Finally, the children's stomachs demanded breakfast. That was our last day on the island. The police station was less than a mile away on Bottom Road. I'd be damned if we were going to sit around waiting to make a statement to the police. We ate, and then prepared to go to the beach. "He quiets the raging oceans and all the world's clamor."

We crossed Gloucester Avenue and paid the entrance fee for Doc's cave. Helen, the writer, had just arrived for her morning swim. "I tried to call you," she said. "I knew your phone was stolen." She was calling to tell me that she'd brought a copy of the book she'd written to the beach for me. I thought it was a gift, until she asked me for ten dollars. I gave her the money and stuffed the book deep inside my backpack.

I looked out at the huge expanse of water searching for comfort, and then jumped in. Water calmed me when ever my nerves became frazzled. I allowed the salty sea to wash over my hair. Swimming soothed my soul. I needed to get away from the commotion of the world that wreaked havoc with my peace. I carried Ashley on my back to the trampolines, as I had done with Kaiden on our early trips to Jamaica. We climbed up onto the floating plastic islands, and jumped off them into the ocean about a hundred times before I glanced towards the shore.

The hotel receptionist was waving her arms madly trying to get my attention. I reluctantly returned to the water's edge with Ashley on my back. "The police are waiting for you to make a statement. They need to speak with you right away." I was not one to ignore the police, but I answered to a higher authority.

"We are on vacation. We waited in the room for hours, but the police never showed up. I will not instantly appear when they have finally decided to make this robbery a priority. If they would like to speak to me, I am here on the beach spending time with my children."

We remained in the water until shortly before dusk when we showered to prepare for dinner. I'd asked Mr. Dixon to meet us at the Pork Pit at five-thirty, wanting to fill Ashley's belly before returning her to Anchovy. I couldn't call Mr. Dixon without a phone, so I decided to feed the kids pizza at the Jamaican Bobsled, where I could use the Internet to make reservations to go home. I was immensely grateful that I'd tucked the computer underneath the big brown suitcase we called 'the beast,' because it had remained unnoticed by our midnight caller.

Mr. Dixon arrived just after the pizza. We were sitting at a raised pub table on the porch. "Hey, there's Mr. Dixon!" Kaiden said. I looked up. Sure enough, Mr. Dixon, a man of his word, had arrived at our hotel looking for us. I felt guilty for not getting ahold of him.

"I'm sorry Mr. Dixon, my phone was stolen."

"I know your phone was stolen. I tried to call you and a man answered." Mr. Dixon held his own phone to his ear as he dialled my number. The same man picked up again, wanting to know who was calling, "Mr. Jones," answered Mr. Dixon.

"Do not be callin' dis number again or I bi pumpin' you full of bullets," said the man on the other end of the line...*my line.* Mr. Dixon lowered his head and shook it back and forth as he walked away from our table towards the Caribic House.

Moments later the receptionist walked out of the hotel to speak with me at our table. "We are going to move your family to a higher floor. We will give you a room without a balcony," she said.

I didn't think it was necessary. I didn't want to pack up and move our bags for only one night. After all, we were taking Ashley back right away, and then leaving in the morning. It was a huge hassle. I guess I didn't get the full gist of the incident immediately. I'd never felt unsafe in Jamaica before that day.

Mr. Dixon explained, on the way up to Anchovy, how it could have been terrible. "We could have read about four dead people in the paper," he said. That's when my eyes popped opened, and I realized how truly fortunate we had been. It was a darn good thing we all been *sooo* tired.

It was a godsend that the bathroom light was on, not for the children to see, but for the intruder to have moved around freely without disturbing us. 'He' was able to get whatever he wanted and leave without an altercation. I've since imagined a dark man, carrying a massive machete, that he would not have hesitated to use. He was the kind of evil man that would not think twice about killing four people for a couple of electronic gadgets, and some cash. We had angels hovering over us that night.

It was dark when we arrived at Anchovy. I changed Ashley's clothes in the van, putting her back into her school uniform with a new 'All We Need Is Love t-shirt' underneath it.

The boys couldn't make up their minds whether they wanted to walk Ashley in or not. Sidney did not want to see her cry again as we left. In the end, they decided to go with me instead of waiting in the van.

Ashley looked resigned as she walked up the residential home steps. I gave explicit instructions to the housemother, Ms. Woodit, that Ashley needed to take her medicine three times a day, every day, for the next week. I explained how important it was for Ashley to receive the prescribed medication to prevent permanent damage to her hearing.

Oddly, I'd crossed an invisible threshold. I no longer thought of myself as her 'special friend.' There were no trumpets blowing, or fanfare, on the day I realized we had bonded as mother and child. Unknowingly, I'd gained trust and respect for taking Ashley to the hospital when it was not seen as my responsibility. Mr. Dixon explained to me how my actions demonstrated to the Jamaican authorities that I now had a vested interest in Ashley.

I'd worried that I might be reprimanded for taking a child that was not officially mine to the doctor. I would never have been so brazen in Canada. It seemed health care was a privilege in Jamaica. Only people with money went to the doctor when they were sick.

I kissed Ashley's forehead, promising to return as soon as I could. Ashley quietly walked away from me.

When the boys and I turned around to get back into Mr. Dixon's van, I had to shield my eyes from the bright headlights coming towards us up the empty road. Ms. Woodit walked with us to the gates, to let us out, and presumably lock up for the night. She told me that the approaching car belonged to Ms. Wilton. *What were the chances?* My husband, the Engineer would have said one hundred percent!

Ms. Wilton got out of the car. I laid right into her about Ashley's medicine. "Ashley's ear and cough have gotten much worse. No one has taken care of her. She needs to take her medicine until it is finished." I used mother speak, not friend speak. And then, I climbed into the van to tell Mr. Dixon that the lady in the other car was Ashley's social worker.

"Ms. Wilton goes to my church," he said.

I described to him the time I tried to get Ms. Wilton to pray with me before a meeting. She'd declined and walked out of her cubicle, leaving me to pray with Ms. Bradford. I said I thought she was not a woman of God.

Mr. Dixon explained that they were Jehovah Witnesses. According to the rules of their church, they were not allowed to practice rituals of other religions. He continued to describe their formal set ways of praying, from which they did not deviate. Ms. Wilton had not turned her back on me. She was being true to the God she believed in. I continued to learn about perception and how egocentric I remained.

Mr. Dixon agreed to pick us up at twelve-thirty the next day to get us to our plane on time. He drove us back to the Caribic House, where the security guard humbly carried our bags to the fourth floor, so no one could climb over a balcony to steal our belongings.

The robbery might have been an inside job. If so, they would think we didn't have anything else worth stealing, not knowing I'd hidden my computer. Thank God, because all of my writing was saved on that computer. Other than our lives, It was the only *thing* I could never replace. If the robbery were not an inside job, the bad crack man with the dirty hands, and threatening machete, would not know to which room we moved.

Much later, I realized that God protected us, preserving our lives, and opening my eyes to the unsavory realities in Jamaica. I'd been walking through Jamaica with blinders on, focusing only on Ashley's adoption. God had given me a warning.

Once again, we retraced our steps back to Calgary. We all slept the entire way home. I woke Sidney up when we landed to walk down the long terminal, because there was no way on God's green earth that I could carry both boys. And then, we rode the escalator to the lower level where Sid waited for us. He'd already loaded a cart with our luggage. We arrived home safely, and we were in good hands.

ELEVEN

HOME STUDY

March 24, 2010, we were assigned a social worker by Christian Adoption Services to complete our home study at last. Wendy deliberated long and hard about who would be best suited for our family. She decided to allocate the task to Amanda, who held the respect of Ann S., the Adoptions Director in Edmonton. Ann S. would make the final decision regarding Ashley's adoption based on Amanda's recommendation. Amanda first contacted us by email the night before she left for a family holiday.

> *Hello Erika and Sidney,*
>
> *I just wanted to send a quick email and touch base before I leave for holidays tomorrow. If you are ready to start the home assessment process in a couple of weeks, I am available to begin on April 15, 19th and 21st at 6:30 pm. Let me know if any of these dates work for you.*
>
> *Thanks,*
>
> *I look forward to meeting you both.*
> *Amanda S.*

I cleared my April schedule, in about two seconds, by dropping a twenty-eight hour layover in Hawaii, leaving all of the dates Amanda proposed free. The day before our initial meeting, we sent Amanda the required 'Home Assessment Self Report Form,' previewing our situation and family. Wendy had filled her in on the areas of concern surrounding Olivia, and alcohol.

I also provided the contact information Amanda requested, of my older children, fulfilling my obligation by leaving them voicemails. I provided my grown children's phone numbers, but had no control over how those request would be received. Jonathan answered quickly, fully supporting the idea of our adopting a needy child. I never expected Olivia to respond to Amanda, and she didn't. Sadly, Erica also avoided my preemptive email and phone calls altogether.

It's still hard to come for me to come terms with adult children who will not speak to me. I have learned to live without contact of either Erica or Olivia. They don't know how heartbreaking it is for me not to be in their lives. I think it's cruel and passive aggressive to refuse to communicate. It is the feelings that are not discussed that grow, and gain a power of their own. I hope their children don't ever break their hearts, like they have mime. To survive, I now focus people who want healthy relationships with me, believing that all will be restored in heaven.

Our home study began on April 15, 2010. We opened the doors to our home and hearts, knowing we were fighting an uphill battle. Everyone told us that our odds of making it past our Canadian Adoption Services board were slim. All we could do was be honest about our lives.

I made myself extremely vulnerable, sharing my life's path, and information about my intimate relationships with a stranger who would decide if I should nurture an orphan in a safe environment. I felt embarrassed by my former life, before Sid, and had never revealed the details of it with anyone else. My past met my present within the context of that home study.

Amanda prepared me beforehand warning, "these home studies are very detailed, and I know they want a lot of personal information, but it is better that we explain situations as much as we can, in as much detail, so that they don't send the report back to us half way through reading it, delaying the process."

I thank God's grace for providing Amanda. She thoroughly examined every nook and cranny, every hard place. She did it with a gentle compassion, asking difficult questions that I answered to the best of my ability. I didn't want to misrepresent anything. I trusted her, because she was fair and kind.

Amanda visited our home four times, April 15, 19, 21, and May 7th, in 2009. The first three sessions the entire family was present; including Kaiden, Sidney, Nadia, Alyssa, Sid and me. The last time Amanda came to the house only the boys and I were home. And then, Amanda conducted two telephone interviews with just me.

Amanda's final report intricately described all members of our family:

Sid: 6 feet 2 inches tall, and has blond hair, and green eyes. Sidney is a Caucasian and a fourth generation Canadian. Sid presents as a quiet, calm individual. He is easy going, considerate, and respectful of others thoughts and feelings. Sid is hard working, intelligent, and analytical. He can present as cautious and reserved. Sid puts great thought and consideration into all the decisions that he makes. He is a giving person, who does not hesitate to place the needs of others before his own. Sid looks for positive aspects in all situations and he strives to find joy and humor in his life. Sid's hobbies and interests include skiing, swimming, listening to music, making wine, and enjoying arts and culture. He plays recreational sports, such as golf and basketball. Sid takes time to relax and enjoy quiet time, when he can pause and rest. He does not like to be overly committed to too many extra involvements. Sid enjoys frequent international travel with his family. He looks forward to spending time with friends and family. He is a kind, non-judgmental individual. He possesses the characteristics required of a good adoptive parent.

Erika is 5 feet 9 inches tall, and weighs 160 pounds. She has brown hair, and hazel eyes. Erika is Caucasian, and of French and English background. Erika presents as an outgoing, sociable, and friendly woman. She is caring, considerate, thoughtful, and hugely honest and open. Erika has a kind heart, and she cares deeply for the needs of others. She is determined and focused. She is driven to reach all of her goals; she is strong willed, and strives to fulfill all that she sets her mind to accomplish. Erika is loyal to her family, friends, and commitments. She is frequently smiling and laughing; she describes her sense of humor as dry.

She is well spoken, and can communicate her thoughts and feelings in a respectful, direct, and honest manner. She enjoys spontaneity. Erika is a deep thinker who places great thought into all that she does. When Erika becomes upset, she takes time alone to think through the issues causing her stress. She finds that physical activity helps. She will garden, clean the house, or exercise to relieve her stress. Erika presented as a positive, energetic and caring individual. She leads a balanced lifestyle, and is well able to balance her career, her family and her home life. Erika possesses the characteristics required of a good adoptive parent.

Nadia was described in the report as responsible, cheerful, and friendly. She is sociable, and enjoys spending time with her close friends. Nadia can initially be shy with people, but once comfortable, she opens up and becomes more outgoing. She has a great sense of humor and is frequently seen with a smile. Nadia enjoys young children. She is caring and nurturing, and she enjoys taking care of children and animals. She hopes to pursue a career working with animals. Nadia was present throughout all of the interviews; she enjoyed participating in the conversations and the interview process. Nadia presented as happy, polite, and caring. She was able to communicate her thoughts and feelings openly. Nadia is an intelligent child, who is doing well academically. At times, she has procrastinated completing her schoolwork, and has had to attend summer school to complete the course. She has learned from the past, and she now works hard in order to receive good grades. Nadia has traveled to Jamaica twice. She has spent ample time in the orphanage with Ashley. Nadia is excited about Ashley's arrival; she hopes to share her bedroom with Ashley.

Alyssa is a happy, sociable and easy-going child. She is frequently smiling, and has a good sense of humor. She is a responsible, kind, caring, and compassionate person. Alyssa excels both in academics and athletics. She enjoys the performing arts, theatre, singing, soccer, physical education, drawing and travelling. Alyssa is a healthy, mature and intelligent child. She has no health or behavioral concerns. Alyssa has traveled to Jamaica four times and has spent ample time with Ashley. She recently spent eleven days with Ashley, while the Isnor's were caring for her outside of the orphanage. Alyssa was very touched by the opportunity to spend time with Ashley. She understands that Erika and Sid are hoping to adopt Ashley and she believes that is a great idea. She enjoys her time with Ashley and is excited to welcome her into the family.

Sidney was described as a mature, thoughtful, and calm child. He is responsible and intelligent, and is excelling academically. Sidney is in elementary school, and attends the 4th grade. He enjoys science, mathematics, reading, building with Lego, drawing, playing soccer, and swimming. He looks forward to traveling to Halifax during the summer to spend time at his paternal grandmother's home. Sidney hopes to become an engineer when he grows up, just like his father. Sidney is a child with no health or behavioral concerns. He is able to communicate his thoughts and opinions clearly. Sidney has traveled to Jamaica numerous times; he has spent ample time with Ashley in Jamaica. Sidney enjoys spending time with Ashley, and he understands that his parents are hoping to adopt her.

Kaiden is in elementary school and attends grade 2. Kaiden is an energetic, kind, and strong-willed child. He is sociable and caring, inquisitive and curious. He enjoys reading, building with Lego, swimming, skiing, drawing, and travelling. Kaiden is a healthy child with no health or behavioral concerns. Throughout our interviews, Kaiden was present; he enjoyed participating in the conversations, while building with his Lego. Kaiden is a smart and focused child. Kaiden will be very close in age to Ashley; he thinks it will be great to have a sister.

Throughout the interview process, the Isnor children were polite, considerate, and well behaved. It was evident that all four children are securely attached, and that their needs are well met. All children have strong and loving relationships with both Erika and Sid. These are happy, intelligent, well-behaved, responsible children.

Erica P. is 29 and lives in Texas. She is married and has a two-year-old daughter. The writer attempted to contact Erica via telephone, but without success.

Jonathan was interviewed over the phone. He believes that Sid and Erika have a strong and loving marriage. He believes that providing an orphaned child with a home and family is an honorable thing that his parents are doing.

Olivia H. is 20 years old, and lives with her half-sister, Erica, in Texas. To the best of Erika's knowledge, Olivia is single, and attends university. She is currently studying Philosophy, and is planning a trip to India to do peace work.

A psychological evaluation report was completed on both Sid and me, including our personal characteristics, our marital relationship, historical information, and family background, concluding ours was a loving and supportive marriage that had experienced, and prevailed, over some stressful times.

Our lifestyle, home, and the community in which we lived were described in detail. Our parenting strategies, past and present, were evaluated. We provided our medical reports, criminal record checks, and four names for personal references. Our guarantors, in turn furnished confidential questionnaire of which we were not privy.

We addressed our need for specialized parenting including family preparation and training activities for the special needs of an internationally adopted child. We addressed inevitable adoption issues, and potential concerns.

Amanda gave heed to all of the personal information we divulged and *still* "recommend approval to adopt a healthy female child, under the age of ten, from Jamaica."

Our application was received May 1, 2010. The home study was completed on June 5, 2010, and we were recommended for adoption on July 12, 2010. Our placement approval was considered 'Child Specific,' meaning we had applied to become 'adoptive parents for Ashley Parkinson, DOB: October 13, 2002. The child currently residing in Garland Hall, in Jamaica."

Our extended family is connected like sporadic stepping-stones across a wide river, making it difficult to gather frequently. The summer of 2010, there were two essential rights of passage to celebrate, my nephew Steve Z.'s marriage, and my father's eightieth birthday. We would only be able to manage one family vacation. After deliberating, Sid and I decided to make the trip to Denver, anticipating more time to mingle with everyone at a birthday party than a wedding.

June twentieth, my mother threw a gigantic birthday celebration inviting people from all over the map for a backyard BBQ. Dad celebrated his birthday flying an AT6 Texan, a powerful advance trainer airplane. He rode tandem with the pilot as they did barrel rolls, loops, and aileron rolls to his great delight. Dad worked as a photographer in the war, but I think he secretly wanted to be a fighter pilot.

I climbed up the crab apple tree that my mother planted in 1972, tying name placards for a visual display of our family tree using the black extension ladder, as the thirty-eight-year-old tree had cleverly grown well above my head.

Dad's birthday party in June was the first time my seven children had been all together since my first born's wedding in 2004. I'd had a picture of us taken then at a family baseball game, each wearing a red cap with their birth order number boldly embroidered in white; my game cap reading 'game over.' I printed the photograph in black and white and hung it on our stairway wall, as a constant reminder of why God placed me on this earth.

I hoped to get an updated picture of my *all* my offspring again in Denver. I was so excited when I learned that Erica, Jonathan, and Olivia were all coming to the birthday party. "Love is patient and kind…" If God could wait more than four hundred years for his chosen ones to come out of the desert, what was it for me to wait a decade, or two, for my children's wandering hearts to return home? We would all be on neutral territory, where I would remain purposefully calm at the benign reunion.

I hadn't seen Jonathan since he'd returned from Iraq. Since then, he'd become a proud father of Vivianna, and sadly his wife had asked for a divorce. I found great difficulty in my inability to shelter my son from the hardships of life. From infancy, I had rushed to ameliorate his pain, anger, and frustration. I had removed myself gradually as arbiter of his discomfort, so that he could develop his own capacity to interact directly and effectively within the world. Jonathan. He'd grown so tall but I could still see the little boy hiding inside.

Erica's two-year-old daughter Isabella was a live wire, exasperating her mother, with a will even stronger than my own. Erica once said, "I'm raising my mother." My heart ached for Erica, wanting to relieve her of the relentless responsibility, but Isabella wasn't familiar with me, and the relationship between Erica and me remained too fragile, so I kept silent in fear of being considered critical.

Olivia drove down from Texas with her current boyfriend. She acted polite in front of others, yet remained intentionally distant to me. She'd grown into a beautifully attractive young woman who looked happy. She spoke softly, and her eyes sparkled when she talked to her boyfriend. Being banished from Olivia's inner circle pained me, but I chose to let it be for a time. That was my father's party.

The night before we returned to Calgary, the family shared a meal at a favorite Mexican restaurant, Los Potrillos, where we practically filled the entire restaurant. We were blessed to have such a large healthy happy family. What a shame it was to waste time harboring old hurts no one could, or would, articulate. We were like the Hatfield's and the McCoy's; spirited stock, locked together in a venomously private feud, fighting simply for the sake of fighting. I yearned to make amends with the past, and live in the present.

Our social worker, Amanda, mailed a rough copy of the home study to us, giving us a recommendation for approval of placement. It was in the mailbox when we got home from Denver. I forwarded it to Wendy for editing and a final review. And then, the report traveled to Edmonton. Christian Adoptions had prepared us for the probability of questions or clarifications from the Adoption Services board in Edmonton. So, we sat back and waited for any response, expecting between four to six weeks for the report to be processed.

I asked my employer about a leave of absence. In Canada, new parents can take up to one year off work for maternity leave. Either partner, according to the desires of the parents can apportion the time, and their jobs are secured for the length of the absence. I was surprised to learn that we could expect up to thirty-seven weeks of paternal leave for the adoption of a child. My employer required a four week notification prior to taking the paid leave of absence. It was hard to plan for an undetermined due date. We expected the decision from the Alberta Adoption Board by the beginning of July, so I turned in my request June 14, 2010.

In theory, we had satisfied the requirements of the Canadian Government. We needed to build three sides of our Bermuda Triangle, and we had one complete. The second edge would be assembled when we fulfilled requirements of the Jamaican Authorities. We also needed positive results from the immigration medical forwarded from Jamaican Government to the Canadian High Commission. Two thirds of the triangle would be complete, with only the final immigration piece outstanding. I thought I needed to make only one more short trip down to Montego Bay to get that done before Ashley would be allowed to leave the island. I planned on being in Jamaica only as long as it took to get the medical done, and then return to Canada and make final preparations for Ashley's imminent homecoming.

In Jamaica, I went directly to the CDA to turn in all of the outstanding notarized documents, including the preliminary home study report. Ms. Wilton was on holiday, so I asked Mr. Green to grant permission to have Ashley stay with me while I was on the island.

Mr. Dixon took me to Garland Hall to get Ashley, and then delivered us at the Caribic House for the first time since the robbery. The only available room was a small one on the ground floor with no refrigerator or balcony. Ashley pointed out the new wooden guard hut that overlooked the stairway.

Ashley required a medical assessment proving she didn't have aids, because no Jamaican child can be adopted who has the disease. Ms. Wilton, despite being on holiday, picked us up at the Caribic House in her personal vehicle with her son and mother in tow. I'd never seen Ms. Wilton dressed so casually, wearing a sundress and flip-flops. She made arrangements to obtain the medical forms, an appointment with the doctor, and showed me where to get Ashley's lab work completed. We expected the lab results in seven days, and I would be back in Canada, so Ms. Wilton agreed to pick up the results and deliver them to Ms. O'Connor, despite being on holidays.

I left the island weary and relieved. I mistakenly thought we had everything we needed. I thought the immigration piece would be a mere formality after both Jamaica and Canada had approved our adoption.

I puttered around the house for a week, cleaning and cooking, happy to be home. I remember it was on a Friday that I wanted to prepare a homemade sit down dinner for my family. I jotted down a grocery list including chicken breasts, tomato sauce, garlic, linguine noodles, and a bottle of merlot. I called the boys in from the park to go the Superstore with me for the groceries.

Forty minutes later, we drove back home past their friend Alex's house. They asked me to drop them off, so they could jump on his land trampoline while I prepared sandwiches for lunch. I waited in the car, watching them run up to the front door to ring the doorbell, making sure that Alex was home. His mom waved to me, giving me confirmation that the boys could stay and play.

There was a delivery notice for 'Mr. and Mrs. Sidney Isnor,' posted on our front door when I returned home. No one *ever* addressed mail to us in that manner. According to the notice, I would be able to pick it up after one o'clock the following day.

Our six-week waiting period was almost over. I called the post office and explained how anxiously we were waiting for our international adoption papers. I asked if there was any chance the girl on the phone could check to see if the package had returned to the outlet yet. "What is the tracking number on the receipt," she asked. I was put on a brief hold before hearing, "the package is still on the carrier's truck. It might be as late as six o'clock before the mail gets to this office."

I hopped into the car and scoured the neighborhood searching for the mail truck. We no longer had individual mailboxes in front of each home. I weaved in and out of the boulevards, looking for the mail carrier filling the islands that were sporadically placed on every other block. I spotted the unmarked vehicle just as the mail person was pulling away from the boxes on the private cul-de-sac of Prestwick Estates. I honked on the horn over, and over again, like a wild woman trying to get her attention. The poor woman startled. She was a tiny woman who could barely see over the top of her steering wheel. I stopped in the middle of the road and jumped out of my van. *"I'm sooo glad to find you!"* I hollered, waving the delivery notice over my head, while quickly explaining my excitement. The blessed woman climbed out of her truck to look for my envelope; she handed me a clipboard, and showed me where to sign before giving it to me.

I looked at the return address stamped in black ink on the upper left edge of the envelope:

ADOPTION SERVICES
ALBERTA CHILDREN'S SERVICES
SERVICE SUPPORT BRANCH
11th FLOOR, STARTING PLACE
9940-06 ST.
EDMONTON ALBERTA T5K 2N2

I wrapped my arms around the tiny woman, thanking her profusely for my package. Tears streamed involuntarily down my face. Our mail carrier remained calm and collected throughout my emotional display. I climbed back into the minivan, threw the brown envelope face up onto the seat next to me, glancing at it over and over again, making certain in would not disappear on the drive home.

I waved to the boys, who were still jumping on the trampoline, as I passed Alex's house. I parked curbside, as usual in front of our house, grabbed the envelope, and bound up our front stairs. I thought I could tell by the thickness of the envelope that it contained an approval. I imagined that if the news were bad, it would have come in a thin letter-sized envelope with a single sheet of paper telling us so.

Wendy told me to expect to find the 'Letter of No Objection,' stapled to the approved home study, advising us that it would come directly to our home rather than to the adoption agency. We would get the news first, just like any new parents.

I waited to read the documents with Sid. I dialled his cell phone hoping he'd pick up right away. He did. "We got the letter!" I stuttered, practically breathless. It felt like one of those dreams when you tried to talk, but no sound came out.

"And?"

"*I haven't opened it yet!*" And then, I ripped into it.

July 12, 2010

THIS DOCUMENT IS FOR THE USE OF JAMAICAN
AUTHORITIES ONLY

TO WHOM IT MAY CONCERN;
Re: Adoption Application of:
Sidney James Isnor and Erika Kay Isnor
62 Prestwick Heath, SE, Calgary, Alberta, Canada
T2Z 4E3

Sidney and Erika Isnor have had an adoption Home Study Report completed by Amanda S., Social Worker and reviewed by Wendy R., Program Director of Christian Adoption Services. Christian Adoption Services is an adoption agency licensed by Alberta Children and Youth Services. Sidney and Karen Isnor have met the requirements for adoption in Alberta.

The above-named applicants wish to adopt the child identified as Ashley Parkinson, born October 13, 2002. The child currently lives in Anchovy, Jamaica. Alberta

Children and Youth Services has no involvement in the facilitation of this placement.

Sidney and Karen Isnor must meet all requirements of the legislation of the child's country of origin and must have the adoption order granted in Jamaica.

Section 73 of the Alberta Child, Youth and Family Enhancement Act states "An adoption effected according to the law of any jurisdiction outside Alberta has the effect in Alberta of an adoption made under this Act, if the effect of the adoption order in other jurisdiction is to create a permanent parent-child relationship."

A Letter of No Involvement for immigration purposes will be provided by Alberta Children and Youth Services upon receipt of the finalized adoption order. The Letter of No Involvement should not be interpreted as a Letter of No Objection.

If it is not possible to obtain the adoption order in Jamaica, Sidney and Karen Isnor obtain a Private Guardianship Order, Mr. and Mrs. Isnor will need to deal directly with Citizen and Immigration Canada to obtain a permanent resident visa for the child before the child enters Canada. Alberta Children and Youth Services has no role in private guardianship matters.

Ann S., MSW, RSW
Senior Manager
Delegated Central Authority
Under the Hague Convention
On Intercountry Adoption
Alberta Children and Youth Services
cc: Sidney and Erika Isnor

"It's done. Thank God. Are you happy?" I asked Sid.

"Of course I'm happy," he said. "Now we don't have to start all over again with another agency."

"Do you think I would do that?" I asked.

"I know you would do that," he replied.

I hadn't explained to Sid that if Anne S. had denied us, I would have considered it the end of the road. I believe there was an appeal process, but it was not something I ever intended on exploring.

"When are you leaving?" Sid asked.

I was packed and ready, as if I'd been waiting for contractions. "I want to go on the red-eye Monday." There was so much more to say, but Sid had to get off the phone. He was at the shop doing inventory on drill bits, and apparently it was crazy there.

I spent the afternoon calling friends and family, informing them that the time had finally come to bring Ashley home. Nadia and Alyssa were already in California with their dad for the summer. I warned them that it might be difficult to reach me for a time, but they could expect to find Ashley home when they returned for the new school year. Once we had Ashley's visa and passport in hand, she was coming to Canada!

The boys expressed disappointment in having to go to Jamaica *again*. They wanted to go to a friend's birthday party. They'd rather go swimming in a wave pool than at the beach in Jamaica.

I prepared a celebratory dinner, searing the chicken breasts in olive oil with white onion and fresh garlic. I placed the poultry in a casserole dish underneath linguine, covering it with marinara sauce and mozzarella cheese. I baked a homemade apple pie using the 'simple flaky' pie crust recipe out of my mother's Joy of Cooking cookbook. The aroma of the comfort foods made the house smell like home. No matter what, wherever my children were, I knew they would think of me when they ate one of my 'comfort foods.' Even Olivia couldn't avoid me when she smelled spaghetti, mashed potatoes, broccoli casserole, lasagna, or apple pie.

I popped open the cork of the merlot wine, that I'd picked up with the groceries, just before Sid returned from work. I filled the wine glasses halfway to give the wine room to breathe, thinking...*my glass always half full.*

We left for Jamaica on Kaiden's eighth birthday, celebrating at the Olive Garden en route to the airport. It would be the last time I took the boys to Jamaica before Ashley came home. The restaurant was excruciatingly busy. I noticed a four-top table in the small bistro bar where the people had paid their bill and were ready to leave. "Are kids allowed here?" I asked the waiter.

"Absolutely. I guarantee the best service in the restaurant," he replied. "What can I get you to drink?" Sidney ordered a strawberry mango slush, and Kaiden requested a cup of hot chocolate. We filled our bellies with Italian food served by a gem of a waiter.

Sid drove us to the Calgary airport, dropping us off with our bags, at the departure level. He joined us in the terminal, after parking the car in the short-term lot. He didn't expect to be at the airport long, but everything concerning the adoption always seemed to take longer than we expected. He moved the car three times before leaving the airport. We checked in twice as many bags as usual because I intended on staying in Jamaica until we brought Ashley home. I didn't anticipate being there longer than a week, however, I was prepared with a humongous jar of peanut butter, a Costco bulk bag of individually wrapped Cheezies, an economy package of fruit bites, plus tons of sunscreen. I never expected to run out of sunscreen before coming home.

TWELVE

SUMMER OF 2010

My boys and I lingered at a breakfast table in the Toronto airport for two hours before we boarded our morning flight. We were the last to get standby seats, unable to sit side by side, but the boys were seasoned travellers. Sidney sat next to me, and Kaiden was behind us. The flight time was a short three-hours-and-thirteen minutes. I figured by the time the pay-per-view movie ended, we'd arrive. I was really tired of planes. I needed a break.

I filled out the Jamaican immigration form like a pro, drank a complimentary Canadian beer, and took one of those drooling naps where my head snapped up every now and again. I'd be ever so grateful for these trips to end. I looked behind me, and found Kaiden sleeping with his head burrowed into the shoulder of the woman sitting next to him. He looked so small. I adored his childish innocence. He always gravitated to a soft shoulder and kind heart.

Suddenly, it dawned on me that I was for all intensive purposes on parental leave. I helped groom the airplane when we landed, while the boys waited at the top of the bridge for me, and then we moved through the yellow hallway that echoed with reggae music. We sailed through customs, and then assembled our five checked bags. We found Mr. Dixon waiting for us outside. He packed the van with our luggage, before even asking where we were going. It was time to pick up my daughter.

"I'd like to go straight to the CDA, and then to get Ashley," I said.

"What time does the CDA close?" asked Mr. Dixon.

"I believe at four."

Mr. Dixon glanced at his watch. It read a quarter past two. Apparently, Polkerris guests were expecting Mr. Dixon at the airport at three, so he didn't have time to go downtown. Mr. Dixon had the patience of Job. He began to lose his composure, understandably, because I paid him local fare while treating him like a charter driver. We would have to find another way to get downtown.

I'd placed a two hundred fifty dollar deposit on Sid's American Express card, reserving a room for four nights at the Polkerris. The rates had been raised by seventy-five dollars per night, making it prohibitively expensive for my budget, yet I refused to return to the Caribic House with the boys. Mr. Dixon dropped us off at the luxurious accommodations, where we were greeted with cold pineapple juice, and a room cooled by forced air.

The first thing we did was to change into summer clothes. And then, I unpacked our suitcases, hanging Ashley's frocks in the closet, and carefully setting out my toiletries on the bathroom vanity. I intended on keeping the lovely room clean and tidy.

I didn't know if we would need to be near Kingston for immigration purposes, or to visit Mr. Bowen. I'd found another hotel on the Internet called Blue Harbour, claiming to be Noel Coward's estate, two-and-a-half hours closer to Kingston, if that was where we needed to be. I'd spoken to the owner in the states, who quoted me a local rate of sixty US dollars per night. She also provided a Jamaican contact name and number to call when we arrived. Also, I figured we could always return to New Moon. I had four days before our finances required a move, but we were set for the time being.

We walked down to the concrete inlet, knowing where the safe JUTA taxis stood waiting to be hired. Ms. Wilton was still on holidays when we arrived at the CDA, but she'd made the necessary arrangements with Mr. Green to provide a letter for me to take to Garland Hall. I'd hoped she could simply make a phone call so that I would not have to make the detour into the city. Towards the end of the adoption, I learned that Ms. Wilton always documented each of our visits in of Ashley's file, keeping record of our interest in Ashley.

"Hello Ms. Isnor," said the receptionist, "Ms. Wilton is not in office."

"Thank you kindly, but I am here to see Mr. Green." I heard an eruption of raised voices coming from the private cubicles. The argument became more and more heated as each moment passed. The voices were Jamaican, so I only understood every other word. I sensed a tone of desperation and detected authority in Mr. Green's voice. I could not help but think about how Maryam had described him as 'useless.' When Mr. Green walked out of the argument and the main door of the CDA, I waited for the dust to settle.

"Someone must 'ave ad der chil took,' said the woman closer to the fan than I. I nodded, emphasizing with the unknown person behind the divider.

Mr. Green walked back inside. "A pleasant afternoon to you Ms. Isnor. Are you here to pick up your daughter?" I must have been hearing things. I could not believe that Mr. Green, of all people, had actually referred to Ashley as my daughter! "Who are you here to see?" he asked, giving me a practiced pearly white grin.

"You actually," I said, sparking a genuine look of surprise. "I need a letter from you so that I can go pick Ashley up, Ms. Wilton told me you would give it to me," I said straight and to the point.

"I will prepare the letter for you. How long would you like the child?" he asked.

"I would like to have her from today until the day I take her home." He glanced up at me looking somewhat perplexed. I assumed he needed a specific date for the letter, and that dating it was merely a formality. "August thirty-first, please."

We were in the midst of a cat and mouse game of negotiation, and Mr. Green wanted control. "I'll make the letter out until the sixteenth of August. At that time, we will renew the letter." Done. I hoped we would be long gone by then.

"What is the last name of the child?" he asked. *Incredulous!*

"Parkinson. Ashley P-A-R-K-I-N-S-O-N." He returned to his private cubicle, where I overheard him putting another two cents into the argument waiting there. And then, he quietly reappeared in the waiting room holding a hand written letter. I took the letter out of the unsealed envelope, noticing it was written on Child Development Agency stationary. Mr. Green stood there watching me read it.

Central House

4 Kerr Crescent, Montego Bay Jamaica
Tel: 979-3446/1024 FAX. 971-1569
The Manager
Garland Hall c/h
27 July, 2010

Dear Mrs. G. Woodit,

Please release Ashley Parkinson in the care of Mrs. E. Isnor for the period between July 28, 2010 to August 16, 2010. Mrs. Isnor has an interest in the child. She has been with her before. The office will inform you of any change made in this arrangement.

Thanks,
Oliver Green
Team leader

"You made this letter out for tomorrow. I want to pick her up today."

"Oh did I?" he said. The argument in the background escalated. The manager was needed. "Yes, go ahead and pick up the child. I will make the phone call to inform Ms. Woodit."

"Thank you Mr. Green. Thank you very much. And, thank you to referring to Ashley as my daughter," I said with genuine gratitude. The boys and I bound down the stairs to look for another JUTA taxi. Instead, we found Mr. Dixon sleeping in his van waiting for us. When he drove us up to Garland Hall to get Ashley, I hoped it would be the last of our trips to Anchovy.

Mr. Green did not call Ms. Woodit. She clucked her tongue and shook her head, complaining about not having the child prepared. I assured her that I did not need a bag of clothes for Ashley. I handed her Mr. Green's note, allowing me permission to remove Ashley from the premises. The only thing I wanted was to get my daughter out of that hellhole; we waited an eternity.

"I have a surprise for you Ash," I told her as we walked down the hill towards Mr. Dixon's van. The boys hoped to trick Ashley. They'd ducked down behind the seats, and then jumped up when Ashley climbed inside, making everyone, including Mr. Dixon, laugh. Ashley's big brothers were already giving her a hard time.

When Mr. Dixon dropped us off at the hotel, I changed Ashley into a purple spaghetti strap sundress, and purple beach shoes. We walked down to the Pork Pit and stuffed ourselves with Jamaican local food. After supper, we retraced our steps up the hill, looking forward to a refreshing night swim in the glistening pool before showering and dressing in our jammies.

I began reading aloud the story of Percy Jackson and the Olympians: The Sea of Monsters, as a bedtime story. I intended on establishing a routine of normalcy, planning on continuing it at home. A bedtime story offered an opportunity for all of us to settle for the night, cuddling together. Ashley fell asleep that night as I read the first chapter. There were three hundred seventy-four pages in the book of twenty-two chapters. I hoped we'd be home well before we finished reading it.

Story time in Jamaica proved to be valuable, primarily for the boys. Little did I know how difficult Ashley's behavior would become when I concentrated on fulfilling the boy's needs. They deserved my undivided attention at certain times. They needed to feel loved, and not displaced, as we assimilated Ashley into our lives. The first night back in Jamaica proved to be the easiest of the whole trip.

The next morning we began our day with a lovely poolside breakfast. The boys ate French toast, fruit, and discovered Milo, a warm drink that tastes much like Ovaltine, or hot chocolate. Ashley and I each devoured a plate of fruit, and one of ackee and saltfish, boiled green bananas, and fried dumplings. Ashley worked on using the dumpling as a pusher, instead of her fingers. She also practiced eating with her mouth closed. Her manners, although improved, left something to be desired. I reminded myself to just to keep putting one foot in front of the other.

We all jumped into the pool immediately after breakfast. I intended on getting as much pool time in as possible while we were at the bed and breakfast. The water kept us cool and entertained. Ashley promptly bit, and popped, the grey plastic blow up elephant I'd bought for her to float on. She couldn't seem to keep anything out of her mouth.

That day, Mr. Dixon picked us up at noon to take us back downtown. Wednesday was Ms. O'Connor only day in Montego Bay. The rest of the week she worked in the town of Trelawny, up the coast, on the way towards Ochos Rios. I gave Ms. O'Connor our official home study, wanting to receive an estimate about how long we might need to stay in Jamaica before Ashley could leave.

Mrs. O'Connor asked about the medical information and Ashley's passport pictures.

"Ms. Wilton is in possession of the medical, and the passport pictures. We took care of those things the last time I was here," I reminded Mrs. O'Connor.

"Ms. Wilton will be in the office next week. How long do you plan on staying on in Jamaica?" Ms. O'Connor asked.

"I would like to stay until we take Ashley home," I said.

"I would not advise that. The paperwork has just gotten to me. There is still much to be done. I need to write the report, and then it needs to go to Kingston. I cannot say how long that will take."

"What about the birth certificate?" I asked.

"The birth certificate has been applied for. It will not impede the adoption. You only need the birth certificate to get the visa to take her home." I left the office with the promise that Ms. O'Connor would complete the report at her earliest convenience.

Mr. Dixon took us back to Polkerris where we ate peanut butter and jelly sandwiches for lunch. We spent the remainder of the afternoon floating in the pool, before walking down to Bottom Road at dinnertime. We visited The Back Page, a little hole in the wall eatery, devouring fried chicken, rice and peas. And then, we retired early, with pinker bodies than we'd arrived with, despite layer upon layer of Hawaiian Tropic 59 SPF. Once again, the kids fell asleep as I read the second chapter of Percy Jackson.

We woke up the next day with a plan, but life has a way, when you try to arrange it, of making a fool of the best-laid plans. We went to the Registrar to try to get Ashley's birth certificate ourselves. Ashley and I each put a frock on. I wore my sleeveless black and white polka dotted sundress, and Ashley donned a green sleeveless one, with white eyelet trim that matched her shoes. I brought wraps to cover our shoulders, if need be, to show respect.

I'd made arrangements for Mr. Dixon to pick us up, hoping for a quick stop at the Registrar, intending on proudly delivering the precious document to the CDA. The office was located in a strip mall on Humber Ave. A large official looking white sign with bold black letters hung over its entrance read;

REGISTAR GENERAL OFFICE

Western Regional Office

Registration and certified copies of births, deaths & marriages, deed polls, record updating

Operating Mon-Fri 9am-3pm

I figured it was not going to be a quick stop when I opened the door. The waiting room was filled with people patiently sitting in row upon row of portable folding chairs. I pulled number 149 from the dispenser on the wall, noticing three employees sitting at desks, each in front of an antique computer. Periodically, one of the three called out a number. They were on number 132 when we got there. *Hmmmmm,* there seventeen people in front of us.

I phoned Mr. Dixon, not wanting him to wait in the hot van for us. I urged him to make some money, as we planted ourselves in a row of seats as close to a fan as I could get. The only thing we could do was to sit down to hurry up and wait.

All I carried in my purse to entertain the kids was a set of multiplication flash cards for practicing math skills with Sidney. We invented a game to see who could come up with an answer to an equation first. I held up the cards one by one. The person who gave the correct answer first got to hold the card. I allowed Kaiden and Ashley to add the numerals together, while Sidney multiplied. Ashley counted her fingers like she was using an abacus.

We'd waited about a half-an-hour when a man in bright yellow shirt leaned around the corner and handed me his number. "You are next, mon." he said, as he walked out of the office. I wondered what the people who'd gotten there before me would think when I answered the call to our newly acquired number.

The nameplate in front of the lady who called us read Ms. Johnston. After we moved, en masse, to share the two seats if front of her desk, I explained that we wanted Ashley's birth certificate. She did some clicking on her computer. According to the records, the CDA had initiated a search for Ashley's records on the sixteenth of July. "Nothing shows as yet," said Ms. Johnston.

"What do you mean as yet? How long does a search take? Is there anything I can do to register the child myself?" I asked hopefully.

"No mon. You must wait for the process to work." The process was obviously broken. Since when did it take thirteen days for Google to do a search? I left the Registrar empty handed, and damned if it wasn't hot as hell outside. I called Mr. Dixon to take us back to the pool.

We ate a lunch of pepperoni pizza at the Jamaican Bobsled, so I could use the wireless Internet in air-conditioning. I emailed Sid to let him know we had arrived safely. He answered immediately wanting to know when we were all coming home, but I didn't have an answer for him. On the way back to the bed and breakfast several people we'd gotten to know over the past few months asked if we were 'takin' Ashley home this time?'

"I hope so. It depends on her birth certificate," I answered.

"You haven't gotten her birth certificate yet?" they asked. I noticed a lot of Patois flying around in the air between the shopkeepers. I recognized the woman that had given Ashley the bracelet so many months before. Her name was Bibsey, and we were standing outside her shop. "I know Mr. Clark at the RGD," she said. "He will help you to register the child."

A group of four or five shop girls assembled around her step. More Patois. "Do you have phone?" Bibsey asked me.

"Yeah mon," I answered, handing over my newly acquired Jamaican Digicel. She called her Mr. Clark to explain Ashley's situation, and made an appointment for him to meet with me the next morning between half past the hour and eight o'clock.

"I'll be there," I promised. The kids and I hiked back up the hill, with a little more bounce in our step, to read another chapter of Percy Jackson before retiring. Once the kids were sleeping, I asked for breakfast to be served at nine-thirty, hoping we would have returned by then. I also called to make arrangements with Mr. Dixon for another early morning pick up. I woke up extra early the next morning, to make sure that everyone was dressed and ready to go before Mr. Dixon arrived at seven.

Mr. Dixon looked surprised when he found out that the office was actually open that early. I didn't take a number, but simply asked for Mr. Clark. The security officer said he was behind the cashier's desk, which looked like a barred bank teller's window in an old western movie. He motioned for us to take a seat in front of his name plate, then asked me when and where Ashley had been born, and what her parents names were. I gave him the best information I had, not knowing how accurate it actually was.

"I believe Ashley Parkinson was born at the Sav-la-mar hospital in Westmoreland. Her birth mother's name was Georgia, and her Father's name, according to Ashley, was Dalton."

"The parents were married?" asked Mr. Clark.

"I do not know," I answered truthfully.

"What is your interest in the child?" asked Mr. Clark.

"We are adopting her."

"Do you have proof of the impending adoption?" I opened the portable red accordion filing cabinet, that I always carried, to retrieve the home study. I showed him the 'TO IT MAY CONCERN' page for the USE OF JAMAICAN AUTHORITIES ONLY,' that identified our wish to adopt the child Ashley Parkinson. The letter satisfied Mr. Clark regarding our interest in the child.

Mr. Clark confirmed that Ashley's birth had never been registered. He photocopied a fifteen-page 'LATE REGISTRATION OF BIRTH' questionnaire on a prehistoric printer, and then advised me to take the papers to the supervisor at the CDA. He programmed his telephone number into my cell phone, while instructing me to have the supervisor call him directly so that he could "inform him of the requirements." Mr. Clark then shook my hand and we were on our way.

We arrived at the CDA just after eight. Operating hours began at eight-thirty, but Mr. Dixon noticed that people had already been entering the office. He suggested I investigate. Indeed, Mr. Green had arrived for work, but according to the receptionist would not be available until after eight-thirty. We sat to wait, again. Mr. Green walked past us, stopped, and then asked why we were there.

"We're here to see you once it is eight-thirty," I replied submissively.

"Come in. Come in now," he said. He motioned us into his corner office.

"I need you to fill out the 'LATE REGISTRATION OF BIRTH' form so that I can get Ashley's birth certificate," I explained.

Initially, he seemed willing to fulfill my request. He called Ms. O'Connor first, and then Ms. Wilton, searching for the Ashley Parkinson file. Ms. Wilton apparently explained to Mr. Green Mr. Bowen's directive; He refused to allow me to get the birth certificate myself.

"May I speak to Mr. Bowen, please?" I asked. Mr. Green promised he would have a conversation with the head of the CDA, and would relay any pertinent information to me by by ten o'clock that morning.

We returned to the hotel just in time for our scheduled breakfast. The kids all ate 'dippin eggs' with toast and guava jam. I'd asked for my favorite Jamaican dish of callaloo and fish. We ate like kings. After breakfast, we swam in the pool before venturing down to Doc's Cave.

We stopped by the Caribic House hoping to pick up Ashley's rubber mattress pad, and another swimsuit that I'd left hanging in the hotel shower earlier in the month. I got the pee pad, but the housekeeper had already left for the day and the swimsuit could not be located.

Ten o'clock came and went. I never once put my phone down for fear that I'd miss Mr. Green's call. I tried calling the CDA several times. Finally, at about four o'clock that afternoon, the receptionist politely gave me a message. "I am told to let you know, Ms. Isnor, that there has been no change in regards to the birth certificate."

I flipped out. What a *wus*! The *useless* man wouldn't even tell me himself!

I immediately phoned Ms. Wilton loudly expressing my mounting frustration. I asked her to release me of my promise not to call Mr. Bowen.

"Mr. Green is my supervisor. I have no problem with you calling Mr. Bowen."

I called Mr. Bowen's cell phone late that afternoon determined to be a thorn in his side. "Mr. Bowen, this is Erika Isnor from Calgary Canada, I need your help. Will you help me? I have been trying to locate Ashley Parkinson's birth certificate. I'm told we are matched to her now, and Ms. O'Connor has promised to send our adoption package to Kingston soon."

Mr. Bowen gave me a lot of blah blah blah about the process.

"Mr. Bowen, we have been down to Jamaica nearly every month working on this adoption. I *need your help.* I have brought my two young boys with me this time. My budget is suffering. My family is separated." I pulled on as many heart strings as I could grab.

"Monday is a holiday. Call me on Tuesday. I'll see what I can do. Can you call me on Tuesday?" asked Mr. Bowen.

I wondered what we would do about accommodations until Tuesday. "I'll call you on Tuesday." I said. We ventured back to the Pork Pit for dinner, and then back to bed with yet another chapter of Percy Jackson.

Our last meal at the bed and breakfast was interesting to say the least; goat stew, and I was game. I was in it for the long haul wasn't I? I wanted to explore every aspect of the child's culture who we intended to assimilate in our home. The best part of eating goat was the savory taste. I'll admit I was a bit surprised to find small bones throughout the stew, served on a plate, rather than in a bowl. The real turn off for me was the tiny hairs I found still attached to small pieces of fat, or skin. I couldn't help but think that I'd been eating Grover, the satyr from our Percy Jackson novel, and the reoccurring prophetic line in the book "you will fail to save what matters most." I put my fork down. The kids had all opted out on goat stew early on, even Ashley. They ordered a traditional breakfast of scrambled eggs, bacon, wheat toast, and fruit. The most exotic item on their plates was the papaya.

We did nothing but swim away the morning leaving the pool only to use the washroom in our room. It amazed me when the maid had thoroughly cleaned our room before ten o'clock in the morning. The beds were neatly spread, with the sheets folded down over the blanket at the top edge. My toiletries were all fastidiously arranged on the bathroom counter, my comb placed in my bristle brush, and the floor was swept and mopped to perfection. I appreciated the orderliness as I sat slothfully by the pool.

Around noon, the maid came to the pool to tell me that I had visitors at the front door. I threw Ashley's Tatiana Disney princess towel around my skimpy red bikini after getting the kids out of the pool. I swiped the security card in front of the laser box on the wall, opening the front door to greet Angie and Kerri. Kerri was Doug's girlfriend, the owner of Angie's villa. They stood in the shade under a breadfruit tree, about twenty-five feet to the left of the main door.

I'd never met Kerri before. She looked absolutely *nothing* like the person of my imagination. Kerri had a waist-length mane of fire red hair, with pale virginal skin seemingly untouched by the sun. She didn't strike me as pretty, until later, when we were sitting by the pool where I began noticing her delicate features. She reminded me of Nicole Kidman. And, there was something oddly sad in her expression.

Kerri's reputation had preceded her. I'd heard ravings about her kindness and generosity. I failed to understand the connection between her and the ogre of a man who owned the villa. Angie confided that he had refused to marry Kerri, despite several years of a monogamous relationship. She'd endured the tumultuous years of his teenage daughters; never having children of her own. I imagined Kerri holding Angie's hand under the mango tree spilling heartache out to her one true friend.

It embarrassed me that I did not invite them into the house right away. I didn't want them to feel uncomfortable in the plush surroundings. "Would you like to come in?" I finally asked in all sincerity, well aware I didn't even have a cool drink to offer them.

"I'd love to go to the lounge for a cold Heineken," said Kerri.

"We don't actually have a lounge here per say, but we can go to the pool," I offered, quickly swiping the security card to get back in. We walked through the foyer, then the sitting room, and out French doors to the verandah and pool.

"Good job guys, you can get back into the pool." The boys both immediately cannonballed into the deep end, and Ashley returned to the second step, to play with her beach girl Polly Pocket doll in the water. I admitted that I didn't have anything to offer them to drink, but would walk down to Bottom Road, to pick up some beer. Kerri decided to go with me, and Angie offered to stay with the kids to watch them in the pool.

Kerri and I made the trek down long stairway. I unlocked the gate at the bottom leading to the alley behind the Rehab Bar. A man offered to "hook Carrie up," but she said she was taken care of. We walked past the Burger King towards the Indian owned store that sold beer for the most reasonable price on the hip strip.

Kerri took six Heinekens out of the red Coca-Cola refrigerator and placed them on the counter. I added three Red Stripes, intending on paying for the entire purchase. Kerri pulled out a thick wad of bills from her bra, insisting on paying for all, and negotiated an ever so slightly lower price due to the quantity of beers on the counter. The Indian cashier placed all the beer into a brown paper bag, and then we retraced our steps back past the dealer man to the pool.

I put some of the beers in the little freezer compartment of the dormitory sized fridge in my room. Kerri and Angie only drank three of the Heineken between them. I tried to send the rest home with them, but Kerri refused. She invited us to the villa for burritos that night, and I accepted, incredibly grateful that we had something different to do. We were all getting bored. Angie said she'd be back to pick us up between five and five-thirty for dinner.

When we arrived at the villa, Kerri asked me whether I'd like a glass of red wine or a bottle of Red Stripe. I opted for the Red Stripe that Duj got out of the bar freezer. Kerri complained about how difficult it was to keep beer cold in Jamaica. She said that she really couldn't drink beer unless it was *really* cold. I admitted to consuming more than my share of warmish beer on the island. It never seemed to slow me down.

Kerri, Angie and I sat together at the breakfast bar while the twins made our dinner. They both thought that the adoption process had taken much longer than it should have. "The bottom line in Jamaica is the dollar. It is the only thing that makes anything move here," said Kerri.

"Do you mean that I should bribe someone?" I wondered. Kerri was far more familiar with Jamaica and its people than me. I felt utterly naive, and she was simply educating me on the way of the land.

"It needs to be discrete, and it must go to the right person. It won't do any good if you give money to someone without authority."

I dreaded the day I'd have to deal with Ms. Tumming. My adoption agent knew first hand that money drove the Adoption Director of Jamaica. I stored Kerri's information not knowing if, when, or who I might bribe to get Ashley home. The possible legal consequences sacred me; I imagined myself separated from my family locked up in a dirty jail, accused of child trafficking.

Rej and Duj made burritos using soft shell flour wraps, shredded cheese, sour cream, and a spiced minced meat mixture. I always wondered which animal minced meat came from. Nevertheless, we all dove into the family style meal at the dining room table.

Afterwards, all the kids jumped into the pool. Keri, Angie, Avion and I all kept our eyes on them. I'd had a running start on the beer, so I'd begun to fade, but Kerri and Angie were just beginning a night that would continue long after I'd taken the kids back to our hotel.

About the time, that I was ready to pull my brood out of the pool, Angie's daughter Suan arrived and offered to braid Ashley's unruly mop. It always took a minimum of forty-five minutes for me to comb out Ashley's unruly hair. I appreciated that it was going to finally be done properly. Kerri extended a gracious offer, asking us stay for the night as Suan weaved Ashley's hair. She said the kids could sleep on the comfortable couches in front of the large screen TV in the living room.

It occurred to me that the last time we'd been invited to stay at the villa we'd been robbed. We were at the villa again under similar circumstances. I had a room that was already paid for, but our last night at Bed and Breakfast that was far more expensive than the Caribic House. I needed to organize my thoughts and make a decision about where we were going to stay long term. We reluctantly declined the invitation and packed into Angie's Toyota for the ride back into town.

Kaiden and Ashley both fell asleep. Sidney swiped the security card for me to let us into the house, so I could carry my sleeping salt and pepper babies, one at a time, into the comfortable secure room. It was still manageable to carry each of them, who were a similar size and weight. I'd always wanted twins and this was as close as I was ever going to get to it.

When we said goodnight, Angie assured me she would call around in the morning to see if she might be able to find us affordable long-term accommodations.

I woke up at 3 am, anxious about our eleven o'clock check out time. My chest felt tight, making it difficult to breathe, let alone sleep. My mind bounced around like a ball bearing in a pinball machine worrying about where we would go.

Thankfully, we did have a few options. My primary concerns were safety and cost. I hoped I would be able to find a long-term arrangement where I paid a monthly rent, we planned on getting out of Dodge as soon as Ashley received her visa. If the rent was prepaid, so be it.

Two hours passed and I hadn't gone back to sleep. When all else failed, I prayed. Dear God, help me. Lord *take* this burden from my heart. Show me what your will is. Tell me where it is you want me to be. Please protect my babies. Keep them safe. Lord let me rest. Flood me with peace so that I can sleep.

The next time I looked at the clock it was nearly eight o'clock in the morning, when everyone woke up starving. We dressed quickly for a breakfast of eggs, toast, and fruit. Afterwards, we donned our sunblock and swimwear for a last dip in the pristine pool. I settled on a lounge chair, planning on hanging out for a couple of hours, so that I could make calls on my Digicel while the kids were swimming. My early morning anxiety had departed leaving me calm and confident that our accommodations dilemma would soon be solved. I knew God had things well in hand even if I didn't.

I could count on one hand the people that rubbed me the wrong way in Jamaica, including the bad man, crack man, room robber that took our stuff. Three of the other people had something very much in common, one way or another they were all involved in Jamaican real estate.

Doug, the owner of the villa where Angie worked, taught me how to make immediate email transfers out of my Canadian bank account. The second time we went to Jamaica I made a reservation on a third party website to reserve his entire villa in Ironshore. Doug agreed that I could pay a deposit on the Internet and then the balance in cash. I had a paycheck due when we would be in Jamaica, and I wanted to use my own earnings. I'd promised Sid I wouldn't exceed a specified amount on his credit card and I intended on honoring that agreement. The entire $2,400.00 US was erroneously billed to Sid's Visa when I made the booking, and Doug refused to reverse the charges. When I spoke to him about reneging on our agreement, his response was "I am a business man first. I took what I was entitled to." Fair enough. I'd thought that we were *friends*. I didn't treat friends like that. I decided that if he were a business man first, and a friend second, that I would take my business elsewhere. I never gave him another dollar.

One day, I met a retired doctor on the beach who owned rental apartments across the street from Doctor's Cave, at the Montego Bay Beach Club. He was a caucasian, white haired, overly tanned, leathery man, who had acquired a fair sum of money in the first fifty plus years of his life. He wore an air of undeserved entitlement.

He made me understand why the natives felt oppressed by white people. When I closed my eyes I could envision him in different times wearing a hooded white robe on a lynching party. He gave me a bit of friendly advice when he discovered our plans to adopt Ashley. "You can take one off the island and raise it in an entirely different environment, but they are all the same. They are internally wired differently than white people. It's because they have spent so much time simply trying to survive. One day they will forget everything you've ever taught them, and they will turn on you like a wild animal."

I can't believe my jaw didn't drop. He called himself a doctor. What kind of quack was he? I couldn't imagine him adhering to the Hippocratic Oath. I couldn't imagine him doing anything for anyone else without benefiting himself first. He actually had the audacity to tell me "The bottom line for everyone in Jamaica is money, that's how it works here."

That Doctor's ears perked up when I said I'd stopped by the office across the street in search of an apartment to sublease. That was when he offered to show me one of his rental apartments "if my children were showered and sandless."

I called on him the next morning with shiny dry children. We rode the rickety elevator up to the eighth floor where he lived. He remained preoccupied on his cell phone when he opened the door for us, waved us in, and whispered to the children not to touch anything. He continued talking on the phone while we stood there, never excusing himself from the phone call.

The Doctor took us up to the twelfth floor to view his vacant studio apartment. He'd decorated the apartment with a cheap beach-flavour of peach and turquoise, that he was as proud as a peacock about. He showed me the imported bathroom tile, bragging about how much he'd paid for it. The tile looked to me like a clearance item you might find on a back table at Home Depot.

His biggest concern was that my kids would destroy his white faux leather couches with crayons. My biggest concern was the twelfth story balcony. It made me think about Eric Clapton's five-year-old son Connor, who'd tumbled to his death out a window a maid had left open.

He wanted a disconcerting $2,4000.00 US for a month's rent, with the first and last month paid in advance, in addition to a damage deposit. The Doctor required a psychiatrist. No wonder his studio remained empty.

I never met the other real estate consultant who specialized in property management rentals for Jamaican 'holidays and long term sales.' Helen, the children's author, gave me her business card. Doreen, the real estate agent, stated that she too had availability in the Montego Bay Beach Club building. I'd emailed Doreen from Calgary, hoping to make arrangements in advance, but she never answered my inquiry.

Apparently, Doreen also frequented a Doctor's Cave beach. I asked the staff and the other regulars to describe her to me, so that if I recognized her on the beach I might speak with her about an apartment. All I was told was that she was "short as Beenie Man."

Mr. Dixon once explained to me how the musical artist 'Beenie Man' got his name. In Patois, someone who was considered small was described as 'beenie,' because they were no bigger than a bean.

I believe I actually saw Doreen once, after we were settled in a long-term agreement. I watched a woman walking back and forth along the stretch of the beach early in the morning. She wasn't any taller than my son Sidney. She too had the leathery wrinkled tanned skin I wanted to avoid.

I spoke to Doreen that last day we were at the bed and breakfast, when she phoned my cell phone. I told her we were staying in Jamaica for an undetermined amount of time, and needed a studio near the water for my three children and me. We'd been staying in a traditional hotel room, but now needed to economize.

Doreen thought the studio she had available at the Montego Bay Beach Club was much too small, having two single beds and a pull out couch. She suggested a one-bedroom apartment. Countering, I said that we intended on spending very little time inside the apartment. We intended on either being at the beach, or fulfilling adoption requirements. All we needed was a place to lay our head down at night, and a kitchen to prepare simple meals.

Doreen's Miami accent grated on me. She kept giving me the typical real estate run down about amenities and *location, location, location...* I was familiar with the art of negotiation, offer the moon at a high rate of exchange and then take something of value away as the bartering price lowered. Her response was "You can't expect to have it all."

"Yes I can," I replied. I've lived my life believing "whether you think you can, or you think you can't, you're probably right."

Doreen tried to get me to look at a one bedroom condominium in the community of Wyndam where "professionals such as teachers and taxi drivers lived." It was twenty minutes out of town, towards Rose Hall. "Considering the inclusion of water, electricity and air conditioning, you could probably get the place for somewhere in the neighborhood of $700 US for the month of August," she said. I wondered what Doreen's cut would be.

"Is there a pool?" I asked.

"No pool." If we wanted to swim we'd have to pay for a taxi to get to water. I wondered how I would entertain three children in the August heat. Reluctantly, I made plans to see the property at noon.

I called David at New Moon Cottages, informing him that we planned on staying in Jamaica until the adoption went through. I needed a weekly rate for a room beginning that night. "I can give you the same rate as last time, but the room will not be available until Monday," he said.

"I can't pay forty-five US dollars a night. I'm on a very tight budget. Maryam told me that she paid $100 a week."

"It's high season now. There is a rush for rooms," David said. He'd also told me it was high season four months ago. When was the low season?

"The most I can pay is one hundred US dollars a week," I said. David promised to get back with me. I dreaded the two-hour trip to Negril, but not as much as dreading the bed bugs.

I also called Blue Harbour, making arrangements with my contact Leroy. The American owner had graciously offered me the local rate at sixty US dollars per night. The *major* drawback was the two-hour drive to the Parish of St Mary's. Leroy gave me detailed directions past Ocho Rios to the little town of Galina. He told me to look for a small corner sign on the side of the road reading Blue Harbour. He gave me his cell phone number to call upon our arrival. I said we expected to leave Montego Bay by the mid-afternoon.

I called Mr. Dixon for transportation arrangements to get to Blue Harbour. It would have been adventurous to explore that side of the island, especially Noel Coward's estate, but we never got there. I'd intended to call and cancel the reservation, but once we found the apartment in Ironshore I concentrated on the process of moving. I burnt a bridge with Leroy, leaving him forever wondering what had happened to us.

Angie gave my number to a Mrs. Parchment, or "Parchi," who according to Angie, had the reputation of having the "cheapest rooms of all for rent." It was worth a shot. I still had a couple of hours before we needed to vacate our present location.

Mrs. Parchment called with an offer I couldn't refuse. Her house was walking distance to Angie's villa in Ironshore. She had a studio apartment on the top floor of her private residence, with a king-sized bed, a twin bed, and a small kitchenette. Ms. Parchment hemmed and hawed over the price and availability of it, considering the cost of water, electricity, and running the air conditioner.

"I won't need to run the air conditioner," I said, speaking words I would most definitely live to regret.

"Considering all of the expenses involved I would like six hundred dollars US for the month of August.

"I can't pay more than five hundred US."

"Well then let us settle in the middle for five hundred fifty US," said Ms. Parchment. Gavel down, deal done sight unseen. She said a friend of hers was currently occupying the apartment, so she would need an hour or two to make final arrangements to get it ready. "I am ninety-nine percent sure that the apartment would be available, but I must check with the property manager to see if there are any arrangements that I am not aware of," said Ms. Parchment.

"I understand," I said. Later, I realized that there was no property manager. She made her friend move so that she could get an income from me.

Mrs. Parchment called back confirming that arrangements for our apartment had been finalized.She would provide directions to her house when we arrived at the Blue Diamond shopping center.

Mr. Dixon arrived intending to take us to Blue Harbour. When I said I'd changed my mind, he packed our suitcases in his van agreeing to take us to Mega Mart before dropping us of in Ironshore.

I needed money for groceries and to prepay our rent. I'd promised Ms. Parchment that I would pay, in advance, for the entire month whether or not we stayed. It was my last bargaining tool and I think it sealed the deal. Mr. Dixon suggested that I get money from the machine inside the Mega Mart, but I knew about the $15,000 JMD daily limit at that ATM. I needed more cash than that for our food and shelter. Mr. Dixon, somewhat reluctantly, turned right on Bottom Road towards Scotiabank, in the opposite direction of the Mega Mart.

I'd become accustomed to doing creative financing with the Scotiabank instant teller, only the teller was anything but instant. I tried my Bank of America card first "You have exceeded the funds available in your account," read the monitor. I tried three more times, lessening the amount requested in increments of $8,000 JMD. It was a no go. Next, I tried to get the entire amount needed for the rent, $46,000.00 JMD using my green TD Canada Trust access card. Once again, I slowly lowered my expectations until I received about $300 dollars in US funds. Finally, I took out a similar amount from my personal account where my paycheck was automatically deposited every other Friday.

There was a growing line of people behind me waiting to use the bank machine. I heard such comments as "It's not working?...Let someone else try,...Give someone else a chance. You are taking *toooo looong,"* One woman banged on the glass door with an accusatory fist. *"Lady....You are being ruuude. Give someone else a try!"* I did my very best focusing on the task at hand as the bank machine slowly relinquished small denominations towards amount I needed.

I held my head up as I passed by the impatient lady on my way out. "I wish the Jamaican government worked as fast as that woman expected me to move." I muttered as I climbed back into Mr. Dixon's van. I noticed a smile cross his face in the rear view mirror.

Mr. Dixon drove us to the Mega Mart to get some supplies. "Mr. Dixon, I have a question to ask you. I would very much appreciate your honest opinion."

"Yeah, mon."

"I have been told by several people that if I were to offer some money that it would expedite the process and get Ashley home. I am told that it is the only way to get her home."

"I can tell you Ms. Isnor that Ms. Wilton would not accept a bribe." Mr. Dixon drove on contemplating his next words very carefully. "Ms. Isnor, I think it is very important to keep it clean. You have done everything that they have asked and you are near the end. It is important to keep it clean."

"Thank you, Mr. Dixon. I appreciate your honesty."

The sky darkened on our way to the discount shopping store; pouring fat rain and thundering the entire time we were inside. I paid just over $7,000 JMD for basic supplies, and then stopped at the small segregated liquor store inside Mega Mart to buy a ten dollar bottle of wine. The kids were hanging on the sides of the grocery cart as we exited the warehouse.

Puddles of rainwater filled the potholes in the parking lot. Mr. Dixon was standing under an umbrella across the parking lot watching for us. He held a palm up, indicating that he wanted us to stay put until he brought the van around so we would not get wet.

I tried to reach Ms. Parchment by phone several times on the way towards Ironshore, to no avail. Mr. Dixon's patience had been tried so I asked him to drop us off at the villa. He always did so much for us for so little. Finally, he suggested that I start using the local taxis to get around, as he helped Rej and Duj unload our suitcases, stacking them under the mango tree. I'm sure Mr. Dixon felt relieved when he left us at the villa.

I found Kerri sitting at the breakfast table by the pool. I stepped one foot onto the white tile porcelain tile, and promptly shattered the bottle of merlot, spewing red liquid and green glass all over the floor. "I brought you a bottle of wine…" I shrugged.

"I had enough wine last night. But thank you for the gesture," said Kerri dryly.

Kerri filled me in on the continuation of their night's festivities. She said they'd all gone out to a bar in the country to drink and dance until the early hours of the morning. I was happy I'd gone back to the hotel and avoided a hangover. I'd bet money they'd gotten home about the same time that I was praying for relief from anxiety.

I sat with Kerri until I finally connected with Ms. Parchment on my cell phone. The kids were running around the grounds playing 'Zombie,' a modern version of the game of tag. Kerri offered to help me move once we got the official green light to get into our new vacation home. Rej and Duj began packing Angie's hatchback, taking the perishables from the bar fridge where they had put them for safekeeping. We'd left my kids playing Zombie, taking Rej and Duj along to help with the move. It took two trips to transport all of our belongings to the new residence.

Mrs. Parchment's home was off the first exit at the roundabout. One hundred seventy-two Paterson Avenue, where the cactus grew along the exterior of an electronic gate. I phoned Ms. Parchment from outside the gates when we arrived. She pressed the button on the remote control device allowing access to the place I came to think of as 'Hotel California.' "You can check out any time you want, but you can never leave." Ms. Parchment became the third real estate monger whose bottom line was the almighty dollar.

Ms. Parchment was a real piece of art, always dressed in traditional African attire that included a different matching headdress for each outfit. Angie said she knew her as 'Parchi,' and she had dressed like that as long as Angie could remember. I once asked Ms. Parchment where she'd gotten her garments. "Africa," she answered, never elaborating. I think Ms. Parchment tried to cover her true nature in her pretentious African costumes. Jesus taught his followers to "beware of false prophets, who come to you in sheep's clothing, but inwardly are raving wolves."

My first impression, when Kerri and I walked up the steps to the rooftop studio, was that it looked reasonably clean. Ms. Parchment admitted it got quite hot in the early evenings. She showed me how to open the window blinds to let the air circulate within the room.

I put the groceries away as soon as Rej and Duj carried them up the stairs, placing a Red Stripe into the freezer compartment of the dormitory sized refrigerator. For the second time, in a matter of two hours, I shattered a bottle of alcohol on the floor. Ms. Parchment looked mildly irritated as she called her houseman, Ashley, to clean up the mess. He used a straw broom to sweep the amber liquid into a pile, and then some scrunched up newspaper as a makeshift dustpan to collect the glass. The floor remained sticky, until the maid cleaned the entire room three days later. We learned quickly that our Sunshine Apartment wasn't the kind of place where our beds were spread, or the floor was mopped while we were eating a gourmet breakfast.

Kerri delivered my children with our final belongings, on her second trip from the villa, at last leaving us to settle in our temporary home. Man it was hot! So, we decided to cool down in the pool, but it wasn't like the glistening pool we'd had at Polkerris. The water looked a bit cloudy, and the bottom surface felt slippery. The temperature of the water didn't feel cold and refreshing; it was more like the milk that had been left out of the refrigerator all night. A warm rain began falling on our heads while we were in the pool. And then, Ms. Parchment joined us, where we waded together in the stagnating water until the sky darkened and the bugs came out.

We returned to our new room and shut the doors and windows to keep the mosquitoes out. We turned on the overhead fan to circulate the quiet air. Then started to read more of Percy Jackson, but Ashley repeatedly interrupted the story with attention seeking behavior. I finally gave up and put the book down. Ashley cried at bedtime, refusing to stay in her toddler size bed. I didn't have the energy to deal with her misconduct. She protested screaming loudly, making the boys plug their ears with their fingers until she finally fell asleep.

Ashley had never given me a lick of trouble on any of our previous trips. I'd felt confident that she was a pretty easy, resilient child who simply needed a helping hand to fulfill her natural human potential.

Ashley started running away from me and laughing at inappropriate times when she was being reprimanded. She snatched things away from the boys, screaming out for the attention she'd never received at every stage of her development. I expected challenges, but was never in a million years prepared for what was in store when she decided to test our boundaries. There were times that I seriously considered giving up and taking the boys home.

I'd read Holding Time, a book recommended by Christian Adoptions that provided strategies to deal with behaviors of institutionalized children. Admittedly, I was reaching for stars using the process as a last resort. The attachment therapy, described in the book as a 'Holding Therapy,' suggests the primary caregiver restrains a confrontational child firmly. The first stage of the process begins when the child protests being held.

I grabbed Ashley as she tried to dart away from me. She struggled to get free. "That is not the way we act in our family. We do not touch things that do not belong to us," I said calmly. Ashley did not want me to hold her. She persisted in struggling to get away, flailing, scratching, and biting me trying to get loose of my hold. I consider myself to be a woman with a strong will, and able body. I used every ounce of strength and tenacity that I could muster to prevent Ashley from breaking away from my embrace.

"You bi hurtin'mi," Ashley screamed and wailed, using a pitch that could pierce an eardrum.

"I am not hurting you. I will hold you no harder than is necessary," I whispered calmly, but with resolve to finish what we'd started. I hadn't expected to take that course of action, but there we were in the middle of it and there was nothing to do but keep going.

I was afraid that someone might hear Ashley and think I was 'hurtin' her,' in fact, Ms. Parchment came into the room to see if she could help. I held on to Ashley as I explained what I was doing. I half expected Ms. Parchment to interrupt us by insisting I let Ashley go. That would put us right back where we started, but Ms. Parchment seemed to understand what I was trying to accomplish.

"She's not hurtin' you Ashley, be still and listen to your mother," she said while gently repositioning one of Ashley's arms." Ms. Parchment's words fed me the strength I needed to complete the task.

"I'm not going to give up," I said. "If I do, Ashley will have won the battle, and I will have to start all over. She is getting so big and strong, if I do not win now I may never win her over."

"I just wanted to see if you needed my help," said Ms. Parchment leaving Ashley in my arms, just as she'd found us, with the boys watching Sponge Bob Square Pants from the end of the big bed.

Two hours and forty-six minutes after the charade began, Ashley's resolve finally dissipated. I held her closely against my breast looking down into her eyes, as I had when I'd breastfed my biological children. She looked up at me intensely with tenderness in her eyes. When I relaxed my hold on her she snuggled deeper into me.

Sidney snapped a picture of that moment. I looked as though I'd just gone through labor with Ashley bundled in my arm like newborn baby. We both looked content. She fell asleep, and we lay there for the next two hours newly committed to our relationship as mother and child.

In theory, when the child's resistance is overcome and the rage has been released, the child is reduced to an infantile state in which he or she can be "re-parented" by methods such as cradling, rocking, bottle-feeding and enforced eye contact. Later, I learned that the therapy remains a controversial practice. Now I think the theory is nothing but hogwash.

It was then I realized how difficult the road ahead might be. Ashley needed to know that I was going to be there through thick and thin. There might be more thin than thick. Ashley had been on her best behavior during my previous visits. I was just beginning to get to know who she really was. The honeymoon period was over.

The next day in the pool, Sidney swam up to me where I sat on my floating chair reading a book. I'd intentionally pushed myself into the deep end away from her for a moment's peace. "I think that all you think about is Ashley," he said quietly. Thank God Sidney was able to tell me how he felt. Ashley required a great deal of my attention. I promised Sidney that we would not allow interruptions when we read Percy Jackson anymore. I promised to make every effort to make certain that he and Kaiden got one to one time with mom.

"Yeah right. She'll just scream," said Sidney.

I promised Sidney that it would be easier when we got home, explaining that we had a bigger house. We would not all be stuck in one hot room together. If Ashley threw a fit, Sidney could go to his own room, or outside to play in the park. I reminded Sidney that I would have more help at home. Daddy would be there, or I could ask Nadia or Alyssa to play with Ashley when I needed a break.

The boys and I watched the sky from the pool each afternoon looking at the departing planes with the winglets that identified my airline. We wished we were leaving Jamaica every single day. Time moved slowly, as did the progress that we made with Ashley. I kept hoping the hard part of the transition would be over before we got Ashley home.

I tried to keep our spirits up, but our surroundings were really starting to get to me. I let the kids swim in that cesspool against my better judgment for the first two days, warning them not to open their eyes underwater. On the third day, I flatly refused to let them swim. Ms. Parchment claimed that she'd been sold a batch of "bad chlorine" that soon resulted in a thick moldy green reduction. We were housed in a dilapidated Tennessee Williams nightmare.

Our experience at Ms. Parchment's Sunshine Apartments has made me eternally grateful for the everyday conveniences that we have at home, primarily the amenity of my Maytag front-loading washer and dryer. Ms. Parchment said that there were no laundry facilities available on the property, yet we walked right past a room behind her kitchen, that suspiciously looked like a laundromat each time we went to the pool. She'd said the closest place to wash clothes was a half-mile down the hill, at the Blue Diamond shopping centre. It wasn't so bad rolling a suitcase packed with dirty clothes down the hill, but dragging it back up was a killer.

It took me three days to figure out how to do laundry in our rooftop apartment. The pile of dirty clothes on the floor kept growing until we were entirely out of underwear. I became the washing machine. I separated the loads between lights and darks, and filled the bathtub with water. I poured a lid full of Springtime Liquid Laundry Detergent, with "brighteners for hand & machine wash" inside the tub. I took off all my clothes, and jumped in to swish and scrub our clothes. I kept the shower on the coldest setting to keep me cool during the aerobic exercise, as I agitated the laundry. I'd empty the tub, and refill it to begin the rinse cycle. I wrung out the clothes, and then slipped into a pair of shorts and a tank top before hanging the clean clothes out to dry on the porch railing. I had to be mindful that they didn't blow into the pool below, or get soaked by an afternoon shower, because that would mean that I'd have to do the hard labour all over again.

The whites took longer to launder. I'd throw them in the bathtub the night before to soak in a bit of bleach, using the little blue bar cake soap for hand washing to get out the tough stains.

I tried not to let the laundry accumulate. I alternated between doing a load of whites and a load of darks every other day the entire time we were there. I'll never complain about doing laundry at home again.

The kitchen in the apartment drove me nuts. First of all, in the kitchen there was no cold water *at all*, and the hot water scalded my hands. I had to fill an empty jug of milk with cold water from the bathroom to do the dishes in the pint sized kitchen sink. The last day we were there I wanted to leave dirty dishes for Ms. Parchment, but I knew she wouldn't be the one to do them. Evelyn, the housemaid would wash them, and I would never leave dirty dishes for her.

The kitchen was equipped with only a single teaspoon, one tablespoon, two dinner forks, one dull knife, a spatula, a small frying pan, two small pots, and a cutting board. I asked for a can opener to open tomato paste and tomato sauce the first night we were there to make spaghetti. The limited accouterments challenged my culinary skills. I had to shoo the kids out of the small space whenever I cooked on the propane-powered four-burner stove in that hell's kitchen.

I prepared a variety of food for dinners, including spaghetti, pork chops, garlic green beans, and an honest to goodness first attempt at rice and peas. We ate a lot of peanut butter and jelly, or grilled cheese sandwiches for lunch.The boys didn't like the taste of Jamaican cheese, so I paid a premium for processed Kraft slices and Hellman's mayonnaise. I grilled pancakes and eggs, or simply filled a paper bowl with cereal for breakfast.

After our trip to Mega Mart with Mr. Dixon, we carried everything home up the hill from the Blue Diamond grocery store. We never got to the early open-air market downtown for the abundant cheap island fruit. We bought our fruit at a wooden shack at the bottom of the hill. We tried eating Jamaican apples, but they tasted like sour grainy crab apples. Ashley loved them! We bought and ate papayas, mangos, pineapple, or watermelon on a daily basis. If there were one kitchen appliance I wished I had, it would have been a blender to make icy fruit smoothies.

I tolerated Parchi's propensity to be cheap until it became just plain unhealthy. The sixth day I turned on the air conditioner in the early evening figuring we were paying for the use of a useless pool. My children were suffocating. The air conditioning flooded the apartment and satisfied us like fast food...instant gratification. I felt a tinge of guilt, so I used it frugally and turned it off as soon as the room cooled down. I think we had the air on for a total of an hour-and-a-half that night. We used the air conditioning only two more times before Ms. Parchment disabled it.

The Monday we first used the air conditioning was the day that Ms. Wilton returned to work from vacation. I'd hoped that when Ms. Wilton's holiday was over the adoption ball would get rolling. I spoke to Ms. Wilton early in the morning, voicing my concerns about finances and the separation of our family. "Would you like to talk on the phone or would you rather speak in person?" asked Ms. Wilton. "I'll be here all the day."

We took a local taxi downtown where I laid our case before Ms. Wilton. The paperwork was in compliance, and Ashley had been officially matched to our family. I'd thought the last obstacle was acquiring Ashley's birth certificate. I'd attempted to get it myself, but was prevented by Mr. Bowen, who assured me that getting the birth certificate was not a difficult task. "Having the birth certificate was not a requirement for the adoption to go through." It was, however, a requirement for Ashley to receive a Canadian visa and leave Jamaica. I thought it was in the best interest of the child to expedite the birth certificate.

I complained about how the entire process had stressed our budget, and how I'd used most of my earnings over the past year to pay for the travel expenses back and forth between Canada and Jamaica. I'd applied for and received parental leave enabling me to stay at home for up to thirty-seven weeks. My leave was scheduled to begin August thirty-first, meaning my disposable income for the next year would require tightening up the purse strings. I wanted to make sure Ashley felt comfortable and safe in her new home before resuming my job as a flight attendant. I told Ms. Wilton that I did not intend on leaving the island without Ashley, planning to hold her to the words she'd spoken when we were getting Ashley's medical. "Don't quote me Ms. Isnor, but I think we can get this through before the end of August."

Ms. Wilton sat patiently listening to all my cathartic complaining. Nothing immediate transpired from that meeting, except for the reprieve from being so close together all day in those Sunshine Apartments.

We caught a taxi down to the Sam Sharpe Square, stopping at Juicy Patty for some fried chicken and Ting soda. We did a little shopping downtown, first picking up a couple of floaties for the pool, groan. And then, quite by accident discovered a small bookstore that sold reading primers with pictures of coloured children for Ashley.

We found another taxi line by the gas station near Trinity Plaza where Ashley had her work medical done. I paid $300 JMD for all of us to get back to the Blue Diamond, and another $180 JMD to get us up the hill to our apartment before the mosquito happy hour. Sweat was dripping down our backs when we entered the room that had been closed up all day, so I turned the air conditioning back on.

Ms. Evelyn the housemaid, had completely cleaned the apartment. Odd, Parchi and I hadn't spoken of maid service when we were negotiating the price of the rent. It felt wonderful to come home to a floor that no longer felt sticky from the beer I'd dropped. Fresh towels hung in the bathroom, and our bed linens had been changed. I couldn't believe that the laundry I'd left soaking in the sink had been washed, dried, neatly folded, and placed on the bed. When Sidney answered a quiet knock on the door, Ms. Evelyn handed him two more items that had been hanging on the line. She placed her index finger over her lips keeping it a secret that she'd done our laundry.

I learned a great deal about Parchi's character during intermittent discussions we shared throughout our stay. Ms. Parchment claimed she'd been instrumental in getting Maryam's Daniel off the island. "They were here for five weeks. If it weren't for me they would still be here," she'd said.

Ms. Parchment explained how she had instructed Maryam to go to the Registrar and apply for Daniel's birth certificate herself. "It was public record," she declared. I didn't explain how I'd already tried that. It didn't work for me. Ms. Parchment said her family had taken Maryam and Daniel in under her wing, but warned me that they were not going to do that again. Duly noted.

"Maryam was required to come back to Jamaica in March for a court date; she never phoned or contacted me," said the African Queen. I understood that Ms. Parchment felt betrayed by Maryam who "never once contacted her since they'd left the island." I also understood why Maryam needed to get out of the city and go to Negril in September. I wanted to suggest that Parchi treat people more considerately if she wanted to build friendships, but I zipped my lips shut.

Parchi owned a three-legged dog that supervised the property. She called the dog Porsche, like the car. The dog got her leg caught in the chicken wire mesh on one of the gates at the property. According to Ms.

Parchment, the Veterinarian taking care of Porsche did a lousy job of fixing the leg, causing an infection that required Porsche's leg to be amputated. I found it interesting how often Parchi placed blame on others.

The next morning, I turned on the air for another half-an-hour before eight o'clock in the morning. I decided that we would spend the day at Doctor's Cave. We packed up our floaties and sunscreen, leaving the confines of our little apartment behind. It must have been divine providence that sent the white taxi with the red plates down Paterson Avenue at the precise moment the gates closed behind us. I hadn't intended on paying for taxis to go to the beach. I'd hoped we'd be saving money by staying at the pool.

We played in the seawater most of the morning. At noon, we walked across the street to the Jamaican Bobsled where we ordered another large pepperoni pizza. The air conditioner cooled our bodies down and raised my level of patience.

We stopped back by the Caribic House hoping to get Ashley's swimsuit. I guessed the maid had taken it home with her, not expecting our return. We chatted with Ms. Blair, the female daytime security guard, who clucked her tongue when I told her how difficult it had been finalizing Ashley's paperwork.

I asked about Matthew B., who was adopted and living in Washington State. "Was it the same for them? Did it take so long for the paperwork to get done?"

"Yeah mon. Jus' like you, comin' an' going mon, jus like you. But hi wez a small one dat boy." The guard put her hand on the top of an imaginary child's head, a little lower than her waist. Matthew B. left Jamaica on January seventh, 2010.

Hearing about other children having been adopted gave me strength. Yet, the network of people involved with Jamaican adoptions still remained small. I'd only connected with Maryam who took Daniel to New York, and Kristi B. who took Matthew to Washington State. I knew of no other child going to Canada.

Our bellies and spirits felt better after that trip into town; Ashley no longer had to wear the one-piece swimsuit with the strap that cut into her neck. We flagged down a red plated taxicab to take us back to the Blue

Diamond shopping center. I bought all the drinks we could carry, and we returned to our room before the expected mosquito attack.

Ashley threw one of her biggest fits that night at bedtime, immediately after I'd discovered that the air conditioner had been disabled. I told her it was time to get into her own bed. I laid the rubber pee pad underneath the sheet and tried to put Ashley on top of it. The boys wanted to hear another chapter of Percy Jackson, but Ashley refused to stay on her bed. She kept jumping up, and then laughed when I returned her to her bed. In frustration, I slapped her clothed buttocks *hard*.

Ashley's mouth opened wide letting out a primal scream. I grabbed her chin with my thumb and forefinger roughly, and told her to be quiet. My actions produced precisely the opposite effect than I wanted. Ashley screamed harder. I'd never seen a mouth open so wide. It looked like a cartoon. I watched her adenoids vibrate.

"I'm through with you," I said. "I've had it."

The boys covered their ears with their hands. They'd had it too. I froze, completely at a lost as to what to do. *I'd had it.* I stared incredulously at 'this child' before me whose will was so much stronger than my own. I understood, for a moment, how she ended up where she was. I picked her up, kicking, screaming, and flailing. I opened up the flimsy screen door that separated us from the mosquitoes and placed her on the patio. Every bone in my body objected to what I was doing, knowing that the last thing in the world 'this child' needed was to be separated from me.

I was not thinking of Ashley at that precise moment. My two boys were cringing at the noise she made. Ashley banged against the outside of the closed door with her fists, making the whole room shake. She beat against the glass window. I expected glass to shatter inside at any moment. I also expected the tantrum to peek and then decline. I picked up the Percy Jackson book and began reading to the boys. "We are not going to let her interrupt our time," I told the boys.

"I can't hear you," said Sidney softly. We lay on the bed directly under the fan, too hot to touch each other, as I forged forward through the book. Ashley opened the door and crawled back inside. She fell asleep on the floor, just inside the door. No one won the battle that night. Sidney picked her up and placed her on her small bed.

I should have known she wanted to be in the same bed as the rest of us, sleeping together on the king-sized bed. Ashley slept alone only because she peed the bed. I couldn't fathom washing sheets in the bathtub every morning. I should have realized that she saw that as rejection. I'd only seen the arrangement as practical.

I lay back down on the big bed once Ashley fell asleep. "Boys, I just don't know if I can do this," I said. "Maybe I've been wrong. Maybe we aren't supposed to take Ashley home. Maybe I should give up on her. This is harder than I thought it would be." The boys remained silent. They knew their mother never gave up. I *never* admitted defeat. We all lay together on our backs, holding hands and looking up at the ceiling fan. Ashley laid limbs sprawled out over her pee pad. Her sleeping face looking angelic.

"My heart says not to give up on her yet," said Sidney.

I picked up the Percy Jackson book. I read and read in the still quiet room until the boys were both fast asleep. I then pushed Ashley off her pee pad carefully, so as not to wake her up, moved it to one side of the king-sized bed, and then placed her on top of it, so that she would be one with us. I lay on the bed surrounded by needy sleeping children.

I woke early the next morning and found Ashley already awake. She was playing with my hair. "Mi dry," she said as if nothing ever happened.

"Good girl," I replied.

It was already getting hot and it wasn't even seven yet. The day was going to be a scorcher. I scrambled some eggs, and tossed some bread in the toaster oven for breakfast. Then, I washed the dishes, immediately wiping down the countertop, knowing if I didn't do it right away the minuscule pesky ants would invade for the tiniest tidbit of a crumb.

"Get your swimsuits on we're going to a new beach," I said while packing a light bag, not wanting to carry much. I planned on exploring the northern part of the island, halfway between Montego Bay and Ocho Rios, having heard about Duncan Bay beach just past the town of Falmouth.

The town originally flourished as a 'pleasant fashionable seaport,' with several representative structures of Georgian architecture dating from 1790 to 1840. It had become a thriving port, exporting the islands commodities of sugar, rum and slaves. Falmouth's demise began at the time of emancipation of the slaves.

We caught a red plated taxi heading north in front of the big lavender all-inclusive Riu Hotel. "How much to take the kids and me to Falmouth?" I asked the driver. "Three hundred for you and half for the children," he said as we all snuggled into the back seat with two other people.

The windows were rolled down allowing the breeze to fly through the car, so I tied my hair back to keep it from whipping me in the eyes. The taxi stopped all along the coast dropping people off and picking others up. We passed the birthplace of Usain Bolt, in Sherwood Content. Bolt was an 11-time world champion holding the world records for races for the 100 meters and 200 meters, both of which he made at the 2009 Berlin World Athletics Championships.

Falmouth was a town precisely and painstakingly planned in a grid like pattern from its conception. Its piped water supply preceded that of New York City. When we arrived, the town bustled with activity. The Wednesday market bartering commotion was in full swing with entrepreneurs selling dry goods, clothing, and artifacts, but very little produce or food items. I saw ceramics, furniture, handmade straw brooms, and hammocks. "Where do we find a taxi to take us to Duncan Bay?" I asked our driver.

"I can take you there."

"How much?"

"Another three hundred for you, and half for the children." This was an honest man who quoted the price that Ashley, our houseman, told me to expect.

"We would like you to take us to Duncan's Bay please."

The driver talked non stop between Falmouth and the beach, but I could hardly understand a word through his thick accent. Eventually, I caught his gist. He was explaining what 'charter only,' meant. I learned that driver's were fined if they did not display a 'charter only' sign on dashboard, when travelling off their route. He pulled out a rectangular shaped piece of cut cardboard from under his driver's seat with the words handwritten in permanent marker. He pointed to the right side of the highway to show us where to hail a cab to return to Falmouth later. Then, he pulled off the main road towards a beautifully barren beach. I paid him $1,200.00 JMD for the entire ride and thanked him for being honest. We tumbled out of his car onto the white sand.

Duncan beach stretched for miles in both directions with not so much as a shack to buy drinks or refreshments. Two local girls, no bigger than my own children, played together in the water several meters away from us. The water remained shallow and calm well beyond the shoreline.

I pulled out the book I'd bought in the Toronto airport that I'd begun reading. The Help, a first time novel by Kathryn Stokett, about black maids in the South, and their relationships with white families. My book took a beating, getting splashed on in the pool, and full of sand at the beaches in Jamaica. I all but finished it the night before we finally abandoned the island. I left it with Ms. Wilton, knowing I could read the last six pages at the library once I returned to Canada. Ms. Wilton confessed that she'd never before read a book for the sheer joy of it, saying she'd considered reading a chore, but she promised me that she'd make her very best effort to get through it, based on my recommendation. I hoped that by giving Ms. Wilton The Help, I would introduce her to a whole new world; reading for pleasure.

A calm summer breeze gently lolled through the postcard perfect turquoise sky. Kaiden splashed to shore wondering if we might be able to get the Buzz Lightyear kite I'd bought at our local dollar store up in the air. Thankfully, it snapped together in three easy steps. I tied the string on it according to the directions, and put it in Kaiden's eager hands.

"Keep walking away from me until I tell you to stop….ok now hold the kite up over your head…let go *now!*" Kaiden followed all my instructions, but the kite disobediently veered from side to side before nestling itself into the bare branches of the only tree on the beach.

The kite was stuck ten feet over our heads, just out of reach. I gently tugged on the line, hoping for it to dislodge before breaking the string. I was so concentrated on freeing the kite from the grip of the tree, that I didn't see the Rasta man walking towards us from the north. He jumped into the tree, untangled the kite, and handed it back to Kaiden without speaking a single word. "Thanks," said Kaiden before making a second attempt at flight. The wind caught it, lifting the kite and Buzz was flyin' "to infinity and beyond." Kaiden zigzagged back and forth along the beach, letting small lengths of string out, bit by bit. Then, there he stood enamored beneath his childhood hero.

The sight of the kite drew the two little local girls in "Wat iz dat?" they asked.

"It's called a kite," I explained.

The larger of the two girls asked if she could hold it, and Kaiden shared his kite willingly. He handed the string to the older girl, and then waded back towards to his brother.

The older girl anchored down the kite for well into an hour while the little sister played with Ashley, scooting around like crocodiles in the water. I settled back on my beach towel in the sand with my book. When the girls drifted down the shore away from me, I waved Ashley back, but she ignored me. I stood, dropped my book on the towel and walked into the knee-deep water to retrieve my daughter.

The tide was out, and Ashley had attached herself to the two girls and their mother wading far out on the horizon. Ashley seemed reluctant to return to me. Strangers had more in common with her than I did. They spoke the same language, and they were all black. My back had begun to turn a toasty brown by the sun. I trekked out where I could stand close to her in the water, and listened to them talking in Patois. I wondered if there would always be some degree of separation between us, or if it would become diluted in time.

"Ashley, we're going on a walk to look for water to drink." I took her hand, retrieved the kite, and said goodbye to the local girls. I reeled the kite out of the sky, and tucked it back inside my beach bag. The kids all carried their own shoes as we walked in the direction the Rasta man had come from, searching for something to drink.

Some tourists who had just been snorkeling passed us. They said they were staying at the Beaches Resort, on the tip of the bay. They carried a live starfish whose tentacles wriggled at our touch. The boys ran their fingers over its belly as I wondered how long it would live out of its natural environment.

They also carried a glass jelly jar containing an honest to goodness seahorse. I've learned that seahorses lived in shallow tropical and temperate waters. Its equine profile appeared proud and bewildered. It had no scales, but rather a thin skin stretched over a series of bony plates. I doubted that the newly captured treasure would ever be set free because guide had proudly stated that it was the first he'd ever caught.

226

There were no convenience stores between our starting place and the Beaches Resort. I walked up to the bar hoping to buy some water, but the bartender said they were only allowed to serve guests staying at the resort. "Is it possible to purchase a day pass?" I asked.

The bartender directed me to the reception area to make the inquiry. We learned that a day pass cost sixty US dollars for adults, and thirty-five US dollars for children. The fee included all food, drinks, use of the pools, land and water sports, and the possibility of a glass bottom boat ride. They did not have an airline discount for the day rate. I asked.

Three kids looked up at me with large expectant eyes. They'd walked past the inviting pools, water slides, and a circus trapeze. "Is it too expensive?" Sidney asked.

"It's expensive, but we're going to stay for the day," I declared. The kids all jumped up and down. I provided my identification, which was Xeroxed, just in case I decided to skip out with their towels. We each received an armband that entitled us to unlimited refreshments. I told the kids to consume as much as humanly possible before we had to leave.

We were allowed to stay at the resort and use the amenities until six-thirty that night. We began our adventure at a water slide that burst into shallow pool water, then moved to the circus workshop hoping for lessons of the flying trapeze, but we were not equipped with the required dry shorts, shirts and socks, so we moved on.

We tried to go on the glass bottom boat, but there were no more spots available. Instead, we took a long ride on a Catamaran with a private guide. Seawater splashed us in the face as we slammed into the waves. I briefly lost my wallet in the murky ocean when we disembarked, that I'd hidden it in my lifejacket, but the wallet had slipped out when a waved knocked me over. I panicked, but somehow retrieved the C wallet that held all my bank cards and money.

We ate an unlimited supply of hamburgers, nasty fake cheese nachos, jerk chicken, and pizza. I drank buckets of beer, intent on getting my money's worth. We stayed well past our six-thirty curfew.

It was dusk when we left. The receptionist at the front desk pointed us in the direction of the taxi stand to get a ride back into Falmouth. There we stood, while the mosquitos filled their bellies with our blood. I watched the large rider lawn mower type machines spraying thick coats of gray clouds as we were walking out of the resort. I'd assumed that the lawn mowers were in need of engine repair, only later realizing that the machines had been spraying pesticides.

We hailed a taxi to take us into the town of Trelawny where we had no business being at night. I asked a man on the street for directions, who led us to another taxi stand. Thankfully, he had no ulterior motive and did not take advantage of my irresponsible intoxication.

Three of us settled in the back seat of a taxi that held six. Ashley and Kaiden fell asleep on either side of me while Sidney sat wide-eyed alone in the front. The driver offered to take us up the hill to our apartment and I did not care what he wanted to charge. I did not want to get out of one cab at the bottom of the hill only to have to wait for another ride. We traversed the roundabout towards home, but I couldn't remember the house number. I told the driver to look for cactus in front of the house gates.

A car next to us started honking its horn trying to get our attention. "It's Angie," said Sidney. The driver stopped to let us out. I immediately relieved myself on the side of the road.

"You peed yourself," said Duj in disbelief.

"How much do you need to give the driver," asked Angie.

"1,000 JMD," said the driver. "You wet up my seat."

"It's in my wallet."

Angie dug through the beach bag to find my soaking wet Coach wallet and paid the driver.

"Thank you, Angie," I said.

"No. Problem," said Angie as she helped move the sleeping kids into her car. We'd passed the cactus and ended up at a different roundabout where Angie had chased us down.

"Ms. Parchment was worried about you. She called the Police and has them out looking for you," said Angie.

"We were fine. We took a holiday at the Breezes Resort outside Trelawny. It took a little longer to get home than I'd expected." Rej and Angie carried Ashley and Kaiden up the stairs to our room. I stripped their beach clothes off to put their jammies on, then tossed my own damp clothes into the bathtub to deal with in the morning. I crawled into my jammies and hoped we'd all sleep in the next day, because I was going to have a humdinger of a hangover.

I could barely move the next day, every bone in my body ached. My stomach flipped and turned, and my head pounded. I had no right to complain for a single moment. The pain I suffered through was self-inflicted torture. Only the passage of time helped. Even the clock's ticking banged on my head like a sledgehammer. The mere thought of a beer sent me to pray in front of a white porcelain god. I lay prone on the bed hoping to exert as little energy as humanly possible. Of course, I had three children under the age of ten to take care of who required meals and supervision. Spongebob babysat all day as we tried to keep cool under the fan. That cartoon theme song still reverberates in my brain. The kids finished all the leftovers of chicken and rice and peas from Scotchies. They inhaled boxed kraft dinner, and polished off all the cold sodas and juice in the small fridge. They ate an entire box of Cocoa Nut cereal for dinner. It wasn't one of my finest moments. I vowed off Red Stripe for the remainder of the trip.

Friday morning the sun was shining and my head no longer hurt. I woke up early to do the laundry that had piled up when I wasn't moving. The cupboards were bare, we had only six eggs, a bit of cheese, and a couple of pieces of wheat bread left for breakfast. I made cheesy eggs on toast for the kids, and drank lots of coffee. The bare cupboards determined the need for a trip to town. I looked out the balcony window at the slimy green pool below. The kids craved physical activity because they had been cooped up for an entire day watching Spongebob

We were on the road just after nine in the morning headed towards Doc's Cave. My Jamaican phone rang soon after settling on the beach. I dug through the Bob Marley bag searching for the source of the reggae music, but I didn't find it in time to answer. I was not familiar with missed call number the phone displayed, and the only people who had my contact number were Jamaicans. I thought it could have been someone working on Ashley's file. If I had known it was Ms. Parchment, I never would have returned the call. She wanted the balance due for the rent. I took in a deep breath. "Ms. Parchment, I have concerns about the safety of the pool, we are at Doc's Cave, as we speak, because we are unable to use the pool. It is not safe."

"We are working on the pool. I was sold some bad chlorine at the store from the Blue Diamond. I need the money you owe me to buy some more chlorine from a different store downtown," said Ms. Parchment.

"Surely you have other funds, besides what I owe you to take care of your pool. What would you do if I were not here?" I asked.

"There is no need to take care of the pool when we do not have guests," said Ms. Parchment. *OHHH ...so* the murkiness was normal.

"I rented the room with the understanding we would have use of a pool. I will not let my children get into the water because it is not healthy. I do not know if we will be staying without the use of a pool. It is so very hot and my funds are limited; I cannot continue to pay for admission to beaches and taxis when we do not have access to your pool."

"I do not know what your funds are like, but you seem to have no problem getting beer," retorted Ms. Parchment. "You are holding my money ransom. I must tell you that I think differently of you now. I will have the pool taken care of, but I expect to be paid the balance of the $130 US that you owe me by Monday."

That witch! I could barely control myself. I wanted to say; you are suffocating my children in this dreadful heat! You have disabled the air-conditioning and are too cheap to take care of your own swimming pool without extorting your guests! I inhaled deeply and said, "You are right about the beer, I have decided not to spend my money so foolishly. I appreciate your taking care of the pool. Hopefully, the new chlorine will work. I guess we will wait to see. I will let you know our plans by Monday."

We ordered not one, but two large pepperoni pizzas for lunch at the Jamaican Bobsled restaurant that day, when a torrential downpour demanded we leave the beach is search of food and shelter. One pizza satisfied us, but the second one stuffed us.

Then, we walked in the warm rain down to the Indian convenience store, where we stocked up on juice and water before heading reluctantly towards Ironshore in a local taxi. The rain subsided by the time we caught a ride to get up the hill. We took a scenic tour through the upper crust of Ironshore, noticing some amazingly well-groomed mansions as our taxi traversed the hills. The driver made a circular pattern that led to the roundabout where Angie had chased us down after my bender. I enjoyed the diversion and handed the driver $300 JMD when he dropped us off in front of our gate.

Ms. Parchment's stoic red four-door sedan stood parked at the bottom of the stairway to our apartment when we got back. She was home early.

We showered off the sand, one at a time, before all climbing onto the big bed to continue reading the story of Percy Jackson. I read, and read, and read, wondering how many of the twenty-four chapters I'd get through before we were home. We were already more than halfway through the book.

Saturday morning we opened both the main door and the balcony door of the apartment to create a cross wind in our room. Ms. Parchment stopped by mid-morning to see if we were interested in spending some time in a pool across the street. We jumped at the chance to cool off in some clean water. We crossed the street, and walked up the driveway to a modest sized home with a 'for sale' sign in front of it. Ms. Parchment explained that some absentee owners who had 'gone foreign' listed the home for sale with her.

Ms. Parchment unlocked the gates and led us towards a crystal clear pool where the water looked cool and inviting. I read The Help on my rubber floaty as the kids pretended to be sharks circling beneath me. Parchi hovered by the edge of the pool, working on her laptop supervising us, until a big black Dodge Ram truck rolled up driveway. I should have know she had an ulterior motive.

A black couple in their mid-thirties arrived with a man I recognized to be one of Ms. Parchment's employees. He'd been working on correcting the imbalanced chemicals in our pool. I watched Parchi, with peripheral vision, as she took her laptop inside the house while giving a viewing. The couple inspected the interior, exterior, and even the roof of the house, before coming to the pool area. Then, Ms. Parchment brought out three tall glasses of ice water to share with the couple.

Sidney said his stomach hurt. He was thirsty, hungry, and wanted to leave. I hoped we might come back another time, but the opportunity never presented itself.

Ms. Wilton called when we returned to the apartment, inviting us out for the night. We showered and put on clean clothes before she picked us up at six-thirty. She drove us to the Coyaba Beach Resort where we were allowed access to the premises through a railroad style gate, once Ms. Wilton identified herself, "Marcia," The gate rose and Ms. Wilton drove her sedan into the valet parking area. She parked the car herself.

We walked through time entering the front doors of the Coyaba Beach Resort, ascending a stairway leading to the restaurant called 'The Polo Grounds.' Old sepia photographs and equestrian memorabilia lined the dark hunter green walls, exuding a feeling of an old-world country club charm. I expected to see Ernest Hemingway sitting in the wicker chair at the next table, or Noel Coward taking the microphone from the lead singer who was cooing out "I'll follow my secret heart..." The chef set out a free buffet with two-for-one drinks between the hours of seven and nine pm. We ordered our drinks before attacking the bite sized hor dóeurves.

Ms. Wilton noticed Ashley scratching her arms and her belly. "Ashley itches a lot," she said. I too had noticed the scratching, and wondered if our time in the sun was drying her skin. I vowed to lather her up with more lotion.

"What are you drinking?" I asked, trying to make myself heard over the cello behind Ms. Wilton.

"Fruit punch," she answered. "I have never acquired the taste for alcohol."

Smart woman, I thought.

"Do you mind my asking how you came to this profession, working with these children?" I asked.

"I was a high school teacher for twelve years. I needed more challenge."

"I guess you found that!" I said and we both laughed.

"Doesn't it frustrate you how broken the system is?" I questioned.

"It's what we have. We have to make do with what we have." Ms. Wilton explained why things moved slowly; There was no money. She had a caseload of over one hundred children, all with their own important manila files. There was one psychologist responsible for all of the children, some of whom she did not even know. A child in dire need may never get the attention they required.

"It is a shame that poverty is so rampant in Jamaica, that mothers feel it is better to give their children up to give them a better life." I said.

"It is not poverty that is the problem. The poor will do whatever it takes to hold onto their children," said Ms. Wilton.

Ms. Wilton explained that although Ashley's birth certificate only cost thirty-five US dollars, because there were no funds, Ms. Wilton could not get it. Ms. Wilton had to wait until the funds "were appropriated."

"Why couldn't someone like me pay for it?" I asked.

"We have to be very careful about child trafficking these days. You do not want any indication in the file that there is a possibility of that. In this situation, I know that is not the case, but we would not want someone else to misconstrue an act of kindness."

I took a deep breath. I had to ask. "I am told that there are bribes expected. That bribing is the *only* way to accomplish what I am trying to do. Is that true or not?"

"It occurs," she acknowledged. "You are so close to the end. This adoption will go through without a bribe."

I heaved a sigh of relief. Ms. Wilton was a trusted friend who was working in the best interest of Ashley and our family. I was ever so grateful that I could speak frankly with her and get an honest response.

We all ordered a second free drink, and then the kids started going a little squirrely in the upscale establishment, so I thought it might be time to leave. I looked around at the room thinking about how much my husband would enjoy the ambiance. Someday, the Coyaba Beach Resort would be a lovely place for adult time.

We piled back into Ms. Wilton's car and returned to our apartment. I appreciated Ms. Wilton's kind gesture in taking us out for the evening, the diversion had refreshed my spirit. The sun had set, so we opened the doors and lit a mosquito coil hoping to ward off some bug bites. The kids dressed in their jammies, and I read yet another chapter of Percy Jackson, putting the book down when they were all asleep.

I lowered my head in prayer. "Dear Lord, please show me the path that you want me to take. I am so tired of being in Jamaica. I feel spent. I want to go home. Lord, I have promised Ashley she will be going with us, and that we will not leave without her. Lord, what am I to do? Should I give someone some money and be done with it? Should we just continue to wait it out? Lord it is *hot*. The boys miss their father and I miss my husband. Please bring this to an end. Give me a sign. Show me what to do." I closed my bewildered eyes and went to sleep.

Sunday morning I toasted bagels, spreading them with cream cheese. "Mi no like da white stuff," complained Ashley. "Mi want eggs."

"You need to finish your bagel before I give you eggs," I said unwilling to waste any of the precious food we had carried up the hill. Ashley finished her food so that she could have the eggs while I cleaned the dishes, wondering what the day had in store for us.

Ms. Parchment knocked on the door. "Do you still want to go to church?" she asked.

I hesitated only a moment before answering. "Of course we do. I am very much looking forward to going to a church here. It will only take us a moment to get ready."

I threw a conservative dress on myself, and pulled out the green and brown linen frock I'd bought for Ashley's plane ride home. The boy's ironed cotton buttoned down shirts hung in the closet. They put them on with white drawstring shorts. I expected the church service would be long and hot, so I wasn't about to require my Canadian sons to wear long church pants. We were all dressed and ready to go well before Parchi descended the stairs wearing her traditional African attire.

We took the interlocking back roads up to Flower Hill Avenue where the church perched on the top of Torada Heights. The Pastor, an aging black Englishman, named Winsome Oban, lead the Jamaican ministry. God in His divine wisdom, had planted a vision in the heart of Dr. Oban, while he was living in England, to go home and set up a Christian Centre.

The worship area of the church was a large rectangle, surrounded entirely by a wraparound porch with white iron railings. Tall white pillars supported the long sides of the parish. In between the posts, were wooden folding windows that when pushed open, let the outside in. Rows of amber colored wooden chairs formed pews that faced the altar. I was relieved to see several fans circulating overhead, keeping the room cool.

The worship service began before we arrived. The people stood with outstretched palms towards the heavens. The boys found an empty row where we could all sit together. Sidney led the way, followed by Kaiden, Ashley, and me, and last Parchi who wanted the aisle seat. The singing continued giving praise to the Lord.

The Pastor asked for any visitors to stand. He welcomed us, and asked us to introduce ourselves. "Good Morning, My Name is Erika Isnor, these are my sons Sidney and Kaiden, and my daughter Ashley." Ironically, my first public declaration of Ashley, as my daughter, occurred in a church. Ms. Parkinson explained to the congregation that we were in the process of an adoption.

The congregation was finally invited to sit and the Pastor began his sermon, *"If you have integrity, nothing else matters...If you do not have integrity, nothing else matters."* There was my sign.

The Pastor continued his sermon describing the long dark forty-eight years of the Israelites who were lost in the desert. "Life is never a straight road," It was not God's intention, he claimed, that the Israelites wandered. The children of Israel endured difficulties and hardship because they had turned their back on God, not because God had turned his back on them. "God intended to bring them back on track, to goodness and faithfulness. It is not God's idea ...what we are doing, thinking, ...the stubbornness. When we are on God's path nothing can stop us. What is desired is given to us as long as long as the foundation is under God."

Well, there you had it, I'd been given my answer directly out of the mouth of a man of the cloth. Clearly, I was not intended to bribe anyone to get Ashley home.

In my efforts to extract Ashley from that God forsaken place, I realized how lost I was. My perspective changed when I finally realized I was not saving Ashley, she was saving me. I found grace along the course by discovering my need to be saved. I did not make the realization in Jamaica, but the seed of desire had been planted there. It continued to grow in Canada, as slow as an ackee tree.

That Sunday, Ms. Parchment took us back to her house after church. We expected the day to be another hot scorcher. Ms. Parchment opened the electric gate and drove the car inside. I pulled out an envelope from my purse that contained the $130 I owed, and gave it to her. I'd decided to keep my side of the street clean whether we stayed in Jamaica for the rest of the month or not.

I wanted nothing more than to get on a plane with Ashley and the boys and go home. I wanted to sleep in our own beds, where we'd have to use comforters at night to stay *warm*. I soon decided that we would leave the island, with or without Ashley.

Sunday afternoon, right after Ms. Parchment got her money, we were given clearance to swim. Ms. Parchment said that they had shocked the heck out of the pool. "Too much good chlorine had been added to the bad batches and the water needed time to balance. A couple of days have gone by and the chemicals test good." I didn't have much faith in Parchi, but the pool was looking clear, so we went back into the water.

Ashley, the groundsman, vacuumed the pool bottom and checked the chemicals every morning before eight o'clock. He skimmed the bugs and bees off of the surface of the water. The boys waited, with their feet dangling over the edge, in their swimsuits for his work to be finished, and I'd sit with little Ashley reading 'Dick and Jane.'

When he gave the green light to go, we'd all dive in the pool to cool off. I sat on the floating lounge chair from Costco reading, as they boys swam laps. Little Ashley played on the steps with her Polly Pocket miniature beach doll until we got water wings for her, and then she was able to swim with the boys in the deep end.

We swam a whole week away, me reading The Help during the day and Percy Jackson in the early evening, under the fan in our sweltering room. Ashley's behavior began stabilizing. I tried praising her as much as possible, while gently reprimanding her when necessary. She had gotten used to being with us, and expected to be going when we left Jamaica.

Ms. Wilton agreed that we should return to Canada and wait for the process to work. "It might be as far away as October before the paperwork is done." She promised to work alongside Ms. O'Connor writing the report, and then sending it to the Adoption Board for review in Kingston.

I decided to go to the Jamaican Bobsled café to use the Internet and make reservations to go home. I tried booking online, but encountered unforeseen difficulties with the Internet connection which worked sporadically. It kept kicking me offline before I could get a confirmation code. I tried for a couple of hours before finally giving up. I called Sid, who was on a business trip in Houston, asking him to make the listing for us.

Ms. Wilton picked Ashley up on Thursday morning after breakfast. We'd completed our morning routine of reading and I'd packed our suitcases under Ashley's watchful eye. She knew she was being left behind. Ashley sat in my lap as I told her that I was wrong about being able to take her home. I promised to come back for her "when the paperwork was done." I dressed her in another 'All We Need Is Love T-shirt,' and gave her another picture of our family. I wanted her to have something to physically hold while we were out of sight.

Ms. Wilton's vehicle stood outside of the electric door. She called me when she arrived, and I walked up to the gates to let her in. Porsche, the three-legged dog barked incessantly at our heels as we walked back towards the apartment together. Ms. Wilton held onto my arm, using me as a protective human shield against the dog. I shooed Porche away knowing she was harmless. I had relied on Ms. Wilton for so long. It felt good to have the slipper on the other foot. Ms. Wilton promised to watch over Ashley in my absence. She helped me reassure Ashley that I would be coming back, 'once the paperwork was done.' Ashley climbed into the back seat of Ms. Wilton's car and rode away.

Angie gave us a ride to the airport on Friday, making me promise that I'd call her if we didn't get on the plane. I gave her the apartment keys to return to Ms. Parchment at the end of the month. I asked her not to leave my reading floaty in the pool for Parchi. My husband had pre-warned me that the Friday plane was sold out, but we went to the airport anyway. Unfortunately, other stand-by guests had listed earlier than we did. We went through security, but weren't able to board the full plane. Sadly, I had to call Angie back. She happily turned her old clunker around to take us back to our Hotel California.

I called Ms. Wilton who said she'd taken Ashley to work with her when they left us. Ashley showed great interest in the books on the shelves at the office. "Mi mommy read to mi all da time. You bi keepin' mi from mi stories," she complained to Ms. Wilton.

We remained on the island two more days, not even trying to get on the Saturday plane. We left Jamaica Sunday, August fifteenth, ironically Nadia's eighteenth birthday. We'd been on the island for only nineteen days, but it felt like it had been an eternity. If I'd stayed there any longer my skin would have turned to weathered leather. We were so brown that remnants of a tan lingered long into the Christmas season.

---- • THIRTEEN • ----

'LICENSE TO ADOPT'

Two days after we returned from Jamaica, Sid phoned my sister Sheri making condolences for being unable join her son Steve's wedding celebration because leaving home seemed unfathomable. The boys had been living out of a suitcase for a month. They needed to play with their neighbourhood friends and sleep in their own beds, and I was sick from exhaustion. The ceremony took place in Iowa on the rolling grounds of the Harvester Country Club and golf course. My sister helped organize the majority of the wedding including arranging accommodations for our extended family and planning an elegant reception dinner. I hear the bride was stunning. Once we made the decision to stay home my body celebrated by shutting down completely. I climbed into my bed and slept through my nephew's wedding day. I think if we had made the trip to Iowa I would have become seriously ill.

A week later, Sid and I celebrated our tenth wedding anniversary. That morning, I found a dozen red roses on the kitchen counter when I snuck downstairs to set out an edible fruit arrangement for him. My husband's face beamed when we exchanged our anniversary gifts, "It's the first and last time you're ever going to have a tenth anniversary," he said taking me in his arms.

"I'll have to agree," I said, "seeing how we don't live in Utah."

We shared the early morning with the chocolate dipped fruit and coffee before Sid left for his Wednesday morning sales meeting.

We had a seven-thirty commitment that evening, but he wouldn't tell me what the plans were. "What are the requirements of this commitment?" I asked.

"No requirements other than we are together," He answered vaguely.

"Will we be dressed casually or dressy?" I probed.

"Classic casual," he answered on the way out the door.

We shared an early anniversary dinner at Gauchos' Restaurant. The waiter paraded an endless supply of succulent meats to our table, slicing from huge hunks, roasted on industrial sized skewers, cooked in churrasco style. We sipped on a full-bodied red wine together, delighting in the tender rump roast, strip loin garnished with fresh garlic and shredded Parmesan, slow roasted baby back ribs, and leg of lamb. The meal was a carnivore's delight that just kept coming and coming, until we finally flipped the poker chip on the table from green to red to indicate that we had had our fill.

The next day, I found new joy in my housework, puttering around organizing our home before the girls returned from LA that night. I changed their sheets, cleared a mountain of laundry from beneath their beds, taking the better part of the afternoon to wash, fold, and put it away. I bit my lip, because I had vowed not to complain about doing laundry the traditional way.

That afternoon, I called Mr. Bowen asking about Ashley's birth certificate. He told me that he would check the Registrar General's Department (RGD) on Friday. He also informed me that he had taken Ashley's file to Kingston and hand delivered it to Ms. Tumming. "If you recall, Ms. Isnor, these things all work concurrently. The birth certificate will come. The file still needs to go to the Adoption Board, and then to court in Montego Bay. We know that you have interest in the child, and the case is proceeding. I brought the file with me myself from Montego Bay."

My heart was beating like a kick drum in my chest when I called Ms. Tummings direct line, and connected on the first try. I wanted to confirm that she had in fact received the file.

"Please spell the name for me."

"P. A. R. K. I. N. S. O. N"

"That name is not familiar to me," said Ms. Tummings.

I informed her that Mr. Bowen had just picked up the file, personally, from Montego Bay. "Once you have the file, what is the normal amount of time before it would go to the adoption board?" I asked.

"Once I have the file it can be turned around in about four weeks," Ms. Tummings replied. I thanked her for her time, wanting to get off the phone before I irritated her.

I'd stayed in Jamaica because I thought that once we turned in all of the paperwork, including the home study, Ashley's file would go straight to Kingston. I expected that it would move through the court immediately, allowing us to assume all responsibility of our daughter.

August rolled into September again, and our kids started another school year. I signed the annual paperwork, and we got into the groove of academic schedules. I focused on preparing school lunches, signing agendas, and attending 'meet the teacher's' night in three different schools.

I continued to make phone calls and send emails to Jamaica all through the fall, having lost any sense of embarrassment for my frequent contacts. I remembered that Maryam said she'd *hounded* them. I called Mr. Bowen every other day. I called Ms. Wilton's cell phone at least once a week, and Ms. O'Connor every Wednesday when she was scheduled to be in Montego Bay. Sending emails to Jamaica were often like posing rhetorical questions. I rarely received responses.

September 14, 2010 2:10 pm

Dear Mr. Bowen,

Thank you so much for confirming that our file to adopt Ashley Parkinson has reached Ms. Tumming. We are truly grateful. I understand that there is a process that must be followed and that our case will soon be seen by the Adoption Board.

Please understand that I have started a thirty-seven week parental leave from my company, so that I can be with Ashley one hundred percent of the time to attach and teach her how to assimilate into our family.

*I am in week two of the allotted time that must be applied for
and approved by our government. I've received parental leave
beginning August thirty-first. It goes through the Government
and cannot be changed.*

*We were very blessed to have spent some of the summer with
Ashley in Jamaica. She is well acquainted with our boys who
will soon be her brothers.*

*I have heard that on rare occasions a visiting permit may
be granted. Is there any possible route to bring Ashley to our
home in Canada until the process is complete?*

*If there is anything at all that you could do to complete the
process for us we would be so grateful.*

Kind regards,
Erika Isnor

On Jonathan's birthday, September twentieth, I phoned and made it
through to Ms. Tummings' direct line. For the first time in days it wasn't
busy. I felt like I'd gotten through on a radio contest, and was waiting to
answer questions for a prize. "Ms. Tumming is not in office. She is off for
a few days and will return on the twenty-third."

September 22, 2010, I called Mr. Bowen dialling the direct number
twice, before making the connection. "Mr. Bowen's office," said a polite
unfamiliar female voice.

"Hello. This is Ms. Isnor from Canada. May I please speak to Mr.
Bowen?"

"Could you hold the line a moment? He is on another call." I waited
until I heard his voice.

"Mr. Bowen speaking."

"Good morning, this is Erika Isnor from Calgary Canada. I am calling
to see if you have obtained Ashley Parkinson's birth certificate."

"Ms. Isnor. I have told you that I have applied to the REG for the
birth certificate."

"Yes, and I am aware that the file is before Ms. Tumming." I said.

"Not Ms. Tumming, the Adoption Board," corrected Mr. Bowen.

"Yes, the Adoption Board," I consented. "I am wondering how long it will take, assuming the 'Adoption Board' grants our approval, for the birth certificate to come?"

"Ms. Isnor, once the file goes to the Adoption Board, it is either approved or disapproved. If it is disapproved, it will be sent back to Montego Bay with the reason why. If it is approved, then it will come to me, and I will apply for the birth certificate. We will need to have photographs taken of the child."

"I have provided passport photos, they are in her file. Can the passport be expedited?"

"It will only take seven days to receive the passport."

"I have learned that it might be possible to get a temporary visitor's visa so that Ashley might be able to be with us in Canada until the process is complete?"

"I don't know about that. I have replied. I will reply to your email as such. It is very unlikely. You would have to go to the High Commission," said Mr. Bowen.

"I have heard that it might be possible to get a letter saying that the adoption application is in process…" I continued.

"People hear what they want to hear," said Mr. Bowen

"Mr. Bowen, my time is ticking. I just want Ashley to be home with us. I want to be her mother."

"I understand Ms. Isnor. You cannot make your anxiety your enemy."

He was right. There was nothing *I* could do, so there must be a higher power in charge. I was never any good at surrendering, but there came a time when I realized that this adoption thing was out of my hands. Initially, I assumed that I was on a course of my own making. The burden lifted when I dropped to my knees and relinquished all control to God.

I learned that it was *never* me that was actually in charge. I realized that God had enabled me, as his instrument; with all the survival tactics I'd picked up in the 'Israel' of my life, to bring Ashley home. I was like a piece of fruit on a tree ripening into maturity.

He set my path straight when I gave it all up to him.

The next morning we attended Sunday services at the First Alliance Church in Calgary. Sid paid a library fine for a book that had accrued one hundred forty days of late fees. I guess that's how long it had been since we'd last attended church services. Our plastic identification cards were still working to check the boys in and out of Sunday school, although we were no longer required to hold pagers because they had gotten older.

I heard Pastor Scott inviting new believers to pick up an information packet at the welcome centre. The book, 'How to Find God,' presented the New Testament; Living water for those who thirst. Its prefix explained how to know God by questioning what was missing in a human heart searching for spiritual contentment.

I couldn't believe the words typed in black and white on the pages before me. "The Bible clearly identifies our serious problem as sin. Sin is not just an act, but also the actual nature of our being. In other words, we are not sinners because we sin. Rather, we sin because we are sinners! We are all born with a nature to do wrong. "For I was born a sinner—yes, from the moment my mother conceived me." Because we are sinners, sinning comes to *all* of us naturally. That is why it is futile to think that the answer to all life's problems comes from 'within.' According to the Bible, the *problem* is within!

God has a dry sense of humor. He brought me to him through the adoption process of a needy child, making me realize that in truth I was the one He saved. "How blessed is God! And what a blessing He is! He is the Father of our Master, Jesus Christ, and takes us to the high places of blessing in him.

Long before he laid down earth's foundations, he had us in mind, had settled on us as the focus of his love, to be made whole by his love. Long, long ago, he decided to adopt us into his family through Jesus Christ. "What *pleasure* he took in planning this. He wanted us to enter into the celebration of his lavish gift-giving by the hand of his beloved Son." (Ephesians 3-6)

September twenty-ninth, I called Mr. Bowen's direct line again, but he was not in office, so I called his cell number. He said, "I cannot talk right now, we are preparing for an emergency. A hurricane..." and the phone went dead.

A tropical storm named 'Nicole' hit Jamaica that day. Winds hammered the island at forty miles per hour. Thursday, September thirtieth, the flooding claimed the lives of two people, with six others still missing and feared dead.

A day later the tropical storm warnings were dropped, but the system continued to dump heavy rain on Jamaica, the Cayman Islands, Cuba, the Bahamas, and southern Florida. Apart from Florida, areas along the coasts of Georgia and the Carolinas in the United States also saw heavy rains and flooding in some areas. There was still a threat of flash flooding and mudslides in the Jamaica. Kingston, St Andrew, and St Catherine on the southeast of the island, and Clarendon were the worst affected parishes.

Floodwaters battered squatter communities that were perched uneasily on the slopes of the gullies that crisscrossed the sprawling capital of Kingston. Emergency shelters were opened for thousands of Jamaicans who lived in tin houses along the gullies. The hospitals treated only the most serious of injuries.

"Don't they have enough problems in Jamaica?" asked Sidney when he learned about the natural atrocities that were happening on the island.

I called to check on the people we knew and cared about in Jamaica. The villa was on high grounds in the hills of Ironshore. Angie, her family, and Avion remained safe, as did Angie's home in Lilliput. Ms. Wilton said that she was unable to make it into Montego Bay because the roads were flooded, but she and her boy were safe. I heard that the roof at Garland Hall had leaked, and there were many landslides on the 'Long Road' leading up to Anchovy. Ashley told me that the TV wasn't working and that she wasn't attending school.

Tropical storm Nicole caused further delays in the adoption process. It took two weeks for business to resume as usual in Kingston.

October sixth I spoke to Ms. Tumming who said she had no plans to look at our file and could not give me a timeline. I phoned Mr. Bowen the same day, but his secretary said he was in a meeting and was not expected to return until one o'clock Jamaican time. I continued dialing his number throughout the day, receiving either a busy signal or an automated message "All circuits are busy now, please try your call again later."

Mr. Bowen answered the phone at two-thirty in the afternoon. "Can you call me back in ten minutes? No, fifteen minutes. Can you call me back in fifteen minutes? I will speak with Ms. Tumming."

"Of course," I replied, wondering if their offices were close enough for them to talk face to face.

I prayed and prayed for God's presence in the conversation between Ms. Tumming and Mr. Bowen. I prayed that God's will be done, that the words that came out of Mr. Bowen's mouth were God's words, that God would not allow Satan in the conversation, that God would move Ashley's file to the top of the stack on Ms. Tummings' desk. I asked the Lord to send Ashley home soon, praying that God would give me continued faith and strength to carry on during the damned 'process.' I prayed that Ashley's file would go to court before her birthday and that I would accept the outcome of the process.

When I called Mr. Bowen back, he reminded me how I must be patient with the process. "The regular process is very specific. You cannot extract a date from me," said Mr. Bowen. I was confused by the change of his tone and demeanor. There seemed to be a discrepancy in the information I was being given.

"You have not yet been matched to Ashley. The regular process is very specific. The mother has not been found, so a question of parental rights remains," he said.

"I was told Ms. Wilton spoke with the mother months ago, and that she had no interest in the child."

Ms. Wilton told me that parental rights had been severed in April. She'd said that she'd helped Ms. O'Connor complete the report stating that we were matched to Ashley. Their report recommended that we be approved for *adoption*."

"The report from Ms. O'Connor only *recommended* you for adoption. I am telling you what I know and what other people are telling you are different. The file goes for review and then returns to court in St. James. The file is in Kingston now. There are two processes that have to happen concurrently," said Mr. Bowen. My stomach dropped as if on a roller coaster plunging downward.

My fingers got busy again.

October 6, 2010

Mr. Bowen,

My understanding is that you see me frustrated by the process and unable to control it. You think the frustration has impeded my perception that the process is moving and in fact working

Are you suggesting that I am so concentrated on understanding the plan of action, that I appear to have little faith? If this is in fact your view, by all means you are correct. I would rather be known as a Christian than a pragmatist.

I do want to make something happen that is out of my hands. I pray constantly for patience and faith to see the process through. I believe that God will bring Ashley home in His time. I just wish it were sooner than later.

Kind regards,
Erika Isnor

Sid went to Houston on a business trip in early October. He phoned me one night shortly before bedtime excited about a purchase he had made. "What was it that you were searching for in the Disney store for Ashley?" he prompted, reminding me that Disney had recently released their first black princess movie.

"You found Tiana's yellow dress from The Princess and the Frog?"

"Yes. Ashley can wear it for Halloween," said Sid.

"What if she isn't home for Halloween?" I asked uncharacteristically.

"She'll be home," said Sid.

"How did you find it? I looked everywhere in Calgary and I couldn't find one."

"Honey, everyone in Houston is black," said Sid.

The gesture was Sid's own way of preparing for his new daughter. What a sweetie! Ashley didn't make it home for Halloween, but her Disney Princess costume hung in her closet waiting for her.

I remained in Calgary on Ashley's eighth birthday. I'd signed up to go as a parent volunteer to go to the Inglewood bird sanctuary with Kaiden's third grade class. While we were there, we spotted a great blue heron perched high in its nest, in the bare branches of a tree. I learned much about that magnificent bird; the most outstanding feature is its environmental presence. The heron is at home in three elements: Water, Earth and Air. It prefers hunting at twilight, which is a symbol of time in-between. The heron will have one foot on land, and one foot in the water, crossing into a space that is neither here nor there.

The comfort I found while looking towards heaven, at the herons nest, reminded me of Psalm 104:17; "The birds of the sky nest by the waters, they sing among the branches."

I quietly thanked the Lord for bringing me to the Inglewood Bird sanctuary where I was surrounded by His 'splendor and majesty.' I imagined I heard the beating of angel wings over my head, replenishing my soul with a calm sense of peace and patience. I was neither in Jamaica nor Canada, but being in the present where God intended me to be, looking up at one of His creatures. I sensed a growing willingness to accept the series of actions that needed to happen before Ashley could come home.

Kaiden and I also saw several semi-aquatic muskrats busily building their winter lodging. Kaiden held my hand as we walked along the trail together in the brisk morning air, "I'm sorry you could not be in hot Jamaica with Ashley today, but I am glad that you are here," he said.

"I am glad that I am here with you."

My parental leave began August 31, 2010. Twelve weeks had passed, and still I had no child in my care. I hadn't yet to fill out the employment insurance form, to receive benefits, because of the uncertainty of the Jamaican process. In the meantime, I did not receive any sort of paycheck.

On October fourteenth, I got down on my knees before calling Ms. Tumming. I prayed that the phone line would connect, and that the Holy Spirit would be all through me as I spoke to her. I prayed that God's word, and will, would come out of my mouth to bring Ashley home as quickly as *He* pleased.

Ms. Tumming answered the phone right away. I said who I was and where I was from. Ms. Tumming said that she was reviewing our file, and asked for my home phone number to call me back. She asked how old my two boys were. I answered, reminding her that we also had two girls at home. Ms. Tumming said we had a lot of children, and questioned why we wanted another. I described how we fell in love with Ashley, and that we wanted the Jamaican culture in our home.

"You will need someone to teach you how to do her hair. All you need to do is a weave," she said.

"I love Ashley's hair. I've practiced on it quite a bit." I said.

"It sounds like you are on the right track," she said. "I will work on the file and call you."

PRAISE GOD. PRAISE GOD. PRAISE GOD.

I spoke with Mr. Bowen on the sixteenth of October, reminding him that I needed the court order before the end of the month. He "expected it to be done in two weeks…or month." We remained cautiously optimistic.

God had been working on me. I became grateful for how long the process was taking, thankful that God had not given up on me.

On October nineteenth, I called Ms. Tumming again. "Good morning, how are you?" I asked.

"I am fine, we are in a meeting. We are recommending an adoption approval for your case, it will be sent back to the St. James Parish to go to court." said Ms. Tumming abruptly.

"Thank you very much, and have a beautiful day," I muttered.

I received Mr. Bowen's response to an email I'd almost forgotten I'd sent earlier in the month. It arrived October 29, 2010 at 9:39 am, one week *after* I'd spoken with Ms.Tumming. It was my impression that the Internet was *instantaneous*…apparently not from Jamaica!

Dear Ms. Isnor

I refer to your memorandum dated 6th October 2010, and on subsequent telephone conversations regarding the proposed adoption of Ashley who is presently at the Garland Hall Residential Child Care Facility.

*You will recall that I informed you that your application has
been submitted to the Adoption Coordinator, Ms. Marjorie
Tumming who will now review and advise accordingly.*

*I understand your anxiety to have this application concluded
but you will also recall that I have repeatedly advised you by
telephone that all cases must go through a process and this is
the situation with respect to Ashley's case.*

*Please be assured that your application is receiving the
appropriate alternatives and you will be informed once a
decision has been made.*

All the best in your endeavours.

*Winston Bowen
Director of Programs
WB*cc*

We continued living life as usual as much as possible. I stayed home
for Canadian Thanksgiving, Ashley's eighth birthday, and Sidney's tenth
birthday. We celebrated Sidney's ten years by having a traditional pizza and
movie party. Kaiden invited his friends too, because he'd missed having a
party in July. Twelve boys, and one girl, watched The Diary of a Wimpy
Kid together, devouring pizza, slurping root beer, and spilling popcorn
on the floor of our basement. We sang 'Happy Birthday' and fed them
homemade carrot cake before sending them all home on a sugar high. It
felt good to be home doing normal stuff.

Monday, November first, I called Ms. Wilton. "I have very *very* good
news! I will call you back in five minutes," she said.

I learned that Ms. Wilton had received permission to go to the REG
to file a late registration of birth for Ashley.

"How long will that take?" I asked.

"Two weeks," she replied.

Mr. Bowen had explicitly told me that he'd filed for Ashley's birth
certificate fifteen weeks ago. It didn't make much sense.

I spoke with Ms. Wilton again on November fourth. She'd not gone to the REG because she had not yet received the money to do so. "Maybe Friday. We are expecting to get a package from Kingston on Friday," she said.

November fifth Jamaica was hit by yet another hurricane. Tropical storm 'Tomas' threatened the Caribbean the entire first week of November. The eastern parishes received the bulk of the damage; "Because of the conditions of a tropical storm all businesses and Government entities in the parishes of Kingston and St. Andrew, St. Thomas, Portland and St Mary initiated twelve to twenty-four hour pre-impact activities, thus shutting down the operation for non essential workers."

Hurricane Tomas narrowly missed the island of Jamaica. It had been a tropical storm, but was upgraded to a hurricane in the early hours that Friday morning. Go figure.

I called Mr. Bowens office the next Monday, but he was not available. I asked his secretary, Ms. Johnson, how the island fared with the weather, "The sun was out," she said optimistically.

I spoke to receptionist at the CDA in Montego Bay, "No one is in office now based on the weather." It was raining hard in Montego Bay.

The connection was filled with static when I reached Ms. Wilton, but I heard her promise to speak to Mr. Green when he arrived at the office in the morning. "I'll have him speak to Mr. Bowen and see if something can be done."

The family assembled in the living room and spoke to Ashley before she went to court. The kids each grabbed a cordless phone so we that could all give her words of encouragement preparing her. "Ashley, the paperwork is done," I said.

"The paperwork is done?" I could hear the excitement swell in her voice.

"Yes, baby. You will need to go to court," I said. I didn't know what that meant to Ashley. I didn't know if she'd gone to court before, and if she had... what the circumstances might have been. I didn't want her to be afraid. "Going to court is a *good thing*. I get to bring you home after court," I said.

"How many days before I go to court?" asked Ashley.

"Four days baby," I could hear her reciting the days of the week under her breath.

"I go to court on Wednesday?"

"Yes." Our conversation was short and to the point.

Ashley asked for some 'red slippers,' (slippers in Jamaica are flip flops) before saying "bye."

A church group was at Garland Hall that day planning on taking the girls to Aqua Sol, and then the beach in Mobay. I was glad that Ashley would be outside and near the water.

Ashley Parkinson went to court on Wednesday, November 17, 2010. Ms. Woodit, the housemother from Garland Hall, chartered a taxi for her. She rode to the family court on 4 Kerr Crescent all by herself. I spoke with Ashley that morning, when she was waiting in Ms. Wilton's cubicle. She didn't say much to me on the phone, but I heard she was wearing a wide toothless grin on her face. Blessed Ms. Wilton kept Ashley with her for most of the day, eating lunch together before the proceedings. After court, Ashley returned to Garland Hall, alone, in another chartered taxi.

I spoke with Ashley again the following Saturday to ask how court went.

"They dint axe mi notin!" she complained. I nearly wet up myself laughing. I imagined her sitting alone on a bench dressed in Capri pants and a plain white cotton t-shirt, waiting to tell the judge how much she wanted to be with her 'white brudder's' and the mommy who 'reads mi stories all da time.'

All in all, it was a rather uneventful day the next week when Judge R. Feurtado Toby approved "a license, under section 24 of the Adoption of Children Act, to authorize the care and possession of 'Ashley Parkinson,' a child 8 years old, born as far as can be ascertained, on the 13th day of October 2002, to be transferred to Mr. Sidney James Isnor and Mrs. Erika Isnor, citizens of a Scheduled Country, resident outside the Island."

The judge decreed, "WHEREAS I, the undersigned, have heard the said application and am satisfied by the report of Amanda S. that the aforesaid are suitable persons to be entrusted with the care and possession of the said child and that the transfer is likely to be for the welfare of the said child."

Five specific conditions and restrictions were included in the order.

- The applicants "will fetch the adoptee Ashley Parkinson to Canada at their own expense."
- We were to contact Christian Adoptions "within two (2) weeks of the child joining the adopters abroad."
- We were required to have our social worker "supervise the placement of Ashley Parkinson until the completion of the Adoption within two (2) years."
- Written reports were to be submitted "every six (6) weeks during the first three (3) months and thereafter every three (3) months until the adoption is completed."
- "In the event that there is a disruption in the home prior to the completion of the adoption, the Adoption Board is to be notified immediately so that suitable alternative placement of the child can be considered with the approval of the Adoption Board, failing this, the child is to be returned to Jamaica forthwith." *Over my dead body!*

The 'License to Adopt' order was issued on October 22, 2010.

FOURTEEN

KINGSTON

My Mother and I were shopping at the Christmas Store in Banff when I received the phone call from Ms. Palmer at the CDA, notifying me of the Jamaican court's decision to approve our application to adopt Ashley Ashanti Parkinson. I danced puppy circles around the store among the Christmas ornaments. I bought a trinket that day commemorating the monumental event, an angel on her knees holding a choir book. The angel was black.

I reached out several times via email to Kristi B., the mother of Matthew, another child successfully adopted from Blossom Gardens. I told her where we were in the process and that I had so very many questions about what to expect. I hoped to learn from the experience of others.

October 23, 2010 9:15 am

Dear Erika

I am so very Happy for you! (Insert hug) It should go very quickly for you now. We had court within a few days of Mrs. Tumming's approval. Yeah!

Kristi

October 25, 3010 9:15 pm

We had court the first week in December and we brought him home January 7[h].

We had to apply for the birth certificate; they still have never given me a copy of the original. The passport we did in Kingston in December, when we were picking him up. Mr. Bowen can help you with this.

We went to Kingston several times. I would suggest just staying there for a week or so. We spent a fortune on a driver, but we were safe! Anything is possible. Did they give you a date for court? It is all up to immigration.

They tell you 7-90 days to process the approval, but she did ours in an hour. God can do anything! We just celebrated Matthew's first birthday with us. He was so happy. He is adjusting slowly. We have a lot of catch up work to do. We could use some prayer for that. Thanks and you will be in our prayers.

Kristi

Ironically, when Mr. Bowen finally received the birth certificate several weeks later, we discovered that the child we were adopting had an altogether different name. This child was born at the Public General Hospital in Savanna-la-mar, Westmoreland; not Cornwall Hospital in Montego Bay. The birth certificate stated that the child's name was, in fact, Ashley Ashanti Farquharson. The reason for the discrepancy was explained this way; "When Ashley arrived at Blossom Gardens, we misunderstood when the child said her last name was 'Parkinson.' Parkinson is a fairly common Jamaican surname. A 'P,' from a child's mouth sounds much like an 'F.'"

The 'License to Adopt' Ashley Parkinson had to go back to court and be legally changed to Ashley Farquharson before a proper passport or visa could be issued.

I believe the reason it took so long to produce a birth certificate was because Ashley was never registered when she was born. Yet, the document the Jamaican Authorities provided states it was recorded November 27, 2002. I can't help but wonder why it never showed up in any of the statistical searches.

Once we received the official 'License to Adopt,' I went to the passport office in Calgary at the Harry Hays building, hoping to get Ashley a Canadian passport and bypassing the need for a visa from the Jamaican government. We were told we needed proof of Canadian citizenship to process a passport. How I hated that word process.

Sid faxed the order of the court for me to Ann S. in Edmonton, expecting to receive the coveted 'Letter of No objection,' required by Immigration Canada to bring Ashley home. We received an email from Ann S. almost immediately.

November 29, 2009

Dear Mr. James [?] and Ms. Isnor,

Thank you for the documentation you faxed to my office. Children and Youth Services requires a copy of the Adoption Order finalized in the country of origin to issue a Letter of No Involvement for privately arranged adoptions. As you have provided a 'Form of License' and not an 'Adoption Order,' please deal directly with Citizenship and Immigration Canada to obtain permanent residency status to admit Ashley to Canada.

Sincerely,
Ann S.
Senior Manager
Adoption and Permanency Services

I refused to believe that we had run into a dead end. There had to be a way to navigate the damned triangle. If the Internet can make communication happen in an instant, why didn't these Government entities talk to each other? The bureaucrats, officials who work by fixed routine without exercising intelligent judgment, blatantly ignored the human element in uniting orphans with forever families. The archaic system has prospective adoptive parents crying out for an immediate reform in the present system.

In Canada, there is a toll-free call center (1-888-242-2100) that can be accessed to answer questions, in English and French about Citizenship and Immigration services and programs.

The automated telephone service is available twenty-four hours a day seven-days-a-week. If you have a touch-tone telephone you can listen to prerecorded information about programs, order application kits, and check the status of your application.

Call center agents are available Monday through Friday, from 8 am to 4 pm, except for statutory holidays. "Agents cannot answer questions about the status of your application once it is sent to a Canadian visa office outside Canada, make decisions on applications or help process applications more quickly." So what *can* they do?

I got really good at pushing buttons to speak to a real live human being. I navigated through the automated messages by pressing 3-4-1-0 without listening to the instructions. We'd listed my husband as the primary person on the 'Application to Sponsor and Undertaking form,' so half the time I would get an agent who would not talk to me because they did not have record of having received the 'Use of Representative' form. (IMM5476)

Often, I hung up and redialed to get a different agent who might speak with me. There was no consistency. I learned to carry signed, notarized originals whenever I visited a Government agency, either in Canadian or abroad. Only one person can be listed as a primary sponsor, and I was not yet a Canadian Citizen, so even though I did the lion's share of the paperwork, and we were married, Sid had to be the sponsor to allow his wife to speak on his behalf.

Eventually, I received a Fax number from officer 'ML' empathizing with our plight. I bombarded that Fax machine in Mississauga, Ontario hoping to connect with anyone who might help us.

Subject: URGENT IMPENDING ADOPTION

Good afternoon,
We are adopting Ashley Farquharson, born October 13,
2002

We have a court order for the 'license to adopt,' her birth
certificate, and the passport is being expedited.

Our 'Application to Sponsor a Family Member' was sent
to the High Commission 24 June 2009. At that point our
daughter was not named. Our client # is XXXXXXXX.
The Kit ID# is XXXXXXXXXXX

We have arranged a medical with Dr. Charles Hastings in
Montego Bay of Dome Street next Monday 10 am.

Please confirm that we have provided all necessary/correct
documents. Please advise hours of operation. Do we require
an appointment?

I will most certainly be available any necessary time. I hope
to arrive on the island Sunday. Ashley has her visa medical
apt. 13th, Monday 10 am (but can come sooner depending
on your availability)

Kind regards,
Erika Isnor

I left Calgary alone on Sunday the twelfth of December, after booking an appointment for Ashley's immigration medical at 10 am on Monday, in Montego Bay. I remembered that Daniel went home a little over a week after his doctor's appointment at Rose Hall, so we were excited that things finally seemed to be coming to a close.

I planned on taking the bus to Kingston. According to the 'Sponsorship of a Family Member' form provided by Immigration Canada, we were required to apply for Ashley's visa *in* Kingston. Kristy B. from Washington, said they got Matthew's visa from the US embassy in an hour. The Knutsford Express left Montego Bay at five in the morning, to arrive before nine o'clock. Maybe we could be on a plane heading back to Canada the next day.

Flight routes from Calgary had changed since I'd been to Jamaica in August. I could get to Montego Bay through Saskatoon in the afternoon, transfer to the red-eye, and arrive in Montego Bay the next morning in time for Ashley's medical appointment. I planned on sleeping on a bench in the airport terminal during the five-hour layover, but another flight attendant offered an alternative.

My airline has created a culture of people unique in the airline industry. We are a tight-knit network of people that act like a family. I sat next to a fellow flight attendant, Ann Marie, on that first flight. She was deadheading from Calgary to operate a flight out of Saskatoon the next day. I mentioned my plans to nap in the airport during my layover, but Ann Marie would have none of it. She insisted I take the crew van to the hotel, where we could share a meal, have a drink, and I could take a shower in her room, if I wished. We joined another crew at the hotel lounge where time passed more quickly and comfortably than if I'd been on a bench in the terminal.

Afterwards, I rode the crew van back to the airport in plenty of time to go through security. I slept soundly in the window seat at row twenty-three, arriving in Jamaica at six-thirty the next morning. Ironically, we landed early because of the tailwinds pushing the plane, despite departing an hour late.

Two immigration officers processed the line of people, meaning that we moved twice as slow through customs. A third officer stood at the beginning of the line, inspecting each immigration form before directing its owner either forward, or back to the raised tables to complete the document in its entirety. I boldly asked if I could join the Jamaican line where Caribic people bypassed the tourists. "We are adopting a girl who has an immigration medical scheduled at 10 am."

"Where is the girl?" asked the officer.

"In Anchovy," I replied hopefully.

"You have plenty of time."

I'd left Canada so quickly that I hadn't arranged for transportation for when I arrived in Mobay, but I knew it wouldn't be difficult to find a new taxi driver at the airport. A man named Rodney agreed to drive me from Sangster International to the Caribic House for ten US dollars, where I asked him to wait outside while I inquired about a room. Luckily, I was able to register and leave the beast bag at the hotel. Then, Rodney and I agreed I would pay him additional thirty-dollar US for him to take me to Anchovy, collect Ashley, and get her to the downtown core for her doctor's appointment. He felt fortunate to secure my forty US dollars at the beginning of his shift. He'd caught his dinner; the rest of the day's income would be gravy for his supper.

I phoned Ms. Woodit on the drive up Long Hill to remind her that I was on my way. Ashley was shinned and ready to leave, with her hair creamed in soft curls when Rodney pulled up to the white iron gates. She looked pretty and *happy;* I could have sworn Ashley had grown another inch since I'd seen her last. She seemed to understand that mommy had come to take her home

Sid insisted on picking up thirty milk chocolate covered marshmallow snowman suckers when he took me to the airport. He wanted me to give the treats to the children we would be leaving behind. Ms. Woodit's compound housed nineteen girls, ten boys, and six workers. I placed the suckers inside a brown paper gift bag surrounded by burgundy tissue paper, tying a lovely crepe ribbon to the handle of the bag.

Ashley arrived thirty minutes early for her immigration medical at Dr. Charles Hasting's office. We filled out the new patient information forms, provided two passport-sized photographs and a copy of her beloved birth certificate before the nurse escorted us in to see the Doctor. I could only make an educated guess answering the questions on the form. "Did the child walk before eighteen months? Did the child connect more than three words together by the age of three? How many alcoholic drinks does the person consume in one day?" Obviously, the form was intended for a wide range of ages.

Dr. Hasting's was one of three professionals on the island approved to provide the required medical. He startled both Ashley and me when he bounced into the examination room, entertaining the two of us with his peculiar mannerisms and expressions. His complexion was fair with very little pigment, making it difficult to discern his nationality. His eyes were crossed, and he moved in a quick staccato fashion. I thought he looked quite like a rat whose face was pointed to exaggeration. He paid meticulous attention to detail while filling out the form, swaying back and forth between inspecting the form and sticking his nose in my face. The Doctor kept leaning in towards me, pointing with his index finger to emphasize his opinion. I had a hard time keeping a straight face, and Ashley flat out laughed in nervousness. Ashley got impatient and wriggled around during Dr. Hastings inspection of her.

The Doctor described the path that the paperwork would follow once it left his office. It would be picked up on Thursday, sent to Kingston, forwarded to Trinidad, where it might be returned to him for clarification over the smallest detail before being returned to Kingston and attached to Ashley's file. I felt like we were trapped in that observation room, until the nurse finally came in to announce the arrival of his next patient.

We left the medical center after paying the fee of $4,000 JMD. It was barely eleven o'clock in the morning, and I'd already spent over eighty US dollars. We walked down Dome Street towards the old water tower where we flagged a Mount Salem, red-plated taxi, to take us to the CDA. We needed to pick up the revised guardianship order before attaching it to Ashley's visa application. The two caseworkers, Ms. Wilton and Ms. Bradford, were on their way out the door for lunch when we walked into the CDA. Ms. Wilton actually laughed out loud when she saw us, "Ms. Isnor, you are a *persistent* woman!"

Ms. Wilton offered to drive us around town to take care of some last minute errands in Montego Bay. We found a photographer who provided a one-hour service for Ashley's permanent resident photos, I topped up minutes on my Digicel phone, and then we ordered patties at the Tastee drive though. I devoured the spicy chicken tenders in under a minute because I hadn't eaten since the previous afternoon. Ms. Wilton saved me a ton of time and money that I would have had to spend on taxis.

When Ms. Wilton dropped us off at the Caribic House that afternoon, I explained our plans to take the Knutsford Express up to Kingston early the next day, hoping to apply for a temporary visiting visa, so that Ashley might be able to come home for Christmas. "I believe you will get the visiting visa," said Ms. Wilton. "With your *will*....you will get the visa!"

"You are a *persistent* woman," Ms. Bradford agreed.

I promised to keep in touch with them when they left us.

I'd arranged for the driver, Rodney, to pick us up at four-thirty in the morning to get to the bus at Pier One. Ashley and I climbed the stairs up to room number eight to get some sleep anticipating a long day ahead of us.

I woke up several times during the night looking at the clock on the rickety nightstand. At three-twenty I finally decided to get up and get dressed, afraid that if I'd gone back to sleep again we would have missed the bus. I showered and packed the small red roller-bag with an extra set of clothes and jammies for each of us. I brought toiletries and my make up, just in case, figuring that if we were prepared, we might not need to spend the night in Kingston. We left the *beast* alone in our room at the Caribic House.

The very thought of Kingston frightened me. Kingston, the capital of Jamaica, carried a rough reputation. I pictured it much like New York City, only worse. That spring, much publicity surfaced about the Jamaican Juan who the United States wanted extradited for drug charges. I'd heard two sides of the story; on the one hand, the man sold drugs and guns which killed people and devastated families. On the other hand, the Juan provided jobs for people in construction, built infrastructure, and fed families. The Jamaican economy relied on that bad man, crack man, Juan.

The ride to Kingston weaved through St Anne's and St Katherine's, two of the most beautiful parishes on the island. The bus honked its horn around each harrowing corner of the narrow road. The rhythmic movement of the bus lulled me to sleep despite my determination to look out the window. Ashley rested on my lap, keeping me warm, wearing a pink gap sweat suit with another 'All We Need Is Love' shirt strategically placed beneath her jacket. The ride continued through Spanish Town, and then rolled into the bus station before Mr. Bowen had even arrived at his office.

I'd taken the accordion file with the adoption papers out of the red rollie-bag, which was put under the bus as checked luggage. I was afraid the bag might accidently be taken off in Ochos Rios, or worse yet stolen. I'd put our adoption paperwork in the overhead compartment of the bus when we boarded, and left it there when we got off the bus. It was only when we were freshening up in women's room that I remembered the documents. We *ran* back to the bus to retrieve the papers.

I called Mr. Bowen when we got to Kington, first trying to reach him at the office, and then on his cell phone. I listened to the operator telling me to "enjoy the bling" to the sound of Jamaican music. Mr. Bowen was not pleased to learn that we were in Kingston, telling me that the letter of authorization had not been prepared, and that the passport was not due until Tuesday, or perhaps Wednesday. He said to call him once I'd left the Canadian Embassy, reiterating that he had planned to go to the country before two o'clock that afternoon.

Ashley and I hailed a local cab driver named 'Mosquito,' to take us to the Canadian High Commission. Mr. Bowen had said "it was not too far and should not cost more than $300 JMD." Mosquito handed me his card when we got out of the cab, suggesting I call him for a ride when we were finished with our business.

I'd fastidiously prepared several copies of each paper, placing each item alphabetically in my red accordion portable file case, including five of the original IMM746 forms. Sid had already faxed officer ML the form in Mississauga, but I never relied on electronic communication to the Government.

We had to pass through a metal detector to get inside the embassy where the security officer asked me what the purpose of our visit was. I stated my intention to turn in Ashley's application for 'Permanent Residence,' for a child to be adopted abroad. He insisted that the application be assembled in a specific order before allowing us to enter the building.

The inside of the embassy appeared clean and orderly. It felt as though I'd gone through a tunnel into an entirely different country, but the receptionist still looked decidedly Jamaican. I passed my plethora of paperwork through the metal drawer for her inspection. We'd stood waiting in line, well over two hours, for the privilege of applying for Ashly's travel visa. I mentioned the name of the officer that I had been conversing with via email. And then, Ashley and I were asked to sit, and wait some more, while they contacted her.

Ashley's behavior was hideous. She was unable to sit still for a single moment. She wasn't interested in the Christmas program on the overhead TV, and my patience utterly abandoned me, yet we continued to wait. The line of people dwindled and disappeared. People were only allowed to enter the embassy until ten am, and it was approaching lunchtime, but still we waited.

I was called to the protected teller window and told that the paperwork in my hands needed to be turned in at Mississauga, Canada *not Kingston*. My eyes burned, I thought I would snap. "In Mississauga?" I asked. "It was explained to me that I was required to turn in the paperwork in *Kingston*. No wonder the teller's window required a protective barrier!

I showed the receptionist the letter I'd received, specifically stating that the "Details of your application have been forwarded to the following Visa Office…The acceptance of your 'Application to Sponsor a Member of the Family Class' establishes that you are qualified to submit a sponsorship. However it has no validity under law until an application is *submitted abroad*."

The receptionist reiterated that I needed to take the paperwork back to Canada and submit it to Mississauga.

My email contact in Jamaica had suggested that I apply for a 'visiting visa' to take Ashley home. She said that I would need a letter from Mr. Bowen allowing me to take Ashley out of the county, a copy of our 'License to Adopt' and a round trip airline ticket proving that we intended to return to Jamaica with Ashley.

We left the Canadian High Commission at noon. I called Mosquito to take us to 48 Duke Street, the head office of the Children's Development Agency. I smiled, remembering Kaiden's reaction when I told him his mother had to go to the CDA. "The Childhood Detection Agency from Monsters Inc?" he'd questioned.

"Mr. Bowen is expecting us," I said, as we checked in with receptionist at the CDA, on the main floor of the building." She phoned his office before directing us towards the elevator to get to the second floor.

Ashley had only ever been in an elevator once before, when we were searching for an apartment. Her eyes grew big and round. She grabbed onto my hand when the wobbly metal box we'd entered lurched to a sudden stop. We stepped out into a hallway that let to a locked glass door, where we were buzzed us inside to meet Mr. Winston Bowen.

Mr. Bowen shook my hand politely, but he was miffed. "You have *agitated* me Ms. Isnor," he said. I got the impression it took a lot to agitate Mr. Bowen. "I told you, Ms. Isnor not to come until I received the passport."

"Yes, Mr. Bowen, but you also told me that you expected to receive the passport either Tuesday or Wednesday of this week. This *is* Tuesday. I also needed to turn in the immigration papers at the Canadian High Commission in Kingston."

"And what did they tell you Ms. Isnor?"

"They would not take the papers from me. They told me that they needed to be turned in in Canada. They also told me that I might be able to apply for a 'Temporary Visiting Visa' to get Ashley home. I require a letter from you allowing me to take Ashley out of the country."

"Yes, but Ms. Isnor that letter is not ready. It will not be ready until tomorrow," said Mr. Bowen.

"All right then. I will take the bus back to Montego Bay tonight and get back on the bus in the morning to come back and pick it up."

"You would do that Ms. Isnor?"

"Whatever it takes Mr. Bowen." Our eyes locked. I wanted him to know that I would submit to any legal condition imposed upon me to get Ashley home. When Mr. Bowen picked up the telephone, and asked his secretary to type a letter for him, I heaved a huge sigh of relief. And then, Ashley and I sat waiting in Mr. Bowen's office, as the letter to the Canadian Embassy was prepared for us.

December 14, 2010

The High Commission
The Canadian High Commission
3 West Kings House Road
Kingston 10

RE: Ashley Ashanti Farquharson
Born: 13th October 2002
F.P.O 25th November 2009

This is to certify that Ashley Ashanti Farquharson was made the subject of a 'Fit Person Order' in the St. James/Hanover/

Westmoreland Family court on 26th March 2009, after she was deemed to be in need of Care and Protection.

She is now being accommodated at the Garland Hall Children's Home, Anchovy St James, and a licence has been granted for her transfer to Canada for the adoption by Mr. and Mrs. Sidney Isnor.

Mr. and Mrs. Isnor have indicated the desire to have Ashley spend thirty days vacation in Canada with the understanding that she will be returning to Jamaica for the processing of application for residency in Canada.

I Winston Bowen, Director of Programmes Child Development Agency, state that by provision of the 'Fit Person,' I am the legal guardian of Ashley Ashanti Farquharson.

I hereby give permission for Ashley to leave the island with Mrs. Isnor and I ask that favorable condition be given to granting her a visitor's visa to enter Canada.

Yours Truly,
Winston Bowen
Director of Programmes

Mr. Bowen's agitation dissipated as money squandered sometimes does. He became the 'Grandfatherly' persona Maryam had described to me months earlier, allowing me use his computer to print off the itinerary for the required round trip airline ticket that Sid bought for Ashley, as proof of our intention to bring her back to Jamaica.

Mr. Bowen continued moving through his workday. He answered phone calls on both his cell phone and the CDA line, forging forward like a worker bee carrying out specific specialized tasks. Wendy Robinson was right. It was obvious that this kind, elderly man cared immensely for the underprivileged members of his society. Mr. Bowen asked what my plans were for the remainder of the day when he handed me the letter.

"I will wait for Ashley's passport and try to return to the Canadian High Commission to apply for a visiting visa," I said.

"Will you stay in Kingston?" he asked.

"If I need to," I said. "Do you have a suggestion of a safe, cheap place to stay?" Mr. Bowen asked his pool of secretaries to do the research for me. They came up with the Medallion Hall, which was close to the Canadian Embassy. The rate would be seventy US dollars for the night.

"The passport *should* be here by two o'clock," said Mr. Bowen "but don't come back until two-thirty. What are you going to do now?" he asked. I hadn't eaten yet, and Ashley only had a bun and a piece of cheese for breakfast.

"Where is the best place to get lunch?" I asked.

"There is a restaurant downstairs. It is not the *best*, but it will suffice," said Mr. Bowen. He told me not to expect to see him when we returned; he was "leaving for the country."

"Where?" I asked.

"St. Anne's," he replied. We had rolled through the luscious country in the bus on the way to Kingston, seeing herds of cows grazing in green fields. The country looked far more inviting that the touristy cities that were familiar to me. I thanked Mr. Bowen for helping me through the difficult process before we left for lunch.

Ashley and I turned left out the front doors of the CDA, walking down Duke Street, towards the sea on the horizon. I'd been told there was a Scotiabank where I could pay the fee for Ashley's visiting visa, and that the bank would provide proof of payment to take back to the Canadian High Commission. We walked hand in hand, cautious, but not fearful of the dreaded city.

We ate rice and peas, and shared chicken out of a Styrofoam container before returning to the CDA at 2:30 in the afternoon. Ashley's passport had not arrived, and Mr. Bowen had not left for the country. Mr. Bowen allowed us to continue waiting in the boardroom where Ashley could finally move around. I tore some pages out of my green journal for her to draw on, giving her something to do.

One of the secretaries' sons stopped by the CDA office after school. Ashley and I showed him the artificial snow I'd brought from Canada. I poured a bit of the dehydrated white powder into the boy's hand, added some cold water, and then watched his face as the mixture expanded into cold 'snow.' I told him to keep the substance in a cup where it would dry out, so that he could repeat the process whenever he wanted to. He said he was going to take the snow to his school on Thursday for show and tell.

Mr. Bowen was heading towards the elevator, presumably towards the country, with his briefcase in hand at three-thirty. He stopped at the boardroom on his way out to ask me if I had met Ms. Tumming. When I shook my head, he motioned for Ashley and me to follow him into the elevator, down to the first floor, where we would find her.

I'd pictured Ms. Tumming looking like the Ursula character from the Little Mermaid Disney movie, but she was not at all as I'd imagined. We found her sitting at a desk in a disheveled office, surrounded by packed boxes, and stacks of books that were pushed away from all of the walls, because her office was being painted. Stacks of legal-sized manilla envelope files covered her desk.

I'd expected an obese slovenly woman. Instead, I found a smiling, soft, even kindly person, who cautioned me to exercise patience with Ashley. "These children have lived in different environments where they may not have had running water, or a table to sit down to for a meal. You must be patient and not expect Ashley to immediately conform to your expectations."

I thanked Ms. Tumming for our gift, Ashley, promising to provide the reports from our social worker and to keep in touch. I noticed a dozen photographs of children of various ages taped to the drywall in her office. "Those are some of the children that have been adopted," she said. I made a mental note to send a picture of Ashley to Ms. Tumming for her wall. "This is a long and hard process," she said. "People must not begin the process if they are not willing to be patient with it."

Thank God we were nearing the end of the damned 'Process.'

The mother of the boy I'd given snow handed me Ashley's passport at a quarter before four that afternoon. It was too late to go back to the embassy, so we took a wild cab ride to the recommended hotel. I paid for a single night's accommodations before Ashley and I walked across the street to go to Friday's for nachos. We were both exhausted from the day's journeys. We retired after our super, hopeful that the next day would provide a visa to take Ashley home for Christmas.

We returned to the Canadian High Commission before eight-thirty the next morning, carrying the required documents which were neatly assembled together in the proper order. We entered the Embassy immediately, joining a queue of people waiting for a single intake worker.

Ashley's behavior had improved significantly since a discussion at dinner the night before. She sat pleasantly in a chair reading her Dick and Jane primer making my mother heart swell with pride. Now and then, she would indiscriminately ask the person closest to her what an unfamiliar word was. I could see the importance of implementing boundaries, but never expected the relentless repetitions that would be needed to do so.

When it was my turn, the intake worker said I needed a DHL delivery envelope to proceed. "Get the envelope and return if you can before ten am, or come back tomorrow." Tomorrow? *Was this the Land of Oz?* It was already 9:32! We rushed out of the building like contestants on the Amazing Race searching for a cab. I asked the security guard, with the four-inch scar across his cheek, where the DHL office was and how to get there. "The man outside the gates wearing the shirt that says "Cricket" is a taxi driver, he will take you there and back for about seven hundred JMD."

We walked out the gates through a half dozen taxi drivers competing for our fare. I looked for the man with the cricket shirt. "Will you take me to the DHL office and be back here before ten o'clock? I can pay you six hundred JMD," I said. He nodded and Ashley and I jumped into his cab.

The Cricket man made a beeline to the DHL office bypassing traffic in the centre lane. We arrived there at 9:37, filled out the waybill, paid the fee of $900 JMD, and returned to the Embassy with three minutes to spare. The same people were still standing in line, exactly where we had left them, they hadn't moved an inch.

It took three minutes to turn in Ashley's application for a visiting visa, the Scotiabank receipt, two passport pictures, and her Jamaican passport. I was told that *if* the Canadian High Commission happened to accept a passport, one was likely to receive a visiting visa within five-to-seven business days. The receptionist asked me when we intended to travel.

"Yesterday, actually," I answered.

"Well since that option is out, what is the next intended date of travel?" she asked with only a hint of a smile.

"This coming Saturday?"

"What about next Wednesday?" she asked.

"Is that the soonest?" I asked. The receptionist nodded.

"Wednesday it is," I said knowing that my husband was going to blow a gasket. I was back in Jamaica, staying another indeterminable amount of time away from home and family during the Christmas holiday. I was beginning to hate Jamaica. I wanted to get out of the country like a bad marriage.

We left the Embassy again at high noon. The cricket taxi man was still standing on the sidewalk. I asked him to take us to the Knutsford Express bus station, where we would take what Ashley called 'the big bus' back into Montego Bay. Ashley slept most of the way home. I made her get up in Ochos Rios to go potty, knowing that she had a bladder the size of a peanut. We ate whole-wheat buns, and triangular shaped pieces of yellow cheese for dinner.

When I called the Caribic House from Ochos Rios, Natalie the receptionist, sounded relieved to hear from me. I'd told her about our trip Kingston, and the possibility of having to stay overnight when we registered at the hotel. During our conversation, Natalie confirmed that we could stay at the Caribic House until we received the DHL package containing Ashley's visa.

Seven days later, I looked up the DHL tracking number online. The envelope had been picked up at 1:39 that afternoon, leaving Kingston at 3:37 the same day. Ashley and I jumped up and down expecting to be on the plane the next morning.

That night, Bibsey braided Ashley's hair with pink and purple beads. Ashley sat with the patience of Job for nearly two hours during the process. I gladly paid $2,000 JMD to get her hair done properly, hoping it would last until I found someone in Calgary to help me learn how to manage her unruly mop.

We showered, packed, and set out our travelling clothes for the next morning. We ate dinner at the Jamaican Bobsled where everyone was ecstatic that Ashley was finally going home. Then, we retired early again, expecting a long emotional homecoming day on Saturday December sixteenth.

I woke up at two o'clock in the morning like a child hoping to see Santa Claus, with my stomach hurting from the excitement. And then, I heard the long screeching sounds of a car's brakes. Metal clashed together, and the sky lit up like the night of our white lightening storm. I knew it was terrible. I heard voices converging at the crash site. A woman screamed. I jumped out of bed thinking of the Christmas poem "When out on the lawn there arose such a clatter. I sprang from the bed to see what was the matter. Away to the window I flew like a flash…"

I grabbed the red travel blanket and threw it over my nighty. People were spilling out of all the rooms in their nightclothes. I picked up the keys and locked my sleeping Ashley inside room number eight. Everyone in the hotel went to the long street side balcony where we could see the remains of three cars. One had overturned, and its wheels were pointing up at an angle, like a searchlight to the sky. I covered my mouth with my hand. There was no way anyone could have survived.

A mass of men started rocking the overturned vehicle, intending on turning it upright to help whoever remained inside. It seems three people were in the car that night. A dazed man sat on the sidewalk, he'd gone through the front of the windshield. A woman in a dark dress and stiletto heels was being held back from the wreckage. Her wailing pierced the night air. I recognized a server from the Jamaican Bobsled, who always wore a long ponytail, consoling the lady with constant prayer.

The driver, a man, fell out the right front door when the mass of men put the car back onto its tires. I cringed knowing it was best to leave an injured person alone in case of neck or back injuries. Later, I learned that Jamaicans are compelled to help immediately at an accident because ambulances take too long, if they ever come at all. I heard that the injured man was talking, but not moving. They carried him on a makeshift stretcher into the back of the police jeep, and off to hospital. The other passengers from the car went with him. All I saw of him were his bare feet. I wondered where his shoes went. I never heard whether he lived or not, and it didn't look like the people in the other two cars were hurt. Luckily, their only injuries appeared to be property damage.

I hoped the crash was not an omen. It became practically impossible to get a good night's rest. Morning came soon, along with the grim news that the DHL office would be closed until Monday. I found out when Angie stopped by to say hello. She'd driven up to the DHL office for me to peer into the locked doors. The office was open Monday through Friday, 10 to 4, except on holidays.

Angie brought along some more bad news. She told me that she had given Parchi the keys to the gate and the room we'd rented at Sunshine Apartments on the last day of the month, in August. Later, she'd run into Ms. Parchment at the Blue Diamond shopping centre, where the wretched woman told Angie that she'd made a complaint against me to the CDA. She'd complained that I was abusive towards Ashley, and drank too much. Parchi described me as having held Ashley's arm behind her back roughly. She said she'd come to Ashley's rescue.

"She's a wicked woman. I didn't want to frighten you, so I didn't tell you. Avian and I knew you wouldn't hurt Ashley. We saw how you are with her and the boys. She's a wicked woman. I'm sorry I ever sent you to her," said Angie.

"Angie, I'm glad you did. We needed the cheap room and it served its purpose," I said. I didn't want Angie to feel responsible for Ms. Parchment's wrath. I was confident that she thought I'd skipped out with her gate remote and wanted to take revenge out on me.

"It's all gone through now," said Angie, "And you know what, Erika? She was mad because they never called her back. She made a complaint and they never called her back. That really made her mad," said Angie with a smile. "I didn't know how wicked she was till then."

Ms. Wilton had received a promotion since my August visit. 'Investigating Officer,' was her new job title. I asked her what she did on a daily basis. "Home investigations of child abuse," she'd said. I'd wondered why Ms. Wilton had recently, repeatedly, asked me if Ashley was ok. Ms. Wilton *knew* Ashley was more than ok. We'd spent enough time together for her to know that I loved Ashley as my own. Ms. Parchment had a higher power to answer to. My side of the street was clean.

Ironically we bumped into Mr. Dixon, on the other side of the street, that morning too. Ashley and I spent the last two days in Jamaica at the beach together. We were wrapped in our beach towels heading back to our room for some leftover Pork Pit grilled chicken sandwiches for lunch.

Mr. Dixon stood against a wall at the entrance of Doc's Cave with the other taxi drivers. Ashley saw him first. I felt kind of embarrassed since I hadn't asked him to pick me up at the airport when I arrived. We told him that we were waiting for Ashley's visa to come on Monday. "I can't thank you enough for all you have done for us Mr. Dixon. I want you to know that I could not have done this without you." Mr. Dixon took my hand and squeezed it, wishing us all the best.

All the little loose ends were getting tied up. I'd met Mr. Bowen, Ms. Tumming, seen Angie, and thanked both Mr. Dixon and Ms. Wilton for their tireless efforts. Things seemed to be wrapping up for us like a good novel. Ashley and I spent the weekend at the beach collecting tiny shells with holes in them to string together on a necklace, as a Christmas present for Nadia.

Ashley had learned to swim. Ms. Wilton told me that Ashley had "blossomed since we were in her life." Ashley's potential was only beginning to bud. I was glad the amazing weather held together those last two days. I wanted Ashley's last memory of her homeland to be beautiful.

The DHL man delivered the envelope that we hoped contained Ashley's visa before noon on Monday. We were already in a taxi headed to the DHL office when Natalie called my cell phone, telling us to come back. The delivery driver needed a signature for the envelope. I asked our taxi driver to turn around, and paid him the full fare I'd promised for the round trip.

I signed for the envelope and tore into it. Ashley had been denied a visiting visa based on our "intent to adopt." I'd stayed on the island away from my family for another six days holding onto the hope that Ashley would join us for Christmas. The Jamaican Government was well aware of our "intent to adopt." They took the seventy-five dollar US fee and made me stay on the island for nothing.

I decided to take Ashley to the airport with me in any case. I believed I had all of the required paperwork. Ashley had a passport, an original birth certificate, and we had the 'License to Adopt.' Obviously this was my child. *If I could just get her on the plane.* I imagined that we'd have a difficult time getting past immigration in Toronto, but that we would get by to sleep in our own beds that night.

We didn't even get checked in. There was no way on God's green earth that Ashley was going to get off the island without a visa. The agent that I checked in with was new. I saw Daniel, a familiar customer service agent, smile as we approached the counter, but his smile soon disappeared when he learned Ashley did not have a visa.

The supervisor, Ms. Beverly, came over and confirmed that Ashley would not be allowed to go to Canada. She looked at the documentation I carried. She called the Canadian High Commission and spoke with an immigration officer who looked up our file. My eyes welled with tears. My eyelids felt like a reservoir ready to burst. I looked down at Ashley who began to cry when she saw my face. I put my sunglasses on inside the terminal to hide behind.

I called Ms. Wilton back to the airport to pick up Ashley. We stood beside each other, waiting on the curb for our social worker to take her back to Anchovy. Ms. Wilton and Ms. Bradford arrived together in Ms. Wilton's sedan. I thanked them for coming for my daughter. I kissed Ashley's forehead, and promised I would be back. "Mommy always comes back," I said.

The last words that little girl said to me before she got into Ms. Wilton's car were "Mommy, don't forget to make Nadia's shell necklace before Christmas," and then, she was gone. I waved goodbye, trying without success to hold my composure together. I went back inside the airport, through immigration and security without incident, and had myself a good cry on the plane going home to Calgary.

I arrived in Calgary five days before Christmas, late in the evening. I felt grateful for the traveling time that allowed me to come to grips with the reality of having to leave Ashley behind. I began focusing on the upcoming holidays with my family.

I was too exhausted to be overly concerned that Sam had made arrangements to have Nadia and Alyssa leave for California the next morning. Part of me felt relieved, and part of me felt deprived of their presence for Christmas. I expected that they'd be packed and ready for the early morning flight. All I had to do was to get them to the airport in the morning in time for an international check in.

Arriving at midnight meant that all the people in the house were sleeping. Only the dogs met me with unbridled affection. It was normal for them to dance on their toenails whenever I returned home. Sid brought my suitcases in and placed them in the hallway for me to unpack in the morning. I kissed the boys foreheads and fell fast asleep in my own bed.

FIFTEEN

AND WE CAME OUT CLEAN

I had to dig down deep in my soul just to put one foot in front of the other the early the next day. The house wore a thick layer of dog hair that needed vacuuming and the girls required a ride to the airport. They were helium inflated with the anticipation of seeing their father over the Christmas holiday. All three of my boys needed cuddling.

I found a letter lying on the dining room table waiting for me from Canadian Immigration; postmark dated December 13, 2010. The document provided both a file number and an actual contact name for an immigration officer named 'ML.' Ironically, it was written the day I last left for Jamaica. I heaved a huge sigh, filled with frustration and relief, before composing a scolding to the Jamaican office in Kingston.

Dec 22, 10:40 am Mountain Standard Time

Good morning Ms.G.,

I have returned to Canada without Ashley, having received a denied visa based on our 'intent to adopt,' despite a letter from Mr. Bowen at the CDA, stating that he approved a thirty-day visit for Christmas.

I now have a file number 0910028224.

I sent another application for permanent residence (form IMM008) for Ashley via Fedex to Mississauga.

I got a letter dated 12, December 2010, from the case processing center stating: "We can tell you that the Visa Office did receive the electronic version of your file from us. The visa office will match it up to our electronic file and create a new file starting with the letter 'B.'"

Blessings,
Ms. Isnor

Surprisingly, I received a response from Ms. G. that afternoon.

Dec 22, 2:27 pm Eastern Standard Time

Dear Ms. Isnor,

I have located the electronic sponsorship. We cannot allocate a B number until we have received the Application Form. [IMM8] Once that has been received we will begin our processing of the application. I have passed the relevant information to our Registry Supervisor to keep an eye out for the Application Form.

Ms. G.

I quickly prepared the new application package and expedited it to *Mississauga.* And then, I had to sit back and wait for the process. Always the process. How does one fix the process? I had to let it go and spend time with my beautiful boys. Ashley would not miss what she did not yet have. "Soon come…..Soon come…."

The next morning, I called Officer ML in Mississauga on the landline he'd provided, explaining how I'd gone to Kingston to turn in the application and was told that the application needed to be filed *inside* Canada. Officer ML reiterated that the process required that the application be filed in at Kingston.

I'd already received tracking notification that new Fedex package had been delivered. Officer ML assured me that he would address the package as soon as it landed on his desk. I didn't think that Ashley's application would get much attention two days before Christmas. The observation of Jesus' birthday deserved its righteous authority.

Our finances and my patience had been exhausted; especially upon learning that Canada required that the application be turned into the visa office *abroad*. No wonder so many adoptive parents dropped off at the wayside.

The idea that an eight-and-a-half year old human being's well being stood in limbo as paper peddlers pushed her future around indifferently, infuriated me. Ashley Ashanti Farquharson's future remained uncertain. I imagined her immigration file as a pewter game piece being moved from one visa office to another, in the fat fingers of an imaginary authoritative giant.

I decided to focus my attention on Jesus, my family, and our time together during the holiday. We spent December the 25th exchanging presents, indulging in an unprecedented caloric intake of comfort foods, and building Lego sets on the living room floor. Sid and I lovingly placed Ashley's presents on her antique white iron bed, that we could see from our master bedroom. I maintained the perspective that although we were missing her in our house, Ashley had no idea what she was missing.

The time spent at home with my three boys between Christmas and New Year re-energized me. I purposefully distanced myself from Jamaica and the quest to bring Ashley home. Once the New Year rolled around, a series of emails travelled back and forth between Ms. G., the Jamaican immigration officer, and myself.

January 6, 2011 9:39 am Mountain Standard Time

> *Dear Ms. G.,*
>
> *I am wondering if you have any news regarding Ashley. I am wondering if the immigration officer, ML, has contacted you via email. Do you have record of receiving*

Ashley's immigration medical from Trinidad? It was done at Dr. Charles Hastings's office December 13, 2010. I have included a copy the office gave me in the application I sent to Mississauga.

I have Ashley's passport. Should I send it to you FedEx once the application has been received from Mississauga, or do I need to bring it in there in person again?

Kind regards,
Ms. Isnor

January 6, 2011 2:11 pm Eastern Standard Time

Dear Ms. Isnor,

I have heard from ML and await receipt of the application forms. Once I have received the application forms, matched them with the electronic sponsorship, I can then check for the medical result and we what action is required next. I will let you know when we require Ashley's passport.

Regards,
Ms. G

January 11, 2011 8:12 am Mountain Standard Time

Good morning,

I was wondering if Ashley's application has made it to Jamaica.

Kind regards,
Ms. Isnor

January 11, 2011 8:17 am Eastern Standard Time

Dear Ms. Isnor,

Not yet. It will take a while, depending on the method used.

Regards,
Ms. G

January 11, 2011 9:32 am Mountain Standard Time

Thanks so much for letting me know, I think ML said that he was going to send Ashley's file via diplomatic mail.

Erika Isnor

January, 11, 2011 9:56 am Eastern Standard Time

That method can take a while.

Ms. G.

January 17, 8:34 am Mountain Standard Time

Good morning Ms.G.,

Any news?

January, 19, 2011 8:42 am Mountain Standard Time

Dear Ms. G.,

I was wondering if you had received Ashley's application yet. I spoke with ML on Monday. He said it was sent out on the 10th of January and agreed that it was a timely process. I am also wondering if Ashley's medical has returned from Trinidad. Again, Dr. Hastings prepared the paperwork on December

*13, 2010. I am concerned that it may get misplaced if there
is no application attached to it.*

Kind regards,
Ms. Isnor

January 19, 2011 10:10 am Eastern Standard Time

Dear Ms. Isnor,

*The application has not been received yet. Do not worry
about the medical as it is submitted here electronically and
will be connected with the application once the file is created.*

*Please be patient and as soon as we have something to tell you
will be notified. Your patience is appreciated.*

Regards,
Ms. G.

Somewhere in the middle of January, I realized that it was much better Ashley hadn't come to Canada on a thirty-day visiting visa. We would have had to pack up her suitcases, and taken her back to Jamaica. It was far better for her to remain where she was than for her to be living in our home for a month and returned, like a library book. She had borne the brunt of too many disappointments in her young life. God knew what he was doing.

I phoned officer ML on January 22, 2011, nearly one month after returning from Jamaica alone. He informed me that a change in the Canadian process had occurred around the time I expedited Ashley's *second* application to Mississauga. The new process rerouted applications to Ottawa *before* being sent abroad to the appropriate visa office causing further delays.

The only point of reference we had for tracking Ashley's application was that officer ML had received it on January 7th. He sent it to Kingston, Jamaica on January 10th. According to the new and improved process, the application arrived in Ottawa on January 14th. Supposedly, I should expect Ashley's fate to reach the hands of Ms. G. in approximately six working days.

I asked Officer ML if I should prepare a third application and send it directly down to Officer G. in Kingston, Jamaica.

"It wouldn't hurt," said officer ML.

"Would you mind sending an email to officer G. so that she will be expecting the delivery?"

"I'll do that," he said.

January 24, 2011 7:48 am Mountain Standard Time

> *Good morning Ms. Griffiths,*
>
> *I have faith that one of these days we will have the excellent news that the application has been received in Jamaica and that we are moving forward to bring Ashley into our family. Any news?*
>
> *Blessings,*
> *Ms. Isnor*

January 31, 2011 9:13 am Mountain Standard Time

> *Dear Ms. G.,*
>
> *I am wondering if Ashley's file has been located. It was sent to Jamaica on January 10th. Surely it must be there by now.*
>
> *Kind regards,*
> *Ms. Isnor*
> *Calgary, Canada*

February 1, 2011 3:47 pm Mountain Standard Time

> *Dear Ms. G.,*
>
> *ML contacted me this morning regarding Ashley's application. Apparently it left Mississauga on January 10th and went to Ottawa due to a new procedure. The processing time from*

Ottawa to Jamaica is approximately 2 weeks once received. It was received in Ottawa on January 14th. Theoretically, it would be in Jamaica around January 28th.

ML supported the idea of sending a new application via DHL directly to you. I am compiling it now. I want to make certain that it is completely correct. I have faxed the application to you first. I would greatly appreciate knowing if anything is missing or incorrect before I send the package. I need to know which of the following items need to be notarized.

- *I have the original 'License to Adopt.'*
- *I have 2 more 'Permanent Resident' (PR) photos of Ashley taken in Jamaica.*
- *I have copies of Ashley's original birth certificate.*
- *I have copies of my husband's passport, Ashley's, and mine. I have a PR as I am American.*

I have a letter from the Canadian Government stating that we have completed the home study, and have been approved. We have a 'License to Adopt,' not an 'Order of Adoption,' so we cannot get a letter of no objection.

I have the electronic file number for Ashley Ashanti Farquharson, born October 13, 2002.

We would greatly appreciate a response at your earliest convenience so that I may get this to you asap.

Kind regards,
Ms. Isnor

February 7, 6:49 am Eastern Standard Time

Good morning Ms. Isnor,

Apologies for not responding before now but I was out of office on medical leave.

All photocopies birth certificates, passports ect. And in this case, the 'License to Adopt,' should be notarized. We do, however, require originals. As you only have one last original of the 'License to Adopt,' you may hold on to this original document until the very end of processing.

All photographs should be the same.

Our telephone and fax communication facilities are not working consistently, so I suggest you just send the package. If there are any errors I can email you about them.

Regards,
Ms. G

I put together the last application package to apply for Ashley's permanent residence in about 4 hours. I had to find someone new to notarize a few outstanding documents. The woman who'd notarized my previous set of documents had adopted from Ethiopia, emphasizing with prospective adoptive parents going through the same process. She worked for a downtown lawyer and didn't charge me for her services. Naturally, a blizzard hit Calgary, causing dangerous road conditions, so I couldn't make the trip into the city center for this final package.

In Canada, one cannot go to a bank to get a document notarized as in the United States. One must go to a barrister's office. The lawyer I found charged me seventy-five dollars CA to confirm that our documents were authentic. I walked into the pretentious office, where I was told it was inconvenient for them to accept a client without an appointment. I paid the bill, received the service, and then raced of out their door hoping to get the package in transit before the cut off time for an overnight delivery. Ashley's application would arrive in Jamaica by Thursday.

I forewarned Ms. Griffiths about the impending package.

February 7, 2011 8:26 am Mountain Standard Time

Good morning,

I hope you are feeling better. I have all things notarized ready to send.

God bless,
Ms. Isnor

February 7, 2011 11:57 am Mountain Standard Time

I know you need the original Police Clearances, but I am reluctant to send them. Please advise.

Kind regards,
Ms. Isnor

February 7, 2011 3:02 pm Eastern Standard Time

Ms. Isnor,

Please send the original police clearances. We no longer require the 'Fit Person Order.' But I do require the original 'Form of License.' Please send the package you have prepared. If anything is missing I will request it later.

Also, please remember we have processing queues and they are dealt with under first in/first out rules, and remember this file has not even been opened yet. If there are no issues or concerns there should not be any unnecessary delays, but please do not expect to have Ashley join you immediately.

Regards,
Ms. G.

I missed the 4 pm cut off time at the post office, so despite my best effort the application would not reach the Canadian Embassy for another seventy-two hours. The tracking information guaranteed Ashley's application would be there by 6pm, local time, Friday afternoon. The parcel arrived at its destination at 5:52 pm Thursday afternoon, with security officer 'J. Oliver' signing for it.

February 9, 2011 5:59 pm Mountain Standard Time

> *Ms. Griffiths,*
>
> *I spoke with a representative at Fedex this afternoon, and they tell me that the package was delivered to the "Security Guard" at 5:52 pm. I assume that you would not see the package until morning and would greatly appreciate knowing it is in your hands.*
>
> *Kind regards,*
> *Ms. Isnor*

February 14, 6:59 am Eastern Standard Time

> *Good Morning Ms. Isnor,*
>
> *The package has been received and the file is being created. You will be contacted if any additional information/action is required.*
>
> *Regards,*
> *Ms. G.*

Monday, February 21, 2011 was a Canadian statutory holiday. We celebrated 'Family Day' embracing "the importance of families and family life."

February 21 12:46 pm Eastern Time

Please Mrs. Isnor, be patient, your constant contact and my having to reply to your messages, takes me away from processing my applications and thus delays me from getting to Ashley's application. This application is not the only one that has been allocated to me for processing. I have hundreds of files in my caseload. This application has been given priority-processing status, but it will not happen in a couple of days and I will get to it soon.

Regards and please be patient.
Ms. G.

February 22, 2011 8:50 am Eastern Standard Time

Our File B0536342812
GCMS F00010946

Dear Ms. Isnor,

Ashley's application has been assessed and is ready for finalization. Please submit Ashley's passport to this office at your convenience. It can be submitted any Tuesday or Thursday between the hours of 1:30 and 2:30 pm. The wait time for the return of the passport after it has been submitted is ten working days. You may submit a prepaid courier airway bill for the return of the passport, as it is not necessary for the passport to be picked up in person. If you prefer to collect the passport yourself or will have someone authorized to collect the passport, please submit a contact number.

Regards.
Ms. G.

February 22, 2011 10:14 am Mountain Standard Time

May I FedEx Ashley's passport to you today, or does this have to be done in person?

Erika Isnor

February 22, 2011 1:51 pm Eastern Standard Time

Hello Mrs. Isnor,

You can send the passport to us by Fedex.

I arranged for FedEx to pick up Ashley's passport and inserted a prepaid return envelope inside. Ian, my friend the Fedex man who had been with us on this journey from the beginning, arrived to pick up Ashley's package. Usually, Fedex requests that outgoing parcels are prepared in advance. Ian took the time to help address the waybill and made sure it was prepared properly.

February 24, 2011 1:46 pm Eastern Standard Time

Dear Mrs. Isnor,

Ashley's passport has been received.

Regards
Ms. G.

I couriered Ashley's passport from Canada on Wednesday, February 23, 2011. Ms. G. received it the next day and attached the visa to it, returning the document to me on Friday afternoon. Over the weekend I tracked Ashley's paperwork through Miami and Tennessee. Monday morning Ian the FedEx man placed the precious visa in my hand.

I ripped into the package open finding the coveted visa securely attached to page seven of Ashley's Jamaican passport. "It is finished," I thought. Time to come home. Hopefully the trip to get Ashley would be uneventful and happen quickly. There was no need to travel to Kingston or dilly-dally on the beaches.

I phoned Ms. Wilton to let her know the good news. "Ashley is leaving on Wednesday? After Wednesday there will be no more Ashley on the island?" The surreal reality of the situation began to hit us all.

I phoned Garland Hall informing Matron Ms. Woodit that I would be taking Ashley to Canada on Tuesday.

Sid took me to the airport about two hours before the flight. We were confident that this would be the last trip to the Caribbean for a very long time. He hugged me tightly *knowing* I'd be home in a day or so, with our daughter.

I'd phoned airline making standby reservations for the red-eye flight through Toronto. There was plenty of availability, with more than sixteen seats open, when I listed. I was third on the priority list.When I gave my reservation number to the customer service agent at the check in counter, I learned I was still third on the priority list, and there were only two seats available. "I can't do that. I can't take that chance. I'm going down to Jamaica to pick up my adopted daughter. I will buy a ticket," I said.

I moved out of the queue to call the employee line to purchase a ticket. Thank God for our fifty percent employee discount policy. It cost $349 CA confirmed, to get from Calgary to Montego Bay that night. I figured I was paying for my sanity

I slept well on the plane in anticipation of a speedy turnaround. I loved Jamaica, but I wanted nothing more than to get home. I looked forward to getting our daughter on Canadian soil.

Thankfully, the plane landed in Toronto on schedule. I'd phoned Mr. Dixon asking him to pick me up at the regular time after I landed. I requested a seat in front of the aircraft on the Mobay flight so that I could deplane as soon as the lead flight attendant opened the front door. I sprinted down the yellow hallway, clearing customs in record time. Usually, I'd find my baggage neatly stacked to the side of the carousel, but I'd come through so quickly that the luggage hadn't even arrived yet. Even Mr. Dixon was surprised to see me so fast.

I waved Ashley's passport over my head showing Mr. Dixon that I had everything I needed to take her home. "You have gold in your hands," he said knowing how hard it was to come by. It made me think again about all the people on the island who yearned for chance to get off of it. He was right, Ashley didn't have an inkling of an idea about the opportunities that lay before her.

I held the passport close to my heart knowing I had very little to do with the getting of it. God had a plan and I was merely an instrument of his service. I had no idea what His intentions were. His intentions were not my business. I felt privileged to have been called into action.

We drove up Long Road and turned onto the narrow rocky dirt path leading to Garland Hall. I left all of my belongings, including my wallet, in Mr. Dixon's van for safekeeping. "I hope I won't be long," I said as I climbed out.

I walked through the tall white iron gates and up the stairs to the office door. Ms. Woodit sat at her desk as if waiting for my arrival. She'd asked me to pick up some Evening Primrose perfume for her when I called to say I had Ashley's passport, admittedly I never even looked for it. Ms. Woodit knew that this was the last time I'd be coming to collect my daughter." *A..S..H..l..e..y,"* she screamed, *"A..S..H..l..e...y* your mother is here."

It seemed like a million years before I saw Ashley's beautiful face peek around the corner. She knew exactly what was going on. The paperwork was done and I taking her home.

The next few minutes Ms. Woodit went on and on about a boil that was on the back of Ashley's head. "It burst," she said, "and I had to take her to the Doctor. It cost $8,000 JMD. I took her to a private Doctor because if I had taken her to the hospital (where it was free) I would have had to wait there all day."

"Does she have medicine?" I asked, remembering the last time Ms. Woodit had reprimanded me.

Ms. Woodit walked around the desk to the small refrigerator standing by the door. "Yes. The child has medicine, antibiotics for her head. She also has something to take away the itching. Why didn't you tell me she was allergic to milk?" asked the woman caring for the orphans.

"I don't *know* that Ashley is allergic to milk," I said. "I suspected that she was because when I gave her dairy products, her skin broke out. I told Ms. Wilton as soon as I suspected that she might be."

"You didn't tell me," she snapped. I bit my lip knowing that the conversation was going nowhere. "The medication cost me a lot of money, the prices is written on the boxes." I was glad my wallet remained in the car.

"Thank you for taking care of my child."

I figured the bill was not my responsibility. Besides, I'd been warned by Mr. Bowen not to give anyone any money. I looked down the hall in hopeful anticipation that Ashley would appear soon so we could get the hell out of there. "May I go inside?" I asked.

I was waved forward down a long dark hallway. I walked through a modest, clean kitchen, into a living area where several partially clothed children sat lounging around. I recognized a girl about the same size as Ashley on one end of a couch. She looked so very familiar... I finally realized it was Julieanne; the healthy twin from Blossom Gardens. "Hello Julieanne. How are you? Where is your sister Jodianne? Do you remember me honey?"

I remembered reading the book Jamaica's Find with the bright-eyed child at the picnic table at Blossom Gardens, but there was no recognition in those dull little eyes. It seemed as if the light had left them. I turned my back on that beautiful child when Ashley appeared behind me. I've had several nightmares since then about Julieanne, Kimeysha, and the others. They are always just out of reach in my dreams.

I took Ashley's hand and said, "Are you ready to go honey? Is there anyone you need to say goodbye to?" Ashley waved goodbye to all the children. She hugged two girls. One was named Alisha and the other Samara.

We'd barely walked through the front door when Ashley suddenly broke away from my grasp and went back inside. Apparently, she ran back to a big Tupperware bin in the laundry room. Ashley returned to me waving the peach-colored French frock I'd purchased for her in Montreal. She'd worn to the airport to go home in December. She was wearing it when Ms. Wilton came back to return her to Anchovy. "Mi Mama bought this frock for mi, and mi gonna take it wit mi!" A smile crept over my face as we walked hand in hand towards Mr. Dixon's van.

Mr. Dixon drove us to the Polkerris Bed and Breakfast where I'd reserved the yellow room by the pool for our last night on the island. I wanted Ashley's last memory of the island to be a beautiful one. We arrived at late in the afternoon after the sun had reached its peak. Clover, the house girl, brought us some freshly squeezed lemonade. We drank it quickly before heading down the hill to hoping get Ashley's hair braided.

I intended on making some final purchases from the people who had been so kind to us throughout the process. We took the room key with us. I noticed that it was different from the original single key on the turquoise coil wristband that Ashley had protected for us in the beginning. The key was digitally programmed for a new security system that had been installed. No wonder the rates had increased by nearly one hundred percent.

We walked down the concrete stairs to Bottom Road, past the double decker Burger King, Margaritaville, and the dilapidated Casa Blanca hotel, heading towards the Scotiabank money machine.

Afterwards, we found Bibsey sitting in her small modest shop where I'd purchased the pink bracelet, and the wooden fish, so long ago. She thought we'd gone to Canada together in December and was truly surprised to see us. I asked if Bibsey would braid and bead Ashley's hair one last time.

My face must have been beaming. The sky darkened and the stars came out above our heads. I don't think there is a place on earth that the stars shine brighter in the sky than in Jamaica. Bibsey continued braiding and beading Ashley's head, but Ashley was getting sleepy and her tummy rumbled for food.

"Do you mind if I leave Ashley with you while I walk down to the Pork Pit to get us something to eat?" I knew Ashley would be safe and in good hands.

"No mon, you go…get some food for the child."

I walked down the street mesmerized by the still night air. I was wearing a sleeveless frock and open-toed sandals, on the first day of March. A foot of snow still covered my backyard patio at home. I'd packed a full-length wool winter coat, long pants, and a turtleneck sweater for Ashley to change into once we got on the plane. Everything on Ashley's planet was about to change, but the weather was what I was most concerned about. How would she like cold Canada?

I ordered a feast of food to share with Bibsey from the Pork Pit. I turned in the little yellow piece of paper at the grill and plopped $500 JMD in the glass jar 'for the boys.' I imagined I would miss the smell of the meat smoking, as I waited outside for our Styrofoam containers of pork, chicken, and rice and peas. And then, walked back to Bibsey's.

I found Ashley asleep, slumped over Bibsey's lap at the shop, but Bibsey's fingers continued braiding and beading Ashley's hair. "Erika, that is not a boil on Ashley's head." Bisbsy's eyes met mine as she spoke the truth I had feared. "Someone burst her head."

"How do you know?" I asked.

"Ashley told me that one of the older girls, a new girl from Granville hit her in the back of the head. She said she was told she must not tell her mother or she would not go foreign. She was afraid to tell you. She wants to go foreign."

I sank down into the chair beside Ashley, placing her fragile head in my own lap to stroke the braids. "No one will ever beat you again," I promised. Ashley wriggled into me. "Mi so tired. Mi want to go to sleep," she whined.

I made Ashley sit up to eat. She dove into the chicken chomping it down to dust. Bibsey stopped the braiding to eat with us. The three of us devoured the meal. We were all ravenous. After eating, we decided to finish Ashley's hair in the morning. I told Ashley to climb onto my back, and carried her down the street, then up the hill to our beautiful yellow room, where we fell asleep nestled together.

The next morning we slept past eight o'clock. We both must have needed it. We were jarred awake by the ringing of the telephone. Clover called asking us what we wanted to eat for breakfast. I ordered ackee and saltfish with dumplings for both of us, knowing the only way I could get it in Calgary would be in a can. Ashley and I shared our last gourmet breakfast together looking out over the waters of Montego Bay. Our life together had technically already started. I pinched myself to make sure I wasn't dreaming.

I called Ms. Wilton, not wanting to leave the island without saying farewell. I'd brought a bronze necklace for her as a gift, wanting her to have something tangible to remember Ashley. Ms. Wilton said that she did not have a vehicle at the moment, but would make sure to stop by to see us before we left. "Ms. Wilton. There is something I am very concerned about," I said. I told her all I knew about Ashley's head, especially how Ms. Woodit instructed her not to tell me.

We walked down the hill after breakfast, one last time to finish Ashley's hair. I picked out several pieces of Bibsey's handmade jewelry to take home for future Christmas and birthday presents. We said goodbye to the people at the Harley Davidson's Jamaican Bobsled, the Caribic House, and to the shop girls along Bottom Road before returning to the house to change into our swimming suits.

We took a last dip in Jeremy's pristine pool water, twirling around, holding on to each other with newfound adoration. Neither one of us had any idea what was in store, except that the paperwork was done and that we were going to Canada.

We postponed getting out of the pool until the very last minute before showering and getting dressed for our trip home. I had not packed the clothes intentionally, but Ashley and I each wore a black dress with white polka dots. I closed the suitcases and rolled them to the top of the stairs to wait for Mr. Dixon.

Clover knocked on our door announcing the arrival of Ms. Wilton and Ms. Bradford. "Come with me Ash. We really need to thank Ms. Wilton for all that she has done, and we need to say goodbye." I held her hand and walked past the pool towards the front door.

Ms. Wilton looked professionally elegant wearing a shin length taupe linen dress that complimented her figure beautifully. I thought the necklace I brought her fit her personality. I handed the box to her expecting her to open it in my presence. She thanked me kindly and tucked the present away inside her purse. I wish I could have seen her face when she opened it.

Ms. Wilton, a child abuse investigator, visited homes where neglect and emotional and physical abuse was suspected. She had experience identifying such atrocities towards children. Ms. Wilton sat Ashley down in a chair and looked at the back of her head. Ms. Bradford, the social worker who had prayed with me, stood beside her. They both got very quiet. "This is not a boil," said Ms. Wilton. "Someone has burst her head. I am so sorry Ashley. You are safe now."

The first thought that went through my mind was how happy I was that I had not had the time to buy the Evening Primrose. Ms. Woodit may not have beaten Ashley, but she sure as heck became an accomplice when she hid it from me. I was glad that Ms. Wilton saw the 'burst' with her own eyes. I recalled Mr. Bowen's words, "There is a difference between what people say and what they do."

We hugged. Ms. Wilton said she could not imagine that there would be no Ashley on the island the next day. I could not begin to express my gratitude to Ms. Wilton's contribution to 'this child.' She left the hotel as quietly as she had come.

Mr. Dixon arrived five minutes before we expected him. He carried our suitcases down the stairs as I paid our hotel bill. *We were leaving...we were actually leaving Jamaica.* I could not believe it! Mr. Dixon drove us to the airport one last time. He took our bags out of his Scooby Doo van and placed them on the curb. He readily agreed when I asked if I might snap his picture with Ashley. I placed two twenty dollar US bills in his palm, hugged him, and said goodbye. Neither of us expected that I would call him back to pick us up. Ashley and I were leaving Jamaica with confirmed airline tickets.

I hoped we would get one of the people I was familiar with when we were waiting in the check in line. We got Daniel. "We have a visa for her," I said. Daniel nodded wearing an ear-to-ear grin.

The immigration line was practically empty, but filled quickly behind us. Our timing was perfect. *Or was it our timing?* We were summoned to booth number nine by a blinking red light. I handed our passports to a tall thin Jamaican man who wore a neatly pressed uniform. "What is your relationship with *this child*"

"Ashley is my daughter. This is the first time she is leaving the island. We are in the process of adopting her." Ashley's head poked up just over the counter.

The immigration officer immediately flipped through Ashley's passport looking for her visa. His kind eyes smiled when he found it. "Do you have paperwork that says you have guardianship"

"I whipped out the 'License to Adopt,' from my red bag. The officer inspected the document and stamped our passports. "All the best to you," was all he said.

Ashley's bag was searched because she'd packed her bottled drinking water inside it, and then we were on the other side, already halfway home.

We stopped at the Red Stripe stand to purchase the hot dog and soda special to go. Thank God Ashley didn't like ketchup. She liked her hot dogs plain. I tucked the meal inside my carry on bag, just in case the airline ran out of food before they got to our row. We stopped one last time at the duty free shop for some 12-year-old Reserve Appleton Rum for Sid. We were the last to board the plane. I still can't believe I forgot the coffee.

We sat across from each other in aisle seats. I held Ashley's hand and took her picture as the plane took off. Her eyes got as big as wagon wheels, so she took the hand of the nice lady sitting next to her. Two minutes later, Ashley fell asleep. I thanked God that we were able to leave the island without further incident. Ashley slept all the way to Winnipeg, where I had to wake her up to get off the plane.

We landed in Winnipeg, Canada; the coldest place on earth, at 8:37 on the evening of March 2, 2011. I expected to miss the last plane to Calgary that left at nine o'clock because we still had to go through Canadian Immigrations.

Ashley and I took our time collecting our belongings and getting off the plane. I'd booked a hotel on Hotwire.com for the night, expecting both of us to be physically and emotionally exhausted. Once again, the immigration line passed quickly. Our turn came and we were sent to secondary security as expected.

There was only one person ahead of us at the secondary security booth. The elderly lady was a United States citizen who continued arguing with the officer about the need to pay fifty dollars for a Canadian work permit. The lady droned on for nearly half-an-hour before finally giving the officer her money. If it had gone on another minute, I would have offered to pay for the work visa myself.

"Next," called the immigration officer. Ashley and I stepped up to the counter. "Passports please." I handed over my US passport, and Ashley's Jamaican passport to the man with the name tag, "Officer Grant," pinned to his shirt.

"This is the first time my daughter is coming to Canada. We are in the process of an adoption."

"I hope you have paperwork," said Officer Grant. I'm sure he did, because if we didn't it would have changed the course of his night. The Montego Bay plane was the last one to land that night. His shift was just about over.

"Do I ever have paperwork," I replied as I handed him our 'License to Adopt.'

Officer Grant reviewed the documents and prepared Ashley Ashanti Farquharson's landing papers. He gave me the receipt that represented the confirmation of Permanent Residence, allowing us to enter Canada legally. As far as I was concerned we were home. Our hearts danced with hope and love. Ms. Wilton and Mr. Dixon were right. We'd gone into the water and come out clean.

> "Love is very patient and kind, never jealous or envious, never boastful or proud, never haughty or selfish or rude. Love does not demand its own way. It is not irritable or touchy. It does not hold grudges and will hardly even notice when others do it wrong. It is never glad about injustice, but rejoices when truth wins out. If you love someone, you will be loyal to him no matter what the cost. You will always believe in him, always expect the best of him, and always stand your ground in defending him. All the special gifts and powers from God will someday come to an end, but love goes on forever."

Love never fails

1 Corinthian 4-8

EPILOGUE

The day our Ashley went to court and we were granted permanent guardianship was one of the happiest days of our lives. Nothing compares to the day a child joins a family, whether it is by natural birth, or supernatural adoption. The day we brought her home from Jamaica, we believed we were changing the course of her life, allowing Ashley an opportunity to fulfill the full potential of her birthright.

We learned that many children of older adoptions are commonly diagnosed with Reactive Attachment Disorder (RAD), Attention Deficit Disorder (ADHD), Post Traumatic Stress Disorder (PTSD), Oppositional Defiance Disorder (ODD), or a combination of any of the above. Parenting an adopted child, especially an older child, requires using different strategies because their needs are special. Unfortunately, despite best efforts, maladaptive behaviours are often manifested, leaving adoptive parents overwhelmed and exasperated.

An infant's ability to handle stress normally develops in concert with the baby's relationship with her primary caregiver, commonly the mother, from birth, when babies' fingers instinctively grasp those of their parents. The body and brain seek an intimate connection between the caregiver and the infant. That bond is made possible by *empathy*, the ability to love and share the feelings of others.

Empathy is a critical ingredient in building healthy relationships. When you don't give someone who lacks empathy what they want, relationships become disposable. Through no fault of their own, the disruption of development on the brain, caused by effects of abuse or neglect during the first five years of life, these children often struggle with the ability to engage in healthy relationships. Sadly, other people become interchangeable objects, because if you can't consider the feelings of another person, you live by the mantra, "It's my way, or the highway."

We learned that the brain develops from the back to the front, beginning with the brain stem. Children who experience a disconnect in nurturing caused by abuse or neglect can have delayed, or even interrupted development until those needs are met. They think with what I have come to know as a 'lizard brain,' rather than a 'wizard brain,' operating on a primal level, and unable to think cognitively.

Someone using their 'lizard brain,' will typically respond with flight, fight, or freeze reactions. Our lovely girl is a fighter first, and a flyer second, but I don't recall ever seeing her freeze. These are normal responses for someone who perceives a threat to their safety and needs to survive, at any cost. It is impossible to reason with someone who is thinking with their lizard brain.

Two-year-olds throw tantrums to get what they want. They bite, scream, and flail their arms, protesting what they perceive to be an injustice to their egocentric world. Naturally, attachment makes the child want to please their parent. In interrupted child development, children learn that tantrums are displeasing, so they find other means of getting their needs met. A sixteen-year-old, who bites, flails, and punches because they never learned appropriate stress responses, can cause significant damage to themselves or to others, even if the perceived threat is only in their own mind.

We believed early childhood trauma could be eradicated by providing a nurturing home and forever family. We thought love was enough. There is more love in our home than you can imagine. Our home remains a safe, predictable environment, where people can make mistakes, and love remains unconditional. Love is not enough.

I believe Ashley first jumped into my lap using the survival skills she learned in her young life. She was intrinsically searching to fulfill basic needs that had long ago gone unmet. We took on the formidable task of trying to meet those needs. Now, it seems we had an impossibly short window of opportunity, to make up for the loss of her early childhood

We fought fiercely advocating and adapting to Ashley's growing complex needs. We spent most of our effort focusing on them since she joined our family, often to the detriment of the other children. We fought for her education and her emotional well being. We supported her through court proceedings for criminal activities with unwavering dedication. And then, we learned we needed to implement boundaries when she brought violence into our home. A good friend likened our efforts to the musicians on the deck of the Titanic, who continued playing their instruments, minute after minute, as the ship quietly sank lower and lower into the sea.

We became involved with the juvenile justice system because she began breaking the law, hurting innocent strangers. It saddens me to think she is choosing to live the hard life we tried so hard to save her from.

Yet, I remain hopeful. I believe that the beautiful girl we found under the mango tree will find peace. She is a survivor who endures. I will always share the privilege of being her mother with another woman, though I often wished I had been there to gaze down into her deep dark chocolate eyes when she was a baby. I still pray for her every night, as we did when we first met. I know there is a glorious Father who watches over her always, when I leave the room.

ACKNOWLEDGEMENTS

Father thank you for Jesus, your perfect gift of grace. I am safe and secure in your unchanging love.

Sid, thank you for always standing beside me…You are my failsafe.

My Children. You are scattered across the continent. You are the reason I breathe.

Ms. Wilton, one of the most Godly women on earth.

Mr. Dixon, so patient.

Auntie Joy, for your ever present kindness.

Ms. O'Connor, Mr. Green, Ms. Bradford, Ms. Palmer, Carmelina, Mrs. Brown, Bibsey, Angie, Avion, Easten, David, Maryam, Ms. Parchment

Mr. Bowen and Ms. Tumming

Christian Adoption Services
Wendy Robinson and Amanda Spade, for showing our family grace.

Embracing Orphans
Meghan and Carl R.

Canadian Immigration Officer ML

Jamaican Immigration Officer Ms. Griffith

Lori Albertson, the best friend a girl could ever have. Thank you for letting me read parts of the book over and over to you, until we thought I got it right.

William F. Rossi, my Dad.

Carolyn Hursh Rossi, my mother, who always said by sheer will I could swim the English Channel.

Printed in the United States
By Bookmasters